The Literacy Game

The story of the National Literacy Strategy

John Stannard and
Laura Huxford

Routledge
Taylor & Francis Group

LONDON AND NEW YORK

First published 2007
by Routledge
2 Park Square, Milton Park, Abingdon, Oxon OX14 4RN

Simultaneously published in the USA and Canada
by Routledge
270 Madison Ave, New York, NY 10016

Routledge is an imprint of the Taylor & Francis Group, an informa business

Typeset in Garamond by
HWA Text and Data Management, Tunbridge Wells
Printed and bound in Great Britain by
TJ International Ltd, Padstow, Cornwall

British Library Cataloguing in Publication Data
A catalogue record for this book is available from the British Library

Library of Congress Cataloging-in-Publication Data

Stannard, John, 1940–
    The literacy game: the story of the National Literacy Strategy /
John Stannard and Laura Huxford
        p.   cm.
    Includes bibliographical references and index.
    1. National Literacy Strategy (Great Britain)   I. Huxford, Laura
    II. Title.
LC156.G7S83 2007
302.2´2440941   2007004716

ISBN10: 0–415–41700–7 (hbk)
ISBN10: 0–415–41701–5 (pbk)
ISBN10: 0–203–94491–7 (ebk)

ISBN13: 978–0–415–41700–6 (hbk)
ISBN13: 978–0–415–41701–3 (pbk)
ISBN13: 978–0–203–94491–2 (ebk)

The Literacy Game

The National Literacy Strategy, initiated in England in 1997, was the most ambitious educational reform programme in the world. While it achieved significant success, there are lessons to be learned at every level from government through local administration to school leaders and teachers.

The Literacy Game is the only systematic exploration of the reform programme, examining the origins, evolution and impact of the National Literacy Strategy (NLS). Invaluable insights from the architect and original director of the NLS and its director of training provide both a vital introduction and a critical appraisal for practitioners and for students.

This illuminating text:

- sets out the political background and context to literacy education in England over a decade from 1996 to 2006;
- explains and appraises the rationale and design underpinning the NLS, thereby rebutting some of the folk-lore that has built up around it;
- provides an example of the principles and practices of large-scale system change;
- links the NLS to wider global research on system change and educational reform;
- evaluates the contribution of the NLS in advancing knowledge of the literacy curriculum in English and the development of pedagogy as a whole;
- considers the impact and consequences of the NLS on standards of literacy.

The Literacy Game provides a fully comprehensive contribution to a wider literature on the teaching of literacy and the management of educational change. This enlightening book will appeal to all policy makers and academics who are keen to know what did and did not work in the NLS and why.

John Stannard was director of the NLS, responsible for national implementation up to December 2000. Since then, he has been involved in evaluating the Strategy nationally, and working on related initiatives in other countries.

Laura Huxford was the training director responsible for the development and introduction of professional development resources and teaching resources from 1997 to 2004, and has had close front-line involvement with schools over most of the lifetime of t' ˢ

Contents

Illustrations

Figures

Tables

Foreword

Sir Michael Barber

The National Literacy Strategy changed the face of primary education in England dramatically and irreversibly.

As a result, the performance of the system is far better than it was. This is evident in the Key Stage results where the percentage achieving level 4 in English jumped from 57 per cent (1996) to 79 per cent (2006) and the percentage achieving level 5 also jumped dramatically. Relying on one indicator in education is always risky even when, as in this case, it is one based on good tests. However, the rise in performance is confirmed by every other significant indicator. International comparisons (PIRLS 2001) showed England's performance in reading among 9-year-olds had risen dramatically (unlike Scotland where there was no Strategy). Secondary school teachers noticed the difference in standards of writing, especially grammar. Most recently researchers showed that primary age children's spelling in 2005 was 12 to 18 months ahead of their equivalents 30 years ago.

Few if any other systems have managed such transformative change across so large a system in such a short time. The story told in this book is therefore significant not just in relation to literacy but also to generating large-scale change in education or indeed public services generally.

At the heart of the strategy driving the crucial first few years were John Stannard and Laura Huxford. Their account here is thoughtful, dispassionate, self-critical and thorough. Its importance lies in the fact that they have explained, at a level of detail, how the Strategy had an impact, classroom-by-classroom across a primary school system with 19,000 schools, almost 200,000 teachers and over three million children. Why is this so important? Because too much of the writing about education reform is at a level of generality and fails to grapple with the central question, which is how to get reform inside the classroom.

In this book John Stannard and Laura Huxford tell a remarkable and courageous story. Admirers will want to read it anyway. Sceptics should make sure they do because much of the criticism of the National Literacy Strategy has been based on misconceptions. The vast majority of potential readers, who are neither admirers nor sceptics but open-minded educators, will find it both fascinating and inspiring. Large-scale educational change is never easy but this book shows that it can be done.

Acknowledgements

We would like to thank Michael Barber for his support and assistance in writing this book, and for providing a foreword. We also thank Michael Fullan for encouraging us and for commenting in detail on an early version of the text. Professor Jill Bourne from Southampton University added to our motivation by pressing us to continue and providing feedback on the book plan and some of the draft chapters. More generally, we wish to express our gratitude to the NLS team of regional directors and the national team of literacy line managers and consultants with whom we have worked over the years. None of the successes of the Strategy would have been possible without them, in particular Steve Anwyll and Kevan Collins who took on successive roles as National Directors when John Stannard retired from the job. CfBT, who worked in the background of the NLS, as its operational and delivery agent for eight years, managing and supporting the national professional and administrative teams, have also contributed to the making of this book. Through discussion, corporate memory and tolerance of John Stannard's absence from his role of consultant for the best part of six months while working on the text, they have helped to bring it about. Most of all, we thank Becky and Richard, our respective spouses for their encouragement, forbearance and support.

Material from official publications is Crown Copyright and is reproduced under the terms of the Click-Use Licence by permission of the Controller of Her Majesty's Stationery Office.

Abbreviations

DES	Department of Education and Science – name of government department responsible for education in England from 1964 until 1992
DfE	Department of Education – name of government department responsible for education in England from 1992 until 1995
DfEE	Department for Education and Employment – name of government department responsible for education in England from 1995 until May 2001
DfES	Department for Education and Skills – name of government department responsible for education in England from May 2001
Framework	The National Literacy Strategy framework of teaching objectives (see Chapter 3)
FS	Foundation Stage: from 2000–2006, the period of two to three years prior to compulsory schooling at age 5; from 2006, the period in a child's life from birth to the start of compulsory schooling
HMI	Her Majesty's Inspector – often used to refer to the inspectorate body
KS1	Key Stage 1 – period of schooling covering years 1 and 2, approximately ages 5–7
KS2	Key Stage 2 – period of schooling covering years 3–6, approximately ages 8–11
KS3	Key Stage 3 – period of schooling covering years 7–9, approximately ages 12–14
LEA	Local Education Authority – locally elected administration, roughly equivalent to a school district in other countries
NAHT	National Association of Head Teachers (professional association for head teachers)
NC	National Curriculum in England
NC levels	National Curriculum levels of attainment: level 2 is the expected level for children at age 7, level 4 at age 11 and level 5 at age 14
NCSL	National College of School Leadership, the body responsible for the professional development and qualifications for head teachers
NFER	National Foundation for Educational Research

NLNS	National Literacy and Numeracy Strategies in England
NLP	National Literacy Project in England
NLS	National Literacy Strategy in England
NNS	National Numeracy Strategy in England
Ofsted	Office for Standards in Education, founded in 1992, responsible for inspecting schools and LEAs; HMI work within Ofsted
PNS	Primary National Strategy
QCA	Qualification and Curriculum Authority – responsible for National Curriculum and assessment
YR	Reception year – the academic year (September–August) during which a child becomes 5 years old (final year of the Foundation Stage)

Introduction

This book tells the story of the National Literacy Strategy (NLS) in England. It was and remains the biggest educational reform programme of its kind in the world. It has been a powerful and formative influence on the structure and professional culture of primary education in England and has also been a cornerstone in the development of knowledge about issues of large-scale educational reform internationally. The NLS has evolved and changed substantially over the years and has been a subject of widespread debate and discussion in England and abroad. Schools, politicians, researchers and critical observers have variously acknowledged its success and pointed to its weaknesses.

We have been closely involved with the evolution of the NLS since its inception. John Stannard was the architect of the rationale, literacy Framework and Literacy Hour and as director of the NLS, responsible for national implementation up to December 2000. Since then, he has been involved in evaluating the Strategy nationally, consulting at local authority and school levels, and working on related initiatives in other countries. Laura Huxford was the training director responsible for the development and introduction of professional development resources and teaching resources from 1997 to 2004, and has had close front-line involvement with schools over most of the lifetime of the Strategy. Inevitably, a reform on this scale and of such political and educational significance will generate a wide range of views and responses. Ten years on, and with the benefit of hindsight, we set out to explain the NLS and its evolution, to evaluate the evidence of its impact and relate this to some of the wider questions of system change and educational reform.

There are a number of parallel and intersecting stories. One is about the teaching of literacy, the underpinning rationale, the content and progression of the literacy curriculum and the fundamental teaching methodologies promoted by the NLS. A second story tells of the political context, motivations and commitments which shaped and drove the reforms, while a third story relates the NLS to the wider research on large-scale reform. Over a decade since 1997, the NLS has changed significantly. It began as a strongly interventionist process of 'informed prescription' (Barber 2002) and, alongside its partner National Numeracy Strategy, evolved into a Primary National Strategy to give increasing responsibility and autonomy to schools. In that time, it moved away from the largely 'top-down' approach, with which it was initiated, towards an approach which 'saw the user, the implementer, as the key figure in the change process and reform as essentially a dialectical process' (Hopkins 2004). It has been a fascinating and challenging journey but never a smooth road to travel. Much has been learned and we have tried to capture this in our narrative.

We have structured the book in ten chapters. Chapter 1 deals with the political narrative, setting the scene, describing the political and educational contexts which gave rise to the NLS. Chapters 2 to 4 deal with the fundamentals of literacy teaching embedded in the strategy – its rationale, content and methodologies. In Chapter 5 we take up the theme of differentiation, briefly describing how the common messages of 'informed prescription' were applied across a vast array of needs and contexts for almost 19,000 schools and the children they served. Chapters 6, 7 and 8 turn to the strategic and practical challenges of implementation, evolution, sustainability and the difficult transition from relatively strong central control to increasing school autonomy. In Chapter 9, we consider the evidence of impact, relating this to the government's declared expectations and targets. In Chapter 10, we take up the political narrative again continuing the story begun in Chapter 1 about context and the effects of the continuing literacy debates. We finish with a plea for clarity and a renewed emphasis on clear implementation of a few key priorities.

Chapter 1

The context and origins of the National Literacy Strategy

A brief history

We called this book *The Literacy Game* because it has an intimate connection with the ambitions for education reform set out in an earlier book, *The Learning Game*, by Michael Barber (1996). *The Learning Game* was written over a period immediately preceding the general election in May 1997 when New Labour came to power. It was a formative text. Barber's ambitions to eliminate failure through guaranteeing standards in the basic skills, the idea of the school as a learning institution, a learning promise for every child, the wider aims of creating a learning society and opportunities for lifelong learning, have all been echoed in ensuing education policies. The National Literacy Strategy, its partner the National Numeracy Strategy, the later, and symmetrical, Key Stage 3 secondary school strategy, the restructuring of the 14–19 sector, and the major redevelopment of early years' education, though not conceived in any detail, all find a place in this original vision. The book sets out an overwhelming moral, social and economic case for placing education at the centre of government policy. Barber's optimistic proposals met with much criticism but, with characteristic persistence and calmness, he listened to and investigated objections, worked out practical solutions and costed the proposals to create an agenda for educational reform that was politically viable and became highly influential in the formation of education policy over the coming years.

The Learning Game provides a detailed critique of education policy over the post-war years, focusing particularly on the preceding terms of Conservative government, at a point when that government was in its final years of power. Ironically, as we write this book, New Labour may be approaching a similar stage in its electoral life. The Thatcher years saw great changes; the two most indelible being the introduction of the National Curriculum in 1989 and the creation of the Office for Standards in Education (Ofsted) in 1993 out of the long-established and rather more benign HM Inspectorate of Schools. The National Curriculum established a framework of statutory, and publicly agreed, standards and expectations for schools. Ofsted, like Ofwat for water utilities and Oftel for telecoms, became the new standards watchdog and regulating body for the delivery of the standards. In the context of the past 50 years both developments are relatively recent but they were and remain fundamentally important as the twin pillars of standards and accountability which define the key structures, responsibilities and working relationships of today's education system.

The conservative project in education, in line with reforms across other areas of public utilities and public services, was to create a market in which parents, as customers, would choose schools on the basis of preference and publicly provided information in the form of national test results and school inspection reports. By the same token, school autonomy was increased with devolved funding for schools, to take to themselves most of the key management functions, including the hiring and firing of staff. Funding was differentiated in various ways with some financial incentives for success, and extra resources for improvement to the weakest. Increasing devolution to schools also, and intentionally, diminished the powers of the local authorities. Many local authorities, especially those in the inner urban areas where school performance was typically weaker, were labour strongholds run by the opposition and frequently a thorn in the government's side. The most celebrated and adversarial conflict with the monolithic Inner London Education Authority was resolved with its break-up in April 1990, and signalled a changed, and much more assertive, relationship between government and local authorities.

Also, over the decade from 1985 to 1995, research into school improvement burgeoned, demonstrating irrefutably that (a) some schools had a big impact on children's success despite differences in socio-economic circumstances, (b) performance varied widely among schools serving statistically similar populations and (c) that weak schools could significantly improve through carefully directed intervention and support. The publication of school league tables along with the hostile practice of naming and shaming weak schools simultaneously raised public awareness and depleted professional morale. It also marked a growing and justified intolerance of school failure which became the hallmark of Ofsted's public success and influence. The fear that schools might be placed into 'special measures' massively strengthened government's leverage across the system and had a major impact on raising public awareness of school performance, especially in the key areas of school leadership and teaching quality. Thus, prior to the 1997 election, government policy on school improvement was framed around four core principles:

- the statutory National Curriculum to define standards and expectations for all children;
- accountability and public reporting through Ofsted to assure quality;
- devolved and differentiated funding to enhance school autonomy and enable each school to direct resources towards continuous improvement;
- parental choice to create a market as an incentive for schools to meet the needs of their 'customers'.

By the mid-1990s, under Gillian Sheppard, the last Conservative secretary of state, this policy framework had settled into a generally accepted modus operandum. The National Curriculum and its assessment was established, most primary heads devoted the greater part of their effort to dealing with management problems generated by the new devolved financial regime and Ofsted's impact was mixed. It had achieved notable success in exposing problems of the weakest schools and local authorities but was having little real impact on school improvement. Inspection reports repeated the same message year after year about good schools being good, weak ones needing to get better, listing the characteristics of each and enjoining everyone to improve but without the wherewithal to contribute more than the most general advice on how to do it.

When Ofsted was created, a clear distinction was drawn between functions of inspection and advice – or pressure and support in the emerging jargon – based on the precept that inspectors should not evaluate their own advice to schools. Over the years, this distinction became increasingly institutionalized and persists today. Distinct and disjoined roles evolved for each function. Inspectors withdrew from any serious participation in support and training and, while auditing and listing schools' strengths and weaknesses, avoided putting their toes in the water of advising schools or prescribing practice, which was strictly a matter for each school to decide in its own way.

The new Ofsted 'hit and run' approach to inspection came to be reflected in the organization of local authority services, where school monitoring began to replace support as their principal school improvement strategy. Local authorities, the main providers of professional support to schools, had their support budgets top-sliced to fund the creation of Ofsted and further reduced through the devolution of funding to schools, seriously depleting their capacity to support schools. Loss of funding, combined with a new emphasis on local inspection and the monitoring of school performance, led most authorities to deploy their remaining resources into school improvement teams. The work of these teams increasingly focused on identifying and monitoring the weakest schools and coaching them through their Ofsted inspections, under pressure from their own elected members, to avoid incurring criticism of the authority, and the threat of penalties for poor performance.

Two other consequences contributed to the malaise. First, local authorities, encouraged by government, attempted to privatize their support services in an effort to claw resources back from the schools. They had to make money or go to the wall. Many failed, while those that survived generally did so on the basis of offering schools what they could sell rather than that which might help or challenge them. Second, the inspection/support division of labour also accorded differences of status to the two roles. Ofsted led the pack, but at the local level, school monitoring teams were the place to be if you wanted a career, while professional support and training progressively diminished. Thus the whole effort to improve was increasingly driven by pressure and the threat of public criticism. This, naturally, exerted itself most palpably on schools, who did their best to comply and stay out of trouble. It was a hard road for school leaders and teachers who felt increasingly exposed and criticized. The constant challenge to improve tended only to depress schools and deepen a growing culture of mistrust and blame.

There was no way that Barber's vision of school improvement, in a learning society with high achievement on a world-class scale, was likely to emerge from this unhappy combination of pressure and low morale. The system had, as Barber argues, important merits. No one in their right mind would seek to disband Ofsted or ditch the National Curriculum. Later, in his role as chairman of the Literacy Task Force, he drew attention to the need for a judicious balance of pressure and support:

> Without too much exaggeration, it would be possible to describe the history of the last thirty years as 20 years of support without pressure and 10 years of pressure without support. If we are to transform literacy standards in the decade ahead, we shall certainly need both.
>
> (Literacy Task Force 1997: 14)

On the positive side, much more was known about the processes of school improvement. There was also a growing understanding that school improvement was largely a function of improvements in the leadership and quality of teaching. The challenge lay in how to exploit this knowledge effectively. In 1996, Chris Woodhead put his finger on it in Ofsted's Annual Report:

> There is no doubt that if standards of pupil attainment are to be raised, then the quality of teaching must be the focus of everyone's efforts. Every government initiative ought to be tested against this key imperative. Will it help teachers to teach better or will it distract them from their key task? This must always be the question. So too, at the level of the LEA and the individual school. Children will learn more when teachers teach better.
>
> (Ofsted 1996a)

Barber agreed but believed the point had much wider implications. The key was system-wide professional development for all teachers and a reciprocal commitment to self-improvement from the profession. Standards and pressure would remain but a massive injection of support was needed to balance out the pressure. Instead of using pressure to berate schools, it would be used as leverage to engage them. In exchange for big commitments in resources, high quality training, professional trust and improved working conditions, teachers would raise their expectations, learn new professional skills and focus seriously on improving their teaching; it would be a deal but not an option. A similar balance of pressure and support would be focused on improving school leadership with priority given to leading the curriculum, teaching and learning. The ambition: nothing less than the elimination of school failure. This brave outlook could only be realized through some serious 're-engineering' of the system where decision makers have to be deliberately ambitious and break with the traditional rules. 'Any government that embarks on re-engineering in education will not succeed if it lacks courage, determination and ambition' (Barber 1996: 251).

In practice, this process of reform would need to begin in primary schools with the basic skills of literacy and numeracy. In a second term of Government, it would move into the secondary sector, creating an upward pressure for change and a developmental pathway to improvement. Michael Barber was invited to advise Labour in opposition on the development of its education policy. Around the start of 1996 he was asked by David Blunkett, the education spokesman, to set up a Literacy Task Force, which was announced at the Whitsun conference of the National Association of Head Teachers. The task force comprised literacy and school improvement expertise, those with experience of system change and large-scale improvement in other sectors plus a number of experienced and successful heads and teachers. Its job was to collect evidence on how best to improve literacy standards, and to make evidence-based policy proposals.

In parallel, at the start of 1996, government frustration with its inability to improve standards boiled over, triggered by Ofsted's report *The Teaching of Reading in 45 Inner London Primary Schools* (Ofsted 1996b). The survey found pervasive weaknesses in the teaching of reading in three inner London education authorities. Inspectors estimated that only about a quarter of the teaching they observed reached a satisfactory level and catalogued weaknesses centred on the quality of teaching and school leadership. Soon after, a similar report was published on numeracy. These were to become landmark documents not just because of their content, but because they were also designed for political impact, calling into question the competence of three under-performing Labour-led authorities.

To their eternal credit, the Secretary of State agreed to a proposal from the Chief Inspector to break with tradition and intervene in these and a number of other poorly performing local authorities with two parallel support projects to improve the teaching of literacy and numeracy through the National Literacy and Numeracy Projects. The projects, although initiated by Ofsted, were run by the DfEE, while Ofsted, along with the National Foundation for Educational Research (NFER) evaluated them. John Stannard, at the time Ofsted's specialist English Adviser, was seconded to create and direct the National Literacy Project (NLP). Fifteen local authorities were invited to participate – none refused. Most but not all served urban disadvantaged areas; three large 'shire' authorities also participated. Demand exceeded supply and a further three were included at their own request while others had to be refused. The National Numeracy Project was developed in concert but with a different group of local authorities, allowing each project to grow and be tested independently. While Michael Barber was developing his proposals in *The Learning Game*, John Stannard and Anita Straker went to work developing pilot programmes for literacy and numeracy with common ambitions and a potentially transferable structure. A striking feature of these early developments was the way that both directors, independently, arrived at similar conclusions about the shape and structure of the support to be offered.

It was evident from the literacy report that merely providing resources for professional development was no answer. In fact the three London education authorities under scrutiny in Ofsted's report, aware of the problems they faced, had been making quite extensive provision but,

> Although there was a great deal of in-service activity taking place it was often random and haphazard in its availability...Except for the initial support offered to most newly-qualified teachers, there was little to suggest systematic provision for the development of individual teachers.
>
> (Ofsted 1996b: §93)

What schools needed was something much more specific and codified for teachers to use which would meet the objective spelled out in the report that:

> ...teachers must be crystal clear as to what their pupils need to know, understand and be able to do to become confident and proficient readers. The fact that almost half of the schools did not meet the requirements of the National Curriculum programme of study for reading suggests that these schools need to review their reading programme with all speed.
>
> (ibid. §12)

This recommendation seemed sensible at the time but, in retrospect, was naive. It was not surprising that these and thousands of other schools across the country were not meeting the National Curriculum requirements. The requirements comprised broad and brief statements intended as a basis for devising detailed school-based programmes. However, constructing such a programme requires subject knowledge and detailed specification which may have been possible in some large secondary schools with specialist departments, but were beyond the ability of most primary schools. Typical of so much change and innovation in England it was conceived as a secondary model and ill suited to the structure and capacity of nearly 20,000 relatively small primary schools, where some 200,000 teachers each had to plan and deliver a ten-subject curriculum. Expecting every school to create its own detailed programme, re-inventing – or failing to re-invent – the wheel was well-intended, but unrealistic, inefficient and unfair. Typically, schools taken into special measures by inspectors had many of the features of those in the Ofsted survey and worse – weak teaching, inconsistency, overload on teachers who, in the absence of adequate structures and professional support, were re-creating the curriculum daily, and the predictable consequences of frustration, diminishing confidence, high staff turnover and pupil behaviour problems.

It was the recognition of these problems that led to the creation of the common structures in the NLP: a detailed framework of term-by-term objectives for teachers, a common approach to teaching through the Literacy Hour, a team of trained and expert consultants dedicated to training and support for all teachers within the common framework plus symmetrical support for head teachers and language coordinators focused on leading teaching and learning, to help them break out of the closed cycle of short-term management and day-to-day survival. The NLP was never intended as just a strategy to improve literacy; its focus on literacy had the twin objectives of raising standards and providing a tool for broader school improvement. This is what was said at the start and it proved to be so in practice.

Risking accusations of over-prescription, and with the authority of Chris Woodhead and Gillian Sheppard behind it, the NLP was launched, to be met with an overwhelmingly positive response. It clearly answered a need and provided stability, support and practical solutions for many hard-pressed schools. Heads were able to implement it with some confidence, not just as a fiat of their own invention, but as a solution with strong credentials and backing. Teachers' skills and the quality of debate in schools about literacy improved dramatically; practice, almost at a stroke, became shareable because of its common language and methodology. Schools reported more interest from parents who, for the first time, could understand what their schools were trying to do. In many classes teachers said the Literacy Hour was having a positive impact on behaviour and discipline. Above all, there was strong anecdotal evidence that children viewed the Literacy Hour positively and that standards of reading were rising. The latter was later confirmed by the NFER tests (Sainsbury *et al.* 1998).

As the NLP became established, an expectation grew that it would be extended. No one was sure how but it was clear that here was the kernel of an approach to school improvement with potential for wider application. Michael Barber, now chairing Labour's Literacy Task Force, invited John Stannard to meet the committee and outline the aims and structure of the NLP. He was impressed and became convinced that the NLP and, in due course the National Numeracy Project, had the potential to be revised and scaled up as a first major step, setting the scene for achieving the broad Labour vision of transforming schools through improved teaching and learning. It was practical, evidently effective, with a clear, supportive and accountable framework. Above all, it was amenable to the large-scale professional development that Barber envisaged. The principles of the NLP were adopted. In February 1997, prior to the election, the outline of a National Literacy Strategy was launched to a key Labour conference at the Islington Business Centre, along with the publication of the Task Force's interim report. A summary of the report was circulated to every primary school in the country with an invitation to respond. Michael Barber, with typical attention to evidence, made a point of responding personally by phone to everyone who contacted him.

The state of literacy teaching in primary schools

Just prior to the publication of 1996 report on the teaching of reading in London, there was heated debate about its content among inspectors (HMI) within Ofsted. Although it was common for reports to be finalized and glossed by the Chief Inspector, some HMI felt it was unfair to pillory these three local education authorities (LEAs). Though no one could argue much with the conclusions, HMI knew perfectly well that most of the criticism levelled at the three unfortunates and their 45 struggling schools could have been levelled at LEAs and schools across the country. The LEAs were a shambles for all sorts of reasons but reading was taught no better in many of the schools served by well-organized and government-friendly authorities. Had the survey been conducted in three more affluent and middle class counties it could easily have produced a similar picture except with higher standards. At the time, differences in school performance had more to do with the children's capacity to benefit from similar teaching approaches than to any systematic differences in the organization or quality of teaching per se. This was a crucial point obscured in the furore over the alleged consequences of 'loony left' administrations in London but salutary for the later development of the National Literacy Strategy (NLS) which was about to challenge every school to do better.

In primary literacy, there are practices and there are theories. For the most part, primary teachers then, and now, have a passing interest in theories and tend to be more pragmatic. Their first concern, quite properly, is with what works and what they should do, rather than with psychological models, social theories or the adoption of ideological positions. For most teachers, successful practice means getting on with the job and doing their best for children with whatever resources are to hand. During the 1990s, in the background of most teachers' experience, the 'reading wars' (as they had come to be called in the United States) began to rage in England. Protagonists were mainly theorists, lobbyists and journalists of various persuasions, while primary teachers, by and large, were the contingent beneficiaries of mixed and partial messages emanating from each side.

At the same time, quite stark differences in practice were evident, between mainstream classroom teaching and the provision for special educational needs in primary schools. The former was populated by teachers, the latter mainly by educational psychologists. Teachers were trained in university departments of education and received a broad, but frequently inadequate, introduction to aspects of reading education. The postgraduate qualification for educational psychologists was taught and awarded by psychology departments. These departments were often in separate faculties and buildings with little or no tradition of common practice or interaction between the two. Most educational psychologists favoured 'bottom-up' approaches to teaching reading, with phonics at the fore-front – well justified for many of the children they were supporting – while primary teachers, with equal justification, took a wider view. The main conduits of reading theory to teachers were the teacher trainers responsible for initial preparation, the professional support staff in local authorities, and publishers' representatives who marketed reading schemes and programmes, and often had the greatest impact on practice.

Traditionally, teachers had regarded psychologists not just as doing a different job but as experts with access to 'remedial' knowledge which, like its medical counterpart, was designed for children with pathologies, rather than those in 'good health'. Methods used by remedial reading services were often perceived (not without justification) as meaningless drills reinforced by the conditioning effects of external rewards. Many teachers' felt, again quite reasonably, that methods such as these were out of step with the professional values they had signed up to. Nevertheless, despite the institutionalized stand-off, there was no great antipathy between teachers and psychologists who co-existed in their complementary roles. Teachers simply perceived phonics as a remedial tool which, like diagnostic testing, belonged in the specialist portfolio of the psychologist. They just did not see it as a big part of their job.

It was no surprise therefore, that Frank Smith's (1971) and Kenneth Goodman's account of the reading process, which sidelined the place of phonics and stressed the importance of active learning and reading for meaning, had a good press among primary teachers. Goodman's famous, and subsequently fatal, characterization of reading as a *psycholinguistic guessing game*, positioning alphabetic knowledge as the last resort for the inexperienced reader, undermined prevailing practices in remedial reading and spoke directly to teachers (Goodman 1970). This new alignment was reinforced by a growing interest in *Reading Recovery* as a programme, which offered an evidence-based, proven and acceptable alternative for young, failing readers. At last it seemed that psychologists and teachers were speaking the same language and the uncomfortable disjuncture between curriculum values and the prescripts of psychology could be put to rest.

From this broad theoretical base, the so-called 'whole-language' or 'language-experience' movement grew up, with strong advocacy from teacher trainers, advisers and the English teaching community. Enthusiasm developed for reading 'real books', modelling and 'apprenticeship learning' and the teaching of reading strategies largely derived from the approaches set out in the *Reading Recovery* programme and, above all, reading for meaning. At the same time great emphasis was laid on the role of parents through projects such as PACT (Parents and Teachers and Children) derived from successful action research projects and the beginnings of 'family literacy' with its roots in school-based adult education (Tizard and Hughes 1984). There was a widespread movement away from using single reading schemes to structure progression in favour of levelled or 'banded' provision which grouped books from a variety of schemes along with other non-scheme texts to expand the range of books available to children at each level. Protagonists of 'whole language' theories such as Meek (1982), Waterland (1985), Holdaway (1979) and Wade (1979) were influential and their books appeared regularly in reading lists in teachers' centres and university departments of education.

Smith and Goodman's work was based on detailed reviews of existing research and strongly influenced by the psycho-linguistic theory of Chomsky and others. The psycho-linguistic influences on their work make very important contributions to understanding literacy which remain highly relevant, as we argue in Chapter 2. Other research was observational and action-based; some was more anecdotal and impressionistic – none passed muster at the doors of experimental psychologists. But nor was it anything like the nonsense it was later portrayed to be. Much of it, including the emphasis given to reading for meaning, motivation, reading response, quality texts, active learning, and the importance of developing self-monitoring and self-correction strategies, was fundamentally important to successful literacy development and remains so today.

Nevertheless, whole-language theories fell prey to two major faults. Firstly, as we argue in Chapter 2, Smith and Goodman were wrong, in fact, about the place and importance of alphabetic knowledge both in early learning and for experienced readers. Secondly, the recommended practices of whole-language theorists were hard to follow without very detailed training, and only a small minority of teachers did anything that resembled them in their classrooms. Most, for example, had never heard of guided reading and virtually no teachers beyond the first year of schooling engaged children in shared reading. When, in 1997, Ofsted set about making a video of good practice in teaching literacy, entitled *Literacy Matters*, inspectors had to scour the country in search of examples of shared and guided reading. There was virtually no evidence, outside of the NLP, that schools used any of these approaches.

But, as critics were quick to point out, reading standards across the country were too low and there was evidence that they were falling in some areas (Turner 1994). In 1996, the same year as the publication of Ofsted's critical report, a campaign of swingeing criticism was mounted by the right-wing Centre for Policy Studies, with considerable support from Ofsted's chief inspector, Chris Woodhead, and an assembled posse of psychologists, lobby groups, right-wing newspapers and assorted promoters of commercial phonics programmes. The attack was led by Martin Turner and Tom Burkard. In a paper entitled *Reading Fever: why phonics must come first*, they catalogued what they described as 'the astonishingly destructive phenomenon of Whole Language policies', even criticizing the National Curriculum for having the temerity to mention the word 'stories' nine times in the first three levels of Attainment Target 2. In a single dismissive sweep of everything that had gone before they claimed:

> Essentially, the tenets of the Whole Language movement have been that language cannot be split up into pieces, that learning to recognize words out of context offends against the wholeness of the text, and that top-down processes moving from the comprehension of the whole to deciding what individual words might be, placing meaning at the centre of the enterprise, are of paramount importance. Such an emphasis upon hallucination rather than evidence readily identifies itself as belonging to the intellectual milieu of the late 1960s.
>
> (Turner and Burkard 1996: 7)

The final sentence is telling. Not only was this an attack on whole-language theories but a wholesale attack on primary school ideology and anyone of a more liberal persuasion who supported it. Phonics teaching was aligned with old-fashioned values of discipline, simplicity and drill, and chimed well with Prime Minister John Major's electoral 'back to basics' mantra. Turner and Burkard's polemical and dismissive tone gave them a spurious authority, especially since most teachers were too ill-informed about phonics to answer back. But there was justice in the criticism. Whole-language theorists were equally ideological, guilty of ignoring phonics and in denial about the growing weight of psychological evidence in its favour. Out of this critique, alongside similarly hard-line positions in the US, grew an uncompromising movement who were to be satisfied with nothing less than total victory for a reductionist agenda. They have not gone away.

For many teachers, the dispute had few immediate consequences. Practices in most schools bore little resemblance to either of the contested paradigms, though the posturing of the opposing camps, like noises off, contributed to a growing sense of professional ill-being.

On the positive side, there were increasing numbers of successful literacy initiatives, though they were widely dispersed through individual projects, and driven by the efforts of particular individuals. The *Literacy Initiative from Teachers*

(LIFT) project, based on successful practice in New Zealand schools, begun in the borough of Westminster and extended into other areas of London, was one example. *First Steps*, a comprehensive approach to teaching reading and writing from Western Australia was becoming established in several areas. *Success for All* from the US was being trialled and *Reading Recovery* was well established in several local authorities with a strong national network and positive benefits for mainstream practice. The work of the inner London *Centre for Language in Primary Education* (CLPE) had been effective and highly influential. A very successful teaching assistant programme, *Talking Partners,* had been set up in Bradford, parental involvement schemes such as *PACT* were multiplying; and, of course, numerous phonics programmes including *Jolly Phonics*, the *Essex Reading Project* and *Best Practice Phonics* were gaining attention. There was growing evidence of success around most of these initiatives. Additionally, there were many gifted and highly successful individuals working as trainers, teachers and school leaders.

In general, however, literacy teaching, along with literacy standards, were on a plateau and neither was good enough. With the exceptions of reading literature to classes and class introductions to creative writing lessons, whole-class teaching was rare in the literacy curriculum. It was often perceived as passive transmission teaching, while interactive learning required individual or small group tutoring. Classroom organization reflected this, with children seated in groups, sometimes with a variety of curriculum subjects running concurrently between the groups. Data from the earlier ORACLE study showed that, although children sat in groups, they actually worked individually and collaborative group work was uncommon (Galton *et al.* 1980). Furthermore, the teacher rarely worked with a group but was more likely to patrol the class, selectively supporting and praising individuals, or to sit at a desk with a queue of children waiting to see her. Children's interaction with each other, on a curriculum focus, was negligible and interaction with the teacher was just a few minutes a day. Teachers spent on average 78 per cent of their day interacting with pupils, whereas pupils spent on average 85 per cent of their day working individually. It was inefficient and stressful. Subsequent school effectiveness research and reports from HMI confirmed these findings (Mortimore *et al.* 1988). While awareness of these issues was growing, it was a nettle many schools seemed unable to grasp.

For most schools, progress and standards in reading were determined by children's passage through levels defined by the school's book bands or reading scheme. It was common to find teachers' day-to-day assessments driven mainly by these criteria. Teaching reading generally amounted to hearing individual readers, and monitoring and recording their progress in relation to how much they had read. In 1997, the School Curriculum and Assessment Authority (SCAA) and Ofsted estimated that schools allocated between 22 and 25 per cent of their time to the teaching of English. Even so, it was estimated that, in a class of 30 children, each child was likely to spend only three to five minutes a week being directly taught by their teacher. Though regular daily reading sessions were timetabled, for the most part, children read independently, to make time for the teacher to monitor individual progress. In the early years, this usually meant trying to hear them every day. As they became 'independent readers', the teacher's support often diminished to make more time available for hearing slower readers. Hearing readers could become a stressful occupation for teachers who had to manage the rest of the class while they did it, and many invested additional hours beyond the timetable in breaks, at lunchtime or after school.

The emphasis on individual teaching also encouraged a growth in the use of exercises, worksheets, comprehension programmes, 'listening posts' (taped stories with accompanying texts) and increasing use of IT-based activities mainly to learn spellings or complete cloze-type exercises. Many slower readers would also receive extra support from an additional teacher or teaching assistant. Teachers invariably devoted regular time each week to reading quality texts aloud to their classes, though these seldom took the form of shared text work. A generation of authors, publishers and teachers had ensured that teachers had up-to-date information about an extensive and high quality range of children's picture books and more extended fiction, via oranizations like the National Centre for Language and Literacy, Centre for Language in Primary Education, Thimble Press, Meek (1982) and Baddeley and Eddershaw (1994). Almost all schools took the business of creating a positive reading environment seriously, though school book resources varied widely, depending on where head teachers had set their financial priorities. A wealth of good reading material was available and the majority of schools had libraries or library areas of some kind.

The teaching of writing had also settled into a widespread pattern. Most non-fiction writing tended to be 'piggy-backed' on other subjects in an over-crowded curriculum. It often took the form of practice with little explicit teaching about how to write non-fiction texts. There was also a strong commitment to teaching creative writing and a common practice was to devote at least one lesson per week to extended story writing with the whole class, in which the teacher would set children a topic or provide a stimulus introducing it with discussion, sometimes brainstorming or helping the class to generate word lists, story openings or outline writing plans. Following an introduction, children would be set to work individually while the teacher supported, encouraged and cajoled. At the end of the lesson, work would be collected and marked, sometimes with the children but usually away from them, and then returned with comments and corrections. This process was depicted in the introduction to *Grammar for Writing* as follows:

the teacher prepares and stimulates ideas for the class

↓

the children write independently

↓

the teacher responds e.g. discusses, marks etc.

Setting the sequence out in this simplified way is revealing. It shows how the teaching of writing can easily be reduced to teaching by correction – teaching after the event – instead of *at the point of writing* … most of the direct teaching is focused on stimulating ideas and preparing … to write while [the child] is left to compose i.e. to draft and revise his own work after which the teacher proofreads and corrects it for him.

(DfEE 2000a: 11)

The twin difficulties with this process were (a) that no one was actually teaching children how to compose and structure texts and (b) that the process of marking inevitably produced a random list of problems and errors which, because of the unsystematic way in which they occurred, left little or no scope to learn from experience. Many children, especially boys, were recycling their own difficulties and failing to progress. A more fundamental difficulty with this situation was that, at the time, no one realized how deep these problems were.

There were approximately 200,000 primary school teachers, almost all working as 'class' rather than 'subject' teachers; each taught the whole curriculum. Although every school had a nominated language coordinator to lead the work in literacy, their professional development was often scant and, for most, there was little or no time to work outside their classrooms. In line with this practice, other teachers would have coordinator responsibilities in other subjects – mathematics, science, IT, physical education, art, music etc. – which took them away from literacy and created equal and opposite pressures on the curriculum, alongside literacy. In small schools, the coordinator was sometimes the head teacher and some language coordinators carried responsibility for other subjects as well. As a professional group, language coordinators had no common professional identity, no common sense of purpose and no common basis of practice. Though most teachers made a big commitment of time and effort to literacy, by and large, they got on with the job by themselves making the best of what they had.

There was a general assumption by government and local authorities that, having created a range of promoted posts for subject coordinators, primary schools would assume a devolved curriculum responsibility structure somewhat along the lines of secondary schools though without the same pattern of departments of specialized teaching. Thus, language coordinators, along with head teachers, were highly accountable through the inspection process, though they received little in terms of professional knowledge, resources or time. What made matters worse was that, despite Ofsted's calls for teachers to be 'crystal clear' about the teaching of literacy, along with most others in the profession they were far from clear about what should be going on in primary classrooms. A survey of good practice published by HMI just after the introduction of the National Curriculum, described the situation for reading at the time:

The basic skills of reading and writing continue to receive a great deal of time and attention. The standards achieved are generally good and continue to improve … published reading schemes continue to be widely used throughout the primary age range … the selection and use of such schemes tends to be more discriminating than at the time of the (1978) Primary Survey … As children become less dependent on schemes they read more widely from good quality fiction and make more use of non-fiction material … Most children have good literature presented to them by their teachers … but the prominence given to literature varies widely. Few schools have consistent policies which ensure that children receive a suitably broad and balanced experience of good literature, including poetry, from year to year.

(DES 1990)

Clearly, too little was known about the place and teaching of phonic skills and many teachers, even some of those inclined to the teaching of phonics, had grown up with the belief that they should not be doing it. Basic reading strategies including word level skills, practice to improve accuracy and fluency, self-monitoring and correction were often untaught, and the comprehension skills of inference, evaluation, information search and retrieval, though acknowledged as important higher level skills, were not defined or systematically taught in the majority of schools. Ofsted's criticism of the professional learning opportunities in the three London authorities, that 'there was little to suggest systematic provision for the development of individual teachers' (Ofsted 1996b: §93), could be applied equally to the national picture. So too could its description of typical practices in the 45 inner London schools:

The National Curriculum programme of study for reading indicates the range of knowledge, skills and activities which should be part of the reading process. Yet, despite the generous allocation of time given to reading, few schools came close to covering the entire programme of study. In particular, insufficient attention was paid to phonic work … to the development of reading beyond the early stages; and to broadening the range of texts beyond narrative fiction.

(Ofsted 1996b: §15)

Nor was England exceptional. Similar patterns of literacy teaching were common in other English-speaking countries. While the NLP and NLS were evolving, issues were surfacing in Australia, New Zealand and the United States with numerous initiatives being developed to address them (Earl, Watson and Katz 2003). What emerged both here and abroad were two predictable and widespread problems.

First, there were serious weaknesses in teachers' knowledge about language at every linguistic level. Knowledge about word and sub-word structure was scant. Phonics was the most obvious example because it had hit the spotlight, but understanding was equally limited in relation to spelling conventions and their relationship with the morphological, etymological characteristics of words. Few teachers had more than a passing acquaintance with grammar, which most had never been taught, and there was little systematic understanding about text range, genre or text types.

Second, despite the existence of successful practice, there were few commonly agreed teaching strategies through which essential literacy skills and knowledge could be imparted. The common practice of individualized teaching pushed teachers into monitoring and managing reading rather than teaching literacy. It was embedded in English primary schools, reinforced by tradition, school organization and parental expectations, and bound up with wider primary school ideologies from the past. It pervaded the teaching of mathematics in a similar way and had its roots in earlier child-centred practices dating back to the Plowden Report (DES 1967). But, for most teachers, ideology was not the great determinant of individualized teaching that critics believed. What drove individualized teaching in most schools was the more mundane, practical and financial investments they had made in commercial reading schemes with individualized readers. The schemes themselves had a variety of rationales reflecting reading theory as far back as the 1950s. Some were based on word recognition, some on rather poor phonics and some enshrined the principles of the much older 'sentence methods'. Publishers had a habit of face-lifting and re-marketing schemes over decades. So long as they sold to a relatively uncritical profession, they continued to be produced. Teachers, for the most part, did not read the teachers' manuals; they just used the individual reading books and had little idea about what, if any, theoretical ideas informed the scheme. Schemes were expensive and money was tight; once bought, teachers were bound to use them, for better or worse.

The broader primary education scenario was also changing rapidly and, by the mid-1990s, research on classroom practice and school improvement (e.g. Galton *et al.* 1980, Mortimore *et al.* 1988, Alexander 1991) was well established and becoming very influential. The publication of a DES-commissioned national discussion paper, 'The Three Wise Men' report (Alexander *et al.* 1992), drew public attention to the weaknesses of individualized teaching. Comparison with much more instructional practices in other countries, in eastern Europe and the Pacific Rim, was generating concern at the economic as well the educational consequences, and starting to revitalize the concepts of whole-class teaching and instructional methods. The primary profession was increasingly aware of the debate but poorly placed to respond to it. It was becoming clear to everyone that, without a national initiative to challenge and support teachers, change on the scale expected would be impossible.

The Literacy Task Force drew on all this evidence. Most importantly, it drew attention to the state of literacy standards. Though data was imprecise, already there was some evidence that standards had become stuck with little upward trend and that in some areas they may have been falling. Standards of adult literacy were a growing cause for concern in a fast-changing knowledge economy, and international evidence on reading standards in schools showed that:

> Britain is out-performed by a group of countries (e.g. Finland, United States, Sweden, France, Italy, New Zealand, Norway) and is located within a 'middle' group (including Germany, The Netherlands, Ireland, Belgium, Spain etc.) which, in turn is ahead of a 'bottom' group (including Indonesia and Venezuela).

> Most disturbing in international studies is evidence of the existence of a 'long tail' in the results among British schools, since performance of lower ability children is substantially below that of other countries.
>
> (Literacy Task Force 1997: §21)

National tests for English were in the early stages of introduction. They had not become such high-stakes expectations as they are today. In 1995, the number of children achieving level 4 or above in reading stood at 48 per cent. By the following year it had leapt to 57 per cent. However, with an ambition to reach 80 per cent by 2002 and then go further there was, as Barber said, no room for complacency.

The case was persuasive; everyone agreed literacy was the top priority. By 1997, in the run up to the election, there was a welcome degree of political agreement about the need to challenge schools through some kind of national strategy. There was a shared ambition to raise standards, and reliable evidence showing that it could be done. On the schools' side, there was much good practice to draw on, growing frustration with their critics and a real concern among the majority about how to improve standards. Schools had learned to live with pressure from Ofsted and expected it to continue but they were also cautiously optimistic about the prospect of political change and a new professional deal to support improvement. For schools, it was a tough but propitious moment.

Stepping up to the challenge

On 13 May 1997, David Blunkett, Labour's new Secretary of State for Education, announced the target:

> Last year, only 55 per cent of our 11 year olds finishing their crucial primary school years reached the standard expected for their age. In English tests, only 57 per cent could read at the same standard. These are weaknesses in absolutely basic skills at vital moments in the lives of our children – and we must tackle them. That's why, today, I am announcing that by the time of the national tests in 2002:
>
> • 75 per cent of 11 year olds will be reaching the standards expected for their age in maths, and;
>
> • 80 per cent will be reaching the standards expected for their age in English.
>
> No one should doubt now that we mean business when we say 'Education, Education, Education'; and that behind that determination is 'Standards, Standards, Standards' … All the international indicators are that we are too far behind our competitors in the three R's. The place to start the recovery is in our primary schools. We are confident that teachers everywhere, who have this future in their hands, will join with us in rising to this challenge.
>
> (Press release, Statement by Secretary of State,
> Department for Education and Employment, 13 May 1997)

By the start of the election campaign, in March 1997, the Literacy Task Force had been on the case for almost a year and were well prepared with policy proposals ready to 'hit the ground running' as soon as the government was elected. The moral case was clear, ambitious and unassailable:

> … we need to begin to take the term **basics** literally and to design an education system which ensures that all children are taught to read well by the age of eleven. Put another way, the education service should do whatever it takes to make this possible. This is the first step towards the creation of a truly literate nation and a pre-requisite of a learning society.
>
> (Literacy Task Force 1997: §4)

The government was embarking on the biggest school improvement programme anywhere in the world – affecting 150 local authorities, 18,500 primary schools, approximately 200,000 teachers working with almost three million children. In Barber's words, 'there was nothing like it on the planet'. The Task Force consulted extensively to ensure that all possible points of view were taken into account and that every problem raised had a response or a solution. There had to be no excuses. There was a strong sense of optimism about the potential to improve based on an extensive review of evidence on:

- national and international comparisons of standards and practices in literacy
- research and inspection evidence on school improvement
- research evidence on teaching, learning and development in language and literacy
- practical evidence of effective teaching strategies and their potential for transfer and system-wide scaling up
- research evidence on large-scale reform, taking account of programmes in other countries, e.g. the Chicago School Reform process, the Learning and Assessment Project in Victoria, Australia, the reform of the New Zealand school system and the focus, within that, on primary school literacy improvement.

On the potential of the NLS proposals the external evaluation team led by Michael Fullan reported:

> Early in our work we commissioned a report about the potential of NLS (Stanovich & Stanovich, 1997). The authors, respected researchers in this field, were quite impressed with the NLS Framework. In particular, they were impressed with those sections of The Implementation of the National Literacy Strategy dealing with educational research and practice. 'Overall', they concluded, 'we find that there is much to admire in the NLS document and very little with which to quibble'. Noting the controversy – even acrimony – in current debates about the teaching of literacy, the authors judge the firm stand and strong advocacy for best practices taken in the document to be '… a bold,

but necessary, step for achieving the ambitious goals the task force has outlined'. They point to the careful wording of the document that, from their perspective, 'reflects a sensitivity to the research literature that is rare in policy documents of this type'.

(Earl *et al.* 2000: 33)

Towards the end of 1996 Michael Barber met with Peter Hill who, at the time, was directing the Victoria Early Literacy Project in Australia. Internationally, this was closest in structure and approach to the proposals for the NLS. Hill was confident, on the basis of his evidence and experience of managing change in the State of Victoria, that the NLS plan could scale up and work nationally. By May 1997, it was agreed that the NLP would to be revised and transformed into a national strategy to be renamed National Literacy Strategy. In July 1997, David Blunkett, the new Secretary of State published the first White Paper of the new government. It set out six big policy principles designed to drive the changes that were to be axiomatic in the development of the NLS:

1. Education will be at the heart of government
2. Policies will be designed to benefit the many, not just the few
3. Standards matter more than structures
4. Intervention will be in inverse proportion to success
5. There will be zero tolerance for under-performance
6. Government will work in partnership with all those committed to raising standards.

(DfEE 1997b)

The White Paper formalized the intention to place raising standards of literacy and numeracy at the forefront of education policy and announced its intention to introduce a National Literacy Strategy. By August of the same year, an outline structure and implementation strategy for the NLS was set out in the final report of the Literacy Task Force (1997). The NLS would have three major elements:

• a framework for teaching – setting out the range and progression of literacy learning
• an agreed and common repertoire of generic teaching methodologies based on good practice and embedded in a daily Literacy Hour
• a national entitlement programme of professional development for every primary teacher up to and beyond 2002.

The NLS would be designed to challenge and support *all* schools, not just those with evident weaknesses. No one was excepted, including those monitoring and supporting schools in local authorities and those who trained them in colleges and universities. Even Ofsted, who sat in judgement of literacy standards, would be expected to improve its capacity and raise its sights. The first challenge would be to get everyone on board and continue improving the weakest; the greater challenge was to raise the performance of the majority of schools from average to good. Average, as then defined, would not be good enough to meet the new expectations.

The introduction of the Strategy was supported by a further range of measures, designed to answer concerns that schools raised and demonstrate that the government's support would be real. In January 1998 some of the National Curriculum requirements were relaxed to meet objections that there was too much pressure on curriculum time to cope with the demands of the NLS. Statutory orders outside the core subjects of English, mathematics, science and IT could be treated with greater flexibility. Advice from the Secretary of State told schools that they did not have to deliver all the statutory requirements of the other five foundation subjects, but that they should 'have regard for them' in the planning and organization of the curriculum. Additional funding was allocated to schools to meet objections that there were too few resources. Time was given for teachers to undertake the training with an additional national school closure day for school-based training. Detailed negotiations were put in hand with publishers and the Publishers' Association to advise on the new expectations schools would need to meet, encourage the rapid production of resources in shortage areas and make adjustments to existing copyright agreements that were inhibiting the use of texts and extracts for shared reading. A number of other important promises of support were made and kept, including the reduction of class sizes, major increases in teaching assistant posts to support teachers in classrooms, improved leadership development, a proper career structure to recognize expert teachers with associated rewards, more investment in school buildings and resources. There were to be no obstacles and no excuses.

As a further important backdrop to the implementation by schools, the government designated the school year 1998–9 a National Year of Reading. Using £50 million of lottery money, it aimed to launch the Literacy Strategy by setting it in the wider context of promoting lifelong learning, to encourage 'all of us to become more creative and practised readers' and to 'kick-start a transforming process which will continue to the millennium and beyond' (DfEE 1998a). The National Year of Reading addressed other concerns frequently voiced by schools that changes in teaching had to be backed up by changes in public awareness and attitudes. Funds were used to promote reading-related activities by individuals and groups across the country, celebrities were recruited to promote reading and improve its image among traditionally reluctant groups. The NLS, particularly the concept of the Literacy Hour, was woven into TV soap opera scripts; there was a growth in book-sharing activities, e.g. volunteer reading support in schools and elsewhere; badges and logos were produced and associated with popular products; national and local reading events, competitions and celebrations were sponsored. There were powerful messages to the public about the importance of literacy, the government's commitment, the need to support children at home, and the Literacy Hour in schools. A national 'read me' logo was incorporated into a wide range of popular products, while industry and commerce were encouraged to sponsor competitions, events and a variety of literacy resources for schools. The National Year of Reading would:

> ... highlight the ways in which parents, employers, school and local authority libraries and community organizations can contribute to raising literacy standards. The parents' contributions will be firmly linked to the work of schools through our proposals for home-school contracts and homework guidelines.
>
> (DfEE 1998a: §29)

With the big strategic decisions – targets, structure, funds, incentives, timetable – settled, we set out to generate the details of a *Framework for Teaching*, the Literacy Hour and the national professional development programme, with less than a year to the implementation deadline in September 1998. Our primary purpose was to avoid the pitfalls of aligning with either side in the 'reading wars', by creating a programme which incorporated and integrated the strengths of each side. Theoretically, this was an entirely justified approach and strongly aligned with the evidence of success in literacy teaching. Despite the recent upsurge of political interest in 'back to basics' and 'phonics first', it remains so today, not least because it incorporates these word level principles into a broader theoretical framework which recognizes the scope of literacy learning, acknowledges its logical connection with values and the curriculum, and cultivates the vital propensity of learners to make sense of the world, work things out for themselves and render their experience meaningful and predictable. Teachers and children deserve the best of both worlds. In the next chapter we discuss this rationale in detail and return to it, in various ways, in subsequent chapters. Not surprisingly it has been a continuing theme.

The issue of whole language versus phonics-first had to be managed with care. It was essential to bring colleagues of differing persuasions together in the interests of teachers and children. Disagreement and ideological back-biting had been festering in the academic community for too long and its impact on primary schools was destructive. We would have little chance of successful implementation if these differences could not be resolved into a broad and credible approach that won support from teachers and offered real-time practical solutions. Imposing a detailed programme of phonics-first teaching on the system at a stroke was clearly no solution. Previous attempts to do this through consultations on earlier drafts of the National Curriculum had met with huge resistance, alienating thousands of teachers. Over-riding all the differences, however, was the necessary and derivative connection between the NLS and the statutory national curriculum which, itself, following widespread consultation had settled on a similarly comprehensive view about the teaching of literacy. Alignment with these national standards and programmes of study was not negotiable.

The NLS in common with other large-scale reform programmes had to run on parallel tracks. One track focused on the specifics of literacy teaching and school improvement with all the associated knowledge, research and controversy surrounding this. A second, more strategic track concerned the wider political and tactical issues of: how to implement; what was likely to work with the profession; what might and might not scale up and transfer; how to condense complexity into sharp, simple, common messages that everyone, including the press, can understand; how to balance the need for short-term 'wins' essential for the maintenance of political focus and momentum with longer term, sustainable improvement; how to evolve and 'learn as you go' without moving the goal posts. These are two necessary realms of knowledge that must be brought together for any effort of this kind to succeed. Neither is sufficient on its own. To be intelligently strategic everyone has to set their personal convictions and ideologies alongside the more pragmatic need for balance and compromise to join in common cause and get the job done. It was never going to be simple.

In the following chapters we examine these parallel tracks. Chapters 2–5 focus on the rationale and content of the NLS, while Chapters 6–8 examine its implementation. In Chapter 9 we have attempted to summarize the very considerable impact of the NLS on schools and standards, while Chapter 10 offers a more subjective perspective on where we have been and where we might be going.

Chapter 2

About learning

The most fundamental aspect of the NLS is its rationale. What it says about the nature of literacy learning is therefore at the heart of everything else it does. From the outset, this was based on the principles of active learning and autonomy and self-extending competence for children. The rationale was captured very simply for teachers in the introduction to the NLS *Framework for Teaching* and incorporated a diagrammatic metaphor of four searchlights. What it did not do was to articulate the rationale in detail and, on reflection, that was probably an error, because it led to misinterpretation and left the Framework something of a hostage to fortune at the hands of a few very vocal critics. In this chapter, we have set out the thinking behind the searchlights and their justification. Despite recent revisions to the Framework and the criticism of this metaphor, we continue to believe it is relevant and helpful as a foundation for the teaching of reading and writing across the primary age range.

The principle of active learning

The National Literacy Strategy (NLS) is founded on the widely accepted assumption that human cognition and learning are active. In the context of primary education, the notion of active learning is rooted in the work of Piaget, whose influence was formative in shaping ideas about the nature of learning and teaching. The theory was attractive to teachers because of its constructivist emphasis on the active role of the learner. However, it failed to recognize the enormous impact of social and cultural values in driving and shaping individual development. As critics were quick to point out, the very notion of development is inherently prescriptive. The concept of 'child development' in education means more than mere change; it is shot through with values. We distinguish development from mere change by implying a movement towards desirable ends, which can only be justified by reference to values. Despite the fact that much of Piaget's detailed theory has been superseded, his account of learning as active remains important and is a central precept in the NLS for two reasons. First, the principle is ethically justified. Active learning should be promoted because it develops desirable attitudes to learning such as imaginative and critical awareness, understanding and respect, appreciation, and self-extending competence. These values form part of the agreed National Curriculum which schools are expected to implement. Second, there is strong evidence and argument to show that effective learning is, as a matter of fact, both active and constructive.

Piaget saw the growth of intelligence as a process of development analogous to biological adaptation. Children, he said, construct and adapt schemas, internalized systems of expectations that we use to make sense of experience. Karl Popper made a similar point in relation to the development of scientific knowledge which, he argued, grows from the interaction between conjectures and refutations, i.e. imaginative leaps of mind to generate hypotheses, which are then subjected to systematic testing in an effort to disconfirm the hypothesis. The extent to which any hypothesis cannot be refuted, he argued, is a measure of the confidence we can have in it as a true account of the world. The human mind is not a bucket waiting to be filled with facts, concepts and theories from the outside, so to speak. The mind is better likened to a searchlight that is constantly expecting, guessing, predicting against a background of expectations from which we project sense onto the world.

> At every instant in our scientific and pre-scientific development, we are living at the centre of what I usually call a horizon of expectations. By this I mean the sum total of our expectations whether these are sub-conscious or conscious or perhaps even explicitly stated in some language … The various horizons of expectation differ of course, not only in their being more or less conscious but also in their content. Yet in all these cases, the horizon of expectations plays the part of a frame of reference: only their setting in this frame confers meaning or significance on our experiences actions and observations.
>
> (Popper 1972: 345)

Miller *et al.* (1970: 5) put a similar point in more everyday terms:

> Consider how an ordinary day is put together. You awaken, and as you lie in bed, or perhaps move slowly about in a protective shell of morning habits, you think about what the day will be like – it will be hot, it will be cold; there is too much to do, there is nothing to fill the time; you promised to see him, she may be there again today … whether it is crowded or empty, novel or routine, your day will have a structure of its own – it fits into the texture of your life. And, as you think about what your day will hold, you construct a plan to meet it. *What you expect to happen foreshadows what you expect to do.* [our italics]
>
> (Miller *et al.* 1970: 5)

Children and adults strive to make sense of their experience, to render the world predictable and bring it under control. Many children, through their early experiences and subsequent schooling, turn this propensity to productive use. Through a combination of instruction and experience, they assimilate new ideas and skills by refining and adapting their understanding and expectations. As they do this, they increase their potential to learn more and so progress and succeed. Other children for a variety of reasons, most often to do with their prior experience, appear experience, appear less active, reluctant to learn and fail to benefit from school. For example, failing children in the classrooms described by John Holt (1969) use different strategies for bringing the world under control. They learn that school is often unpredictable and brings risks of failure. Their lives are less certain and more insecure so they opt for strategies that keep them out of trouble. It is more predictable and thus safer to know you will fail than to think you might or might not succeed. These students say *Yes* when the teacher says *Do you understand?*; they wave their hands when the teacher asks the class a question because they guess they are less likely to be asked; if they are asked, they repeat the question and hesitate until the teacher, impatient to see them succeed, gives them enough clues or tells them the answer; they will choose to wait in a queue at the teacher's desk for help with spelling to avoid facing the challenge of the task, and so on. These children are not passive but they have put a different construction on schools and learning, one that frequently manifests itself noticeably and early in failure to learn reading and writing.

The theoretical basis of the NLS

The National Literacy Strategy is focused on the learning and teaching of reading *and* writing. Although there is a substantial body of research on writing, theories of literacy tend to cluster more around the psychological research on reading, where there is controversy about theories of learning and even greater controversy about implications for teaching. We referred to disagreements about teaching in Chapter 1 and will return to the teaching of reading and writing in Chapter 4. Broadly speaking, there are three stories about learning to read and, by implication, about learning to write. The first two, aligned with the more polarized 'whole language' and 'phonics-first' models of teaching, are well known. These are commonly characterized as 'top-down' and 'bottom-up' theories. Both have been shown, for different and opposite reasons, to be invalid but both emphasize crucially important aspects of literacy development.

Top-down theories, espoused by Frank Smith and Kenneth Goodman, were widely influential in the teaching of reading and writing in England over the 25-year period from 1970 to 1995. The burden of the arguments was more pedagogical than psychological. They characterized the fluent reader as an active hypothesis tester who worked out words as he proceeded through the text by sampling visual information in order to test hypotheses, about what words meant.

> Readers have non-visual information about the choices available to an author, and make full use of their knowledge to reduce their own uncertainty about what successive words might be ... In other words, the reader knows so much that for every letter the author supplies, the reader can provide the next himself, without even looking.
>
> (Smith 1997: 24–5)

Thus, when reading unfamiliar words:

> The first alternative and preference is to skip over the puzzling word. The second alternative is to guess what the unknown word might be. And the final and least preferred alternative is to sound the word out. Phonics, in other words comes last, and with good reason, for phonics is the least efficient choice.
>
> (Smith 1997: 54)

Smith sees reading as driven by higher level conceptual processes rather than the more atomic processes of grapho-phonic associations. As we noted in Chapter 1, the attraction and persuasiveness of this account to teachers is obvious. It fits comfortably with the active account of learning, it rejects highly didactic rote teaching which is what a lot of phonics teaching consisted of, and it promotes a rich, creative and motivating experience with 'real books' which is worthwhile in its own right and much to be desired.

The problems with this theory are well rehearsed. There is now sufficient evidence to show that, as Adams puts it, 'the single immutable and non-optional fact about skilful reading is that it involves relatively complete processing of the individual letters of print' (Adams 1990: 105). In fact it seems that one of the characteristics of fluent readers reading relatively simple texts, is that they depend to a lesser extent on these higher level processes for decoding words, which they recognize automatically, than less fluent readers (Stanovich 1980). What is also true, however, is that skilled reading, because it is so automatic at the word decoding level, is highly dependent on readers' response and interpretation and that higher order cognitive processes are vital to success.

Bottom-up theories take the opposite view. They give much less weight to the effects of higher level processes and focus on the necessity for fluent reading of getting the micro-processes learned and habituated. These theories assume that reading and writing are comprised of a hierarchy of skills of which the smallest bit, i.e. the spellings and phonemes, are the fundamental parts. Everything must be built up on them. On the face of it, it seems reasonable to argue that speaking and writing are the result of a relatively simple chaining i.e. think of the first word, then the second, then the third and so on, such that each word, spoken or written, forms the basis on which the next is generated.[1] What is true for speaking and writing would also be true for listening and reading i.e. hear or decode word 1 then word 2 and so on, until you have heard a phrase, then a sentence and the meaning will be complete. By working across the page, as it were, we aggregate up the levels until we have a word, then a sentence and then, by 'listening to what we have read', switch on our comprehension machinery to understand the text.

Chaining such as this would imply that the structure of meaning and grammar is sequential but we know that this is not the case. Miller and colleagues, drawing on earlier work on generative grammar by Chomsky, show why this cannot be so. They

---

1   This can become a serious problem in children's writing; because their writing skills are too slow, they are driven back to thinking about what to write on the basis of what word comes next which often produces very poor composition and is a major inhibitor of writing progress – see Chapter 4 for a more detailed discussion.

identify two lines of argument 'to dissuade one from using a left-to-right model of the sentence planner'. The first shows that it is impossible to *learn* a language in this way. Because the left/right 'planner' relies on a grammar that says 'having produced the words *x* up to this point, you must continue by selecting from the set *y*'. To learn this, a child would need to hear all of the rules for generating acceptable sentences at least once, i.e. which words could acceptably follow which other words in sentences of up to, say, 20 words long. They go on to show that this hypothesis is ridiculous by calculating that 'a child would have to hear about 3×10^{20} sentences per second in order to be exposed to all the information necessary for the planner to produce sentences according to these left-to-right rules of grammar', and this would take about 100 years with no interruptions for eating or sleeping (Miller *et al.* 1970: 147).

They also demonstrate that many common sentences are impossible to generate by a simple left-to-right grammar. For example, in complex sentences, clauses can be 'nested' within clauses potentially ad infinitum. The grammatical dependencies even in relatively straightforward sentences such as *The man who said 'I quit' thought it might rain tomorrow*, reach across the sentence. They can be neither constructed nor understood by applying a simple chaining grammar because the interpretation of prior words depends on words or phrases that follow, not just on those that immediately precede them. What is true at the level of sentences is also true of words, e.g. *scan, scene, scent*.

The hierarchical complexity of language is evident at every level in listening, speaking, reading and writing. Our capacity to blend sounds into words is governed largely by our awareness of what is permissible in pronounced English and by the extent of our vocabularies. It is faster and easier to decode words rapidly if, in the process of decoding them, we recognize them as words. Similarly, recognized words will be read and understood much more efficiently if they are parts of syntactically recognizable phrases of sentences, and sentences are read more intelligently and rapidly when they form part of a predictable or engaging text. Adams, in her extensive review of research into the learning and teaching of reading, while re-emphasising the importance of phonics and spelling, makes a similar point.

> Each of these sorts of knowledge and skills is a real asset for the skilled reader – all the more if they work in concert rather than displacement of one another. As we shall see, that is in fact how they do work. The force of the theory and research … is that they operate in parallel. Depending on the situation, they operate in dominance, complement or deference to each other. Such coordination is possible because they are commonly anchored in the knowledge and processes involved in individual letter recognition.
>
> (Adams 1990: 105–6)

The process of writing demonstrates the integrated and simultaneous relationships that must obtain between each of these sources of knowledge even more clearly. It is common to find children trying to write by a part-to-whole strategy because that is what the process of transcription demands of them. The result is often that the composition breaks down at a variety of levels. It is hard to think out the spelling of a word while remembering the place of the word in the sentence and the purpose of the sentence in the text and the overall structure of the emerging text itself. The syntax of sentences, as we showed above, frequently does not run from left to right, so there are syntactic complexities to be managed that, in turn, have to serve the overall purpose of creating text. Although most texts read from first to last, they too may have structures of meaning which run non-sequentially, or non-chronologically. Writers and readers need to learn to handle all these levels interactively and simultaneously.

The problem with both these kinds of serial-stage models (top-down and bottom-up), as Stanovich points out, is 'that they usually run into difficulty because they contain no mechanism whereby higher level processes can affect lower levels'. He proposed a third class of theories:

> ... formed by those models that posit neither a strictly bottom-up, nor strictly top-down processing but instead assume that a pattern is synthesized based on information provided simultaneously from several knowledge sources (e.g. feature extraction, orthographic knowledge, lexical knowledge, syntactic knowledge, semantic knowledge).
>
> (Stanovich 1980: 22–3)

This is the direction the National Literacy Strategy took. This alternative explanation is conceptually powerful. It takes a variety of forms but the principle remains the same i.e. that successful reading requires us to activate knowledge from a range of sources, inherent in the text by bringing to bear our own knowledge of language and our wider knowledge of the world. These sources are not activated in a sequence but interact in a simultaneous and variable way. The same principle has been modelled in varying ways by Rumelhart (1977), Ehri (1988) and Adams (1990).

The searchlights metaphor

In the NLS we used a simple diagram to show each of the sources of information available for reading and writing and represented them as a system of essential but connected knowledge that readers and writers use in comprehending and composing texts (Figure 2.1).

The diagram illustrates the various linguistic levels that have to be integrated for skilled reading and writing. The sources of information mirror the text, sentence, word and sub-word levels of language used to structure the *Framework for Teaching*. They are also, in a slightly different form, written into the curriculum for the teaching of reading and writing in the mandated English National Curriculum which defines the reading standard for 7-year-olds as follows:

> Pupils' reading of simple texts shows understanding and is generally accurate. They express opinions about major events or ideas in stories, poems and

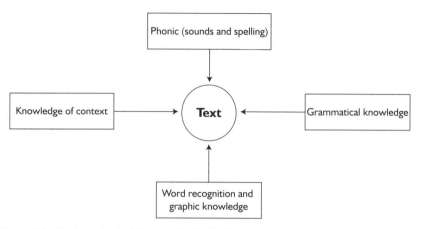

Figure 2.1 The 'searchlights' (Source: DfEE 1998b: 4)

non-fiction. They use more than one strategy, such as phonic, graphic, syntactic and contextual, in reading unfamiliar words and establishing meaning.

(DfE 1995: 19)

The linguistic levels in the diagram are broadly defined as follows:

Contextual information is linked to text level knowledge and includes what individual readers bring to the text, i.e. their prior knowledge of the subject and their expectations of what the text is likely to be about, and their expectations of the type of language typical of the text they are reading. It also includes the meaning of the text prior to the sentence they are reading and the meaning, as far as it can be gleaned, of the sentence in which the word is embedded, the words prior to or following the word under scrutiny, and pictures or other graphics. For skilled readers, context is what enables them to understand authors' intentions, images and inferences.

Grammatical information is linked to sentence level knowledge and includes the reader's knowledge of syntax of the sentence in which the word is embedded and the application of that knowledge to predict or check words that are decoded for sense. For skilled readers, grammatical awareness enables them to read fluently and fast, and also bears on their understanding of text-types, style, language choice and cohesion.

Word recognition and graphic knowledge is linked to word level knowledge and refers to the words which are present in the reader's lexicon and can be identified automatically. Graphic knowledge connects with the overall visual shapes of words and their critical features. For skilled readers, most of this happens quickly and below the level of awareness, releasing more cognitive effort for responding to and comprehending the text.

Phonics is linked to sub-word level knowledge and refers to the decoding of words using knowledge of the alphabetic system at a number of levels: single grapheme to phoneme blending (where a grapheme means a single letter, e.g. 's' or combination of letters to denote a phoneme, e.g. 'sh') and chunking of various sizes: 'str'-'ing', 'l'-'ight', 'men'-'tion'. Phonic knowledge is a way of stepping up to word recognition. Although skilled readers scrutinize each word as they read, they only resort to phonic decoding to help them read unfamiliar words.

For reading, each of the above information sources has a bearing on the comprehension of a text. As Adams (1990) argued, they will bear on comprehension differentially according to the circumstances of the reader's knowledge and skill and what information is available in the text itself, at every level of learning and fluency. We also use the diagram, by inversion, to illustrate the framework of decisions that writers need to make when composing texts. The process of fluent writing involves much fuller knowledge and control than is required for reading because of the need to accurately reproduce and construct a text, as distinct from the relatively easier task of recognizing and understanding a given text.

The special importance of phonics

In broad terms, reading and writing consist of two connected aspects: comprehension and composition on the one hand; word recognition and spelling-plus-transcription on the other. Humans are equipped to produce and comprehend spoken language easily but they are not equipped to process written language so easily. In speech, almost all humans have a natural propensity (learned or given) to process sounds, heard and uttered, directly into meanings. This happens below the level of consciousness, is automatic, fast and readily learned. Written language depends on intervening visual representations of the spoken word, which are conventions specific to particular languages. Children need to learn these conventions explicitly. As they learn, they build an internal lexicon of automatically recognized words. They do this through identifying words and committing them to memory. The identification of words might take a number of forms, for example a child may be told the word, shown a corresponding picture or deduce the word from other contextual features including the grammatical place of the word within the sentence.

The most propitious way of identifying words is by using the orthographic system through which the word is constructed, so that 'the sound structure of words dovetails with graphemes in the spellings of words' (Ehri 1998: 16). The orthographic system in English consists of phonemic and morphemic elements. Growing familiarity with these elements helps readers to become autonomous in two ways. First, it helps them learn new words, as Share (1995) puts it, they become increasingly able to 'self-teach'. Second, by connecting words with similar phonemic or morphemic features schematically, they build up an internal lexicon of remembered words. Reading fluency is built on the reader's ability to identify new words rapidly, and remember and access them automatically when they see them in print. Spelling depends even more heavily on knowledge of, and familiarity with, these sub-word parts. Automatic spelling is essential to writing composition but requires more explicit understanding of sub-word elements, to control and manipulate them explicitly in building words.

It is for these reasons that phonics has a special place in the diagram, and the particular importance of phonics in learning to read English, as opposed to other alphabetic languages, is its relatively complex phonology and orthography. There are about 44 phonemes in English compared with about 36 in French and fewer in Finnish. Also, letter-to-sound and sound-to-letter correspondences are relatively inconsistent in English, with numerous awkward spelling exceptions, some of which children need in the very early stages of reading e.g. *was, the, once*. English orthography, because of its particular conventions and structure, is harder and slower for children to work out for themselves and, reciprocally, harder for teachers to understand and teach. Learning to decode in English requires greater memorization and practice to consolidate and apply than French or Finnish.

This more relativistic account of phonics puts it in perspective. In some languages the sound-to-spelling system is taught quite quickly with a light touch and learned with equal facility. (For example, in Ontario, Canada, children in francophone schools, many of whom do not have very fluent oral French, do well in spelling and writing but poorly in reading. The reasons are not lack of phonics but inadequate oral language skills which impede reading fluency.) The point of learning phonics is to crack the alphabetic code. Other systems have been invented in the past to do the same job; the *Initial Teaching Alphabet* was one such example, and it is possible that there may be new and different ways of teaching decoding in the future. Phonics is an invented, heuristic device and, for word identification in English, it is demonstrably effective. However, there is nothing psychologically fundamental about *phonics*, it is used to help children step up to word recognition, and as an aid to efficient spelling.[2]

As Stanovich has noted:

> … just because phonological awareness enables phonological recoding in beginning reading, it does not follow that this mechanism determines reading ability at all developmental levels. To the contrary, there is a growing body of evidence indicating that there is a developmental trend away from phonologically mediated word recognition in early reading stages toward direct, nonmediated visual access at more advanced stages of reading … It appears that for fluent adults the vast majority of words that are encountered in print are recognized by direct visual access … Phonological information appears to be activated prior to lexical access only for low frequency or very difficult words.
>
> (Stanovich 1986: 375–6)

Basically, by showing how 44 identifiable phonemes can be represented by 26 letters in about 140 common spellings, we can provide children with a powerful and

---

2   Adams (1995: 69) makes the point that the phonemes themselves are not discrete audible sounds in words but have to be invented: '… there is no way that, say, the word *cat* is composed of three separate phonemes except by having somehow learned that it is. The three phonemes in *cat* are audible percepts only because they are such well learned concepts. They are not acoustically discrete. No matter how hard you pay attention, you will not hear them separately, one at a time, unless you think of them separately one at a time.'

reasonably efficient mnemonic – a means to an end. This is a good thing for children to learn because it has been shown to work and, combined with other strategies, such as inference, analogical thinking, generalization and bringing the reader's knowledge of language to bear, early systematic phonics teaching can be readily assimilated, and turned to productive use in the service of word recognition and comprehension, spelling and writing.

Using the diagram above, we depicted the relationship between its parts meta-phorically, as a set of 'searchlights'. The metaphor echoes the underlying commitment to active learning and originates in an image from experiences in John Stannard's childhood:

> I grew up in the second world war, during the 1940s, and lived in a suburban home on the outskirts of London, under the flight-path to Northolt Aerodrome. In those days, during and just after the war, they did not use radar to get the planes down at night; they used searchlights. I remember lying awake listening for the sound of the approaching planes. As they came close, I would hear the sound of its engines. About the same time, a searchlight would begin to sweep its beam across the sky until it picked up the plane, like a small silver cross. This was the main beam from a light at the end of the runway, down which the plane would fly. But the searchlight was not stable, and it was difficult to keep it steadily focused on the plane, especially when the visibility was poor. So as soon as the plane was picked up, a second light would appear from another direction to cross over the first beam and begin to track the plane as it flew down the first beam. Almost simultaneously, a third light was switched on, and sometimes, a fourth, to keep the plane in focus, catching it in the intersection of the lights and bringing it down safely.

This metaphor has also often been called a 'model' but it is not a psychological model. The searchlights were never intended to depict hypothetical mental processes but to describe integrated reading behaviours. Its purpose was pedagogical; it helped us to underline four important and complementary aspects of skilled reading behaviour and their bearing on the process of becoming a reader. It also reinforced the core principles set out in the National Curriculum Programme of Study for English. We used the metaphor to underline a number of important principles for teachers.

The complementary nature of each 'searchlight'

First, we used the metaphor to underline the importance and complementary nature of *each* of the searchlights. Readers and writers at every stage need to access and use all this information. It does not follow, of course, that they need to be able to do this independently at every stage. Chapter 4 discusses how we guided teachers in managing the learning process by 'scaffolding' some aspects while children attended to others, and how children could be helped systematically to bring all this knowledge together in the service of fluent reading and writing. However this is to be done, no part of it can be omitted. There is a logical congruence between the parts because they represent different and integrated levels of written language.

As well as stressing congruence between language levels *within* reading and writing, the metaphor underlines the value of building strong connections *between* reading and writing. For readers, we characterized the levels as searchlights but for writers, they are more akin to decisions. The NLS was designed to capitalize on learning about spelling, sentence construction, text cohesion, style and structure in reading, to help children understand how texts are written. Teaching children to think about reading in these ways also provides many opportunities to use phonics and word recognition in the service of spelling and has a significant impact on the growth of sentence and text knowledge for composition. In learning to write, children need to call up this knowledge and apply it in a coordinated way under much greater control. Because writing requires children to compose and represent ideas it also causes them to reflect on and reconstruct knowledge gained through reading. This process of reconstruction, in turn, helps them to articulate, test, practise and consolidate their knowledge of reading. Reading and writing should make complementary and reciprocal contributions to children's literacy development at every stage. Clay has always stressed the importance of this reciprocity, which has been a strong and productive feature of Reading Recovery Programmes. One senses some frustration in her recent comment that:

> Most theorists in the field of reading acquisition ignore the fact that children are learning and practising writing at the same time. The two literacy activities are kept far apart. Experience with teaching reading and writing together has enabled early intervention teachers to support their most difficult students in important ways.
>
> (Clay 2001: 4)

The principle of redundancy

The second point flows from the first, and applies particularly to reading. The metaphor illustrates the principle of *redundancy*. The more searchlights we switch on, the more 'redundant' each becomes, i.e. it is less critical if it fades or goes out. The metaphor likens reading to a sophisticated process of searching and illustrates how information from different but related sources is used and coordinated to maximize accuracy, speed and comprehension for skilled readers. Rapid, successful reading aims to maximize information by switching on all or as many of the searchlights as possible so that if one is dim, or temporarily goes out, there are others to keep the text in focus, until it comes on again. One of the aims of fluent and comprehending reading, therefore, is to maximize redundancy by switching on as many searchlights as possible in an effort to create a mutually supportive, no-default system. In practice, this means activating all our knowledge of language at every stage and, in the process, extending it at every level too: spelling, vocabulary, grammar, text and general knowledge. To put it another way, redundancy increases reliability. High-reliability systems, like modern day air traffic control systems, have built in fail-safe mechanisms to monitor, provide feedback, resolve uncertainty and self-correct. The term 'orchestration' has also been used – another metaphor that captures this process quite effectively.

In reading development, redundancy operates at different levels for comprehension and word recognition. For skilled readers, who have a wide and automatic word recognition repertoire, the process of reading works much like that of listening. The written representations that skilled readers use, extensively and almost completely, are transparent to them; they see directly to the meanings of words and only resort to breaking words into parts when meeting an unknown word. This may look like a top-down process, because so much of it is automatic – but it isn't. As skilled readers we bring word recognition skills with other prior knowledge about language and the world, to bear on the texts we read. As we read, we regulate the balance of these inputs depending on the simplicity or complexity of the text. If the text contains new words, we may focus explicitly on decoding them, and then check their meanings by reference to the context. If the text is familiar but handwritten and visually unclear, we may rely more on knowledge of syntax, or our assumptions about the purpose or the writer's intentions to supplement the limited visual information. If a phrase or sentence is ambiguous, e.g. ... *they are cooking apples* ... we may use assumptions from other parts of the text to make the correct interpretation, and so on. Sometimes, a text may seem readable, but may still be impenetrably hard to understand, because we lack the necessary knowledge to make sense of it.[3] Mostly, for skilled readers, decisions of this kind are automatic and occur below the level of awareness.

The same principle works at the word level for inexperienced readers. With only a limited word recognition repertoire, they need to focus more of their effort on decoding unfamiliar words. In doing this they are obliged to use grapho-phonemic processes which can be supplemented by knowledge of context and grammar. Stanovich (1980) describes a similar process in terms of an interactive-compensatory model, where information from one source can compensate for absence of information from another. He found that less-skilled readers tend to compensate for limited decoding ability by relying on contextual and syntactic predictions to work out unknown words '*when the context was adequately understood*' [his italics, Stanovich 1980: 59]. There are two major implications to be drawn from Stanovich's research which relate to the searchlight metaphor. First, he found that use of context facilitates reading speed for skilled as well as for less-skilled readers which underlines the importance of the context searchlight at all stages of reading development. Second, he found that poorer readers, although they had inefficient comprehension systems, relied more on contextual information than skilled readers for word identification, thus

---

3   For example, try reading the following:
      'We cannot prove the statement which is arrived at by substituting for the variable in the statement form "we cannot prove the statement that is arrived at by substituting the variable in the statement form *Y* the name of the statement form in question" the name of the statement form in question' (Polanyi 1958: 118). Most fluent readers would need to re-read this many times and probably still have no idea what it means – according to Michael Polanyi, Bertrand Russell took it in at a glance!

compensating for limited decoding skills, which confirms the importance of the phonics searchlight to increase the decoding capability of inexperienced readers.

Tacit knowledge

A third feature of the searchlights metaphor concerns what Michael Polanyi (1969) calls *tacit knowledge*. Knowledge can be of two general kinds: 'knowing that ...' and 'knowing how ...'. The first is sometimes described as propositional knowledge and includes knowledge such as facts and theories. The second refers to skills such as using tools, riding a bicycle or driving a car. Reading and writing are examples of highly specialized skilled performance of the latter kind. They do, of course, involve propositional knowledge, such as conventions, concepts and facts about grammar, language and texts on which readers and writers may draw, but fundamentally, reading and writing are sophisticated *skills*.

Consider the skill of bicycle-riding: a skilled rider knows how to balance, steer, pedal, brake etc. automatically, without thinking. It is this habituated learning that enables him to concentrate on the road. The more skilled and confident a cyclist is at managing the bike, avoiding hazards and negotiating obstacles, the more his attention is freed to think about where he is going, enjoy the scenery, think about what he may do on arrival and so on. If he switches focus to the subsidiary elements, e.g. by looking at what his feet are doing, or how he is steering the machine, like the skilled pianist who suddenly becomes aware of his hands, the skill may start to disintegrate. The music stops; the cyclist falls off the bike. The bicycle and the piano become tools for doing something beyond themselves; they become 'transparent', means to ends, or extensions of the body – we watch the nail when we aim the hammer, not the hand that holds the hammer. These are common features of skilled behaviour, which have special relevance to reading and writing. Polanyi uses an anecdote to illustrate the point:

> My correspondence arrives in various languages ... but my son can only speak English. Having just finished reading a letter, I may wish to pass it on to him, but must check myself and look again to see in what language it was written. I am vividly aware of the meaning conveyed by the letter, yet know nothing of its words. I have attended to them closely but only for what they mean and not for what they are as objects. If my understanding of the text were halting, or its expressions or its spellings were faulty, its words would arrest my attention. They would become slightly opaque and prevent my thought from passing through them unhindered to the things they signify.
>
> (Polanyi 1969: 57)

The effective execution of complex skills lies in the extent to which they can be over-learned so that their subsidiary elements go underground. They are not forgotten but they work automatically in an integrated fashion to enable the skilled performer to focus on the purpose or meaning of the task. Focal awareness is progressively freed to attend to higher levels of meaning in the degree to which the subsidiary elements are internalized and habituated. Reciprocally, the integration and rapid cross-wiring of these subsidiary elements *depends* on our ability to shift attention to the wider horizon of meaning for their integration: 'Keep your eye on the hole, not on the ball', says the golf instructor, 'everything will fall into place'. Thus subsidiary and focal awareness are mutually dependent and interact in the process of learning. Skill learning is neither 'top-down' nor 'bottom-up' in the customary jargon.

The levels of language in our metaphor work in this way for skilled readers and writers. The link between subsidiary and focal awareness is crucial to effective reading and writing and so, by implication, is the way we manage the development of these levels in the process of teaching. The need to do this is evident in the behaviour of children learning to read and write, where the parts have not yet been made subservient to the whole. Thus, when children get stuck on words or read too slowly, their attention is taken to the detail and they fail to grasp the flow or sense of the text. Young writers often struggle to write word by word too slowly and cannot keep a sentence in their heads. They have no 'horizon of expectations' to steer them because all their focal awareness is saturated by the minutiae of transcription. Habituating learning and making knowledge subsidiary for children helps drive them increasingly towards fluency. The need to make sense of sub-parts by reference to the more meaningful wholes also generates a 'protensive' pull which draws learning forward: the more we get children's attention on to the wider horizon, the more they become able to 'subsidiarize' the lower level elements.

Thus, learning to be skilful has three inter-connected aspects: (a) practising and over-learning the contributory skills, (b) practising and bringing them together at speed and (c) integrating them at a subsidiary level of awareness by using them for purposes beyond themselves.

Autonomy and self-extending competence

A fourth feature of the searchlights metaphor brings us back to the principle of active learning. As children learn to read fluently, they learn to exploit the connections between the different sources of information to increase capacity and autonomy. A rich seam of evidence about this comes from the work of Marie Clay. Much of her research is based on close observation of young readers and writers, and how they become proficient through the evolution of reading strategies. She defines reading as a

> … message-getting, problem-solving activity which increases in power and flexibility the more it is practised. My definition states that within the directional constraints of the printer's code, language and visual perception responses are purposefully directed by the reader in some integrated way to the problem of extracting meaning from cues in a text, in sequence, so that the reader brings a maximum of understanding to the author's message … As we progress along the lines of a text it is not unlike the process of finding footholds when climbing a cliff-face, yet the achievement is in the single completed task.
>
> (Clay 1991: 6)

This definition illustrates the dynamics of literacy learning. Our caveat is that, for reasons already given, in the early stages of reading acquisition, we would stress the special importance of switching on the phonics searchlight, through focused and systematic teaching. With all the searchlights switched on, children can learn to use them *strategically*, exploiting the redundancies between different information sources to develop increasing 'inner control'.

The development of inner control is crucial to success in literacy. Stanovich's allusion to the 'Matthew effect' in learning to read is relevant. He draws together evidence on reading success from top-down and bottom-up theories, to show that early success grows from children's ability to crack the orthographic code, which releases more cognitive capacity for higher level processes. At the same time, however, children with a wide early-reading experience are likely to crack the orthographic code more easily and often will be well on the way to doing this by the time they start school. Reciprocally, greater capacity for making sense of texts tends to increase children's reading vocabularies, knowledge of syntactic structures and metalinguistic functioning. There is a cycle of success begetting success. The converse of this is that the poor may get poorer because they have too little skill in cracking the orthographic code nor can they resort to the use of contextual support because they are too slow and the texts they are reading are too difficult. They become trapped at the word and sub-word recognition levels, failing to develop the higher level skills needed to expand and accelerate word recognition. Clay's work illustrates how young readers can exercise increasing strategic control over their own reading and writing development. She draws up a list of desirable goals for a typical 8-year-old.

> Through engaging with many reading and writing opportunities the child would have learned how to call up and use a range of strategies (hidden from our view) for understanding texts such as:
>
> * using feedback, monitoring and self-correction strategies in both reading and writing
> * having direct and rapid access to words in a reading vocabulary
> * having direct and rapid access to a writing vocabulary
> * using ways of getting to know new words in reading from words already known
> * using many cognitive processes to learn about reading and writing
> * using equivalent processes in each language if one is a bilingual child learning to be biliterate.
>
> … competent readers achieve all these things easily while average readers are well on the way.
>
> (Clay 1991: 10–11)

Learning and applying strategies such as these enables young readers to develop self-teaching and generative skills that develop literacy independently. The growth of strategic control is a key component of the NLS approach which is also reflected in the objectives set out in the *Framework for Teaching*.

Many successful young readers learn 'inner control' easily through sensitive and responsive parenting and teaching. Their competence grows through rich and repeated experiences of oral and written language, frequent opportunities to watch and imitate adult reading and writing behaviours, frequent and enjoyable practice, opportunities to play and experiment with reading and writing, contextualized but often quite specific teaching of the alphabet and its uses, and frequent but sensitive corrective feedback. As these children mobilize what they know, they increase and refine their own capacity for knowing more. We have said much about the importance of connections in this chapter: the linkage between the searchlights, the importance of cross-wiring reading and writing, the use of redundancy by skilled readers and the developmental momentum gained from driving sub-skills to a tacit level in the service of more integrated levels of meaning in reading and writing.

Objections to the 'searchlights'

Throughout the life of the NLS, the 'searchlights' has been criticized, principally by individuals and groups espousing a phonics-first approach to teaching early reading. Ofsted, in their final report on the NLS, despite much good news about the teaching of phonics, also criticized the 'searchlights' metaphor as,

> ... not effective enough in terms of illustrating where the intensity of the 'searchlights' should fall at different stages of learning to read. While the full range of strategies is used by fluent readers, beginning readers need to learn how to decode effortlessly, using their knowledge of letter–sound correspondences and the skills of blending sounds together. The importance of these crucial skills has not been communicated clearly enough to teachers. The result has been an approach which diffuses teaching at the earliest stages rather than concentrating it on phonics.
>
> (Ofsted 2002a: §58)

It was certainly the case that, in the early stages, there was much emphasis on shared reading and encouraging children to read strategically. But there was also very clear emphasis on the role of explicit phonics teaching and why it mattered. The introduction to *Progression in Phonics* set out the principle:

> The importance of systematic teaching of phonics and spelling needs to be underlined, not least because it is often treated with suspicion. Young children do not learn to discriminate the sounds of words naturally. This is a skill, tied to our particular way of writing language, which uses an alphabet of 26 letters to represent the sounds (approximately 44 phonemes) which make up the words we speak and write.

... Most beginning readers will have, at best, only limited knowledge of how spelling patterns are used to represent words. The alphabetic nature of our spelling system does not reveal itself to children simply through repeated exposure to books. Beginning readers are more likely to treat written words as images, each differentiated by its overall shape and pattern, than as letter strings corresponding to sounds. It is essential, therefore, that pupils are taught from the outset that words have to be 'spelt', not merely 'drawn', that they are composed of letters set out in particular combinations and orders to correspond with spoken sounds.

(DfEE 1999b: 2)

Nevertheless, there was a growing critical consensus that, despite what had been achieved, too many teachers of younger children gave phonics instruction insufficient attention as a discrete aspect of their daily teaching progamme. More fundamental criticism of the 'searchlights' was signalled in the report of a Parliamentary Select Committee in 2005, recommending:

... a review of the NLS to determine whether its current prescriptions and recommendations are the best available methodology for teaching reading in primary schools. Further large-scale comparative research on the best ways of teaching children to read comparing phonics 'fast and first' with other methods (for example analytical phonics and the searchlights model promoted in the NLS) is necessary to determine which methods of teaching are most effective for which children.

(House of Commons Education and Skills Committee 2005: 36)

A subsequent government enquiry into the teaching of early reading conducted by Jim Rose recognized that reading is fundamentally about the comprehension of texts and that phonics is a necessary but not sufficient part of the broad range of knowledge and skills that children need to become motivated and competent readers. However,

...for beginner readers, learning the core principles of phonic work in discrete daily sessions reduces the risk attendant with the so-called 'searchlights' model of paying too little attention to securing word recognition skills. In consequence, the review suggests a reconstruction of the searchlights model for reading.

(Rose 2006: 4)

There was nothing of significance in the NLS to which the review took exception, except the 'searchlights', which, it says, 'seeks to incorporate the whole complexity of reading. At the time it was introduced, this holistic approach was in line with current accounts of reading development that were accepted by practitioners and teachers' (Rose 2006: 4).

Rose proposed replacing the 'searchlights' with a *simple model* of reading propounded by Morag Stuart, based on distinguishing between word recognition (i.e. phonics) on the one hand and comprehension on the other.

> Rather than viewing reading development as a process involving a continuous increase in the child's ability to apply and orchestrate different 'cuing systems', researchers looked at ways in which children's word recognition skills developed … this new research involved studying these two essential components of reading separately in an attempt to better understand the development of each.
>
> (Rose 2006: §121)

Stuart argued that because it is possible to describe readers who are good decoders but poor comprehenders and vice versa, and to measure how far skill in each 'component' predicts skill in the other, these 'components' *must* be distinct, and are 'confounded' in the searchlights model. Later in the same paper, she implies that the two components mirror distinct psychological processes (Rose 2006: §48) and that the balance of learning needs across the two dimensions changes as children become more fluent.

> … when children begin to learn to read, they have already made considerable progress in their language development … they have not been 'taught' language. *However the time-limited task that is word reading is generally achieved as a result of direct instruction.* [italics in original]
>
> (Rose 2006: §20)

Particular emphasis is laid on the interactive-compensatory model of reading developed by Stanovitch, referred to earlier in this chapter. He showed how children with limited word recognition skills tend to rely more heavily on context to decode or infer unknown words, than those with good word recognition skills. Stuart concludes that this natural propensity must be counter-productive for young readers.

> *These findings refute the idea that poor reading results from failure to use context. They also strongly suggest that it is not a good idea to teach children to use context to read words on the page; children who read well do not need to use context to aid word recognition.* [italics in original]
>
> (Rose 2006: §43)

This conclusion is heavy with presupposition. It should surprise no one to find that when young readers interpret the print around them, they bring all their language experience to bear. If they have not been taught phonics they will inevitably rely on 'guesswork' to infer the visual and alphabetic characteristics of words. This is a serious disadvantage, although it has not proved fatal to many fluent young readers who evidently were not taught phonics at school (Clarke 1984). But if children *have* been taught phonics, the propensity to use additional information is most likely to enhance and extend competence rapidly, not to confuse or inhibit learning. This is the big message of the 'searchlights': teach children phonic decoding systematically and explicitly *and* encourage them to use their knowledge of language and other general knowledge to consolidate and apply their skills of decoding in reading for meaning. Stanovitch himself takes a less partial view about the implications of psychological theory:

> … to emphasize the centrality of word recognition is not to deny that the ultimate purpose of reading is comprehension. Neither does an emphasis on the fundamental role of word recognition in models of reading necessarily translate into particular instructional practices. The interface between models of reading and instructional practices is so complex that instructional prescriptions cannot be assumed simply from a knowledge of which processes receive emphasis in a particular model of reading.
>
> (Stanovich 2000: 208)

Stuart summarizes her position as follows:

> … less skilled and poorer readers have been shown to rely more on context to recognize words. Skilled and good readers have been shown to rely more on context to construct an accurate representation of the meanings of the text. These opposite uses of context by skilled and less skilled readers make a strong case for the need explicitly to acknowledge that there are indeed two separable dimensions of reading, word recognition skills and language comprehension. Each dimension is necessary. Neither dimension is sufficient on its own.
>
> (Rose 2006: 46)

Debate about the *simple model's* credentials can be left to psychologists. However it is also advanced as an alternative model of *pedagogy*, implying that the two distinct components of reading should be distinguished in the organization and processes of teaching. Thus, the 'simple model' appears as a disguised version of the old-style 'bottom-up' theories, this time with two parallel streams of learning where phonics is not only distinct but also psychologically prior; in other words, phonics 'fast and first' and *only* with a rich experience of stories in parallel but 'on the side'. Switch off the other searchlights because they teach children to 'guess' at words and cause confusion. But while properly stressing the importance of phonics, this prescription over-estimates its efficacy as a decoding tool. More importantly, it teaches children to ignore other sources of knowledge about language and texts that will help them develop the self-extending competence we described above. Claims that the 'searchlights' confuse or distract children, while strong on polemic, gain no support in the evidence.

Rose is sensitive to these implications and his conclusions for practice, while less stark, are more ambiguous. No one disagrees that children should begin to read independently as early as possible, certainly in their first year of schooling. Nor is there any fundamental disagreement about the importance of early explicit phonics teaching. However, the more tricky questions are about what, and how, young children should be reading. He steps back from the logical conclusion, recommended by some, that beginning readers should read only texts comprising words they can decode phonically. Such books may be useful, he says, if the quality is good. They can supplement a reading programme to give children 'quick wins' and develop confidence but,

> ... there is no doubt that the simple text in some recognized favourite children's books can fulfil much the same function [and] ... it may be possible to use these books in parallel or in place of them. In any event, the use of decodable books should not deny children access to favourite books and stories at any stage and particularly at the point when they need to read avidly to hone their skills ...
>
> (Rose 2006: 84)

So a basic question arises: if children are reading books that are not 100 per cent decodable, what should they be taught to do when they get stuck on a word? The first resort, as everyone agrees, is to try decoding it phonically, but what if this fails? Should they just wait until someone tells them the word? Most won't, of course. They will do what Stanovich's poorer decoders do and use other strategies of the kinds in the 'searchlights'. If they don't, we would argue, they should be taught to do so – anything less is unacceptable. If children are already tuned into the alphabetic system through learning phonics, they will capitalize on these strategies to recognize the spelling features of a wide range of words quickly and effortlessly. This is the common story of children who progress successfully, and teachers are entirely justified in trying to replicate this pattern of experience for others who are slower to progress. As soon as children tackle texts with vocabulary beyond the reach of the phonics they have learned, they must use additional strategies or fail to read. So when and how are these to be developed across Stuart's two distinct dimensions? The argument cuts both ways. Some children will fail without phonics but their chances of success may also be seriously diminished with *only* phonics.

The NLS characterized reading as a complex skill in which a range of strategies linked to decoding and comprehension interact and mutually support each other in the process of getting to the meaning of a text. Far from being mutually contradictory, these strategies are complementary, necessary and the principal means for developing reading autonomy. If there is any clarity at all to be gained from the wealth of psychological, sociological and ethnographic evidence, it is that good literacy teaching, especially for the most disadvantaged children, promotes active learning in all its forms including practice, play, analogical thinking, problem-solving, predicting, informed guessing, creative, imaginative and critical responding, self-monitoring, error recognition and self-correction. We reject entirely the contention that this breadth of experience will confuse children, or teach them inadequate strategies, which has no basis in evidence and is, in fact, atypical of the profile of a successful young reader.

The 'searchlights' has now run its course and, as we write, is being replaced by the 'simple model'. What matters, for teachers and for the record, is to be clear about its main messages:

- Each of the searchlights matters and there is no benefit in extinguishing any of them in the interests of focusing on others.
- In the early stages, in order to maintain each of the searchlights, reading and writing experiences should be scaffolded – especially writing. For example, through shared reading, and oral story reading, the teacher may carry most of the decoding burden while the children focus on understanding and interacting with the text, learning about text features, reading behaviours, how written language is structured and so on. For independent reading, children should have books with high facility levels (around 90–95 per cent) and be introduced to each text prior to reading to switch on the context searchlights and enable them to focus on decoding the text.
- The exception to this rule is that word recognition, via the teaching of phonics, should be taught and practised separately and then applied in independent reading. Children should, when they encounter unknown words, try phonic decoding as their first option, not their last resort. However, they should also bring other knowledge to bear to check and make sense of what they have read. If a word is not, or only partially, phonically decodable, they should try to predict it from the context and then check it back phonically. These strategies quickly become automatic with the propensity to interact so that comprehension contributes to word recognitions and vice versa.
- While there may be little value in blind guessing at words, there are huge and well-substantiated benefits in analogical thinking, inferring, generalizing, hypothesizing and testing, monitoring and checking. Strategies such as these are needed to develop, habituate, extend and connect word recognition skills. They should be fostered and applied at the word recognition level e.g. generating and consolidating knowledge of spelling/meaning patterns, by bringing to bear other knowledge to check that what is decoded makes sense, and to generate and test hypotheses about undecodable words, as well as for the comprehension of texts.
- The searchlights are equally relevant to understanding the decisions and processes involved in writing and underline the crucial importance of integrating learning systematically across both aspects of literacy.

In its original appraisal of research, the NLS paid attention to Adams' comprehensive investigation into the effectiveness of reading instruction programmes in the United States. In reviewing the most effective of these programmes she has this to say:

> … none of these programmes embodies the misguided hypothesis that reading skills are best developed from the bottom up. In the reading situation, as in any effective communication situation, the message or text provides but one of the critical sources of information, the rest must come from the reader's own prior knowledge. Further, in the reading situation, as in any other learning situation, the learnability of a pattern depends critically on the prior knowledge and higher order relationships that it evokes. In both fluent reading and its acquisition,

the reader's knowledge must be aroused interactively and in parallel. Neither understanding, nor learning can proceed hierarchically, from the bottom up. Phonological awareness, letter recognition facility, familiarity with spelling patterns, spelling–sound relations and individual words must be developed in concert with real reading and real writing, and with deliberate reflection on the forms, functions and meanings of texts.

(Adams 1990: 422)

David Bell, as Her Majesty's Chief Inspector of Schools, made a similar point, more simply. Summarising Ofsted's evidence on successful literacy teaching in 2005, he reminded us of the advice in the Bullock Report that 'there is no one method, medium, approach, device, or philosophy that holds the key to the process of learning to read'. He comments:

This principle is still ignored by some schools that continue to focus on a narrow range of approaches to teaching reading. Our evidence confirms Bullock's findings and shows that the most successful schools do indeed recognize the importance of introducing pupils to a broad range of strategies including the teaching of phonics.

(David Bell, HMCI Ofsted;
speech to mark World Book Day: 2 March 2005)

Literacy skills must be taught but the successful integration of reading and writing skills has to be driven by the actions of learners themselves. This principle of active learning with which we began the chapter pervades everything we shall say about literacy learning and underpins discussions of the literacy curriculum and teaching in the next two chapters.

Chapter 3

The literacy curriculum
A Framework of teaching objectives

The concept of teaching is predicated on there being something to teach. Teaching is a process, and in common with other processes, its effectiveness depends in part on the clarity of its objectives. This truistic observation matters because, when we began the NLS, there was little explicit content in the literacy curriculum of most schools. Research on reading and writing development (e.g. Clarke 1984, Meek 1982, Heath 1983, Wells 1986) had stimulated professional interest in the conditions of learning, creating a literate environment, encouraging motivation and enjoyment, involving parents and the community, but there was uncertainty about what children should be taught as they progressed through school. Moreover, interest in conditions of learning, though very important, tended to reinforce a view of literacy as a process of development where the teachers' main role was to foster and stimulate rather than instruct.

In Chapter 1, we commented on the state of literacy teaching current in schools, its strengths and weaknesses; there were problems but also a solid foundation of commitment and practice on which to build. In terms of the balance sheet, the biggest deficit was probably teachers' knowledge about language and its relevance to the curriculum at every level: word, sentence and text. The immediate purpose of the *Framework for Teaching* was to generate a common and practical progression of objectives to support teachers and steer their planning, but its wider purpose was to create an agenda for professional development. What was in the Framework in terms of its content and structure was ahead of the knowledge of many teachers at the time. It would be challenging and sometimes frustrating to work with but it would also drive professional development forward.

Our starting point was the National Curriculum, introduced by the Conservative Government following the Education Reform Act 1988 and implemented in schools from the autumn of 1989. The National Curriculum represents the best efforts of government to bring together a consensus of views from politicians, the public and the teaching profession, aspiring to:

> ... define and defend the core of knowledge and cultural experience which is the entitlement of every pupil ..., ensure that pupils develop from an early age the essential literacy and numeracy skills they need to learn, provide them with a guaranteed, full and rounded entitlement to learning; foster their creativity; and

give teachers discretion to find the best ways to inspire in their pupils a joy and commitment to learning that will last a lifetime.

(DES 1989: 3)

English is defined as a 'core' subject in primary and secondary schools under the three aspects: speaking and listening, reading, writing, each plotted as a progression through ten levels of attainment. These 'level descriptions' cross-cut the age-related structure of school organization to provide criteria for the assessment and testing of children at different stages. The descriptions are founded on evidence about past and typical performance, benchmarked against expectations for similar age groups internationally and levelled in relation to the demands of the curricula and public examination requirements for older students. Level 4 is the critical threshold of attainment for 11-year-olds. It reliably predicts success in secondary education and pathways into further and higher education. By level 3, children are fluent, accurate readers and their writing is organized, imaginative and clear. The demands of level 4 are as follows:

Reading Level 4
In responding to a range of texts, pupils show understanding of significant ideas, themes, events and characters, beginning to use inference and deduction. They refer to the text when explaining their views. They locate and use ideas and information.

Writing Level 4
Pupils' writing in a range of forms is lively and thoughtful. Ideas are often sustained and developed in interesting ways and organized appropriately for the purpose of the reader. Vocabulary choices are often adventurous and words are used for effect. Pupils are beginning to use grammatically complex sentences extending meaning. Spelling, including that of polysyllabic words that conform to regular patterns, is generally accurate. Full stops, capital letters and question marks are used correctly, and pupils are beginning to use punctuation within the sentence. Handwriting style is fluent, joined and legible.

(DfEE/QCA 1999: 57&59)

All schools are required to teach the National Curriculum but the details of teaching methods and the school curriculum are for them to decide. They must make these decisions within a broad framework of *general teaching requirements* designed to ensure that: all children are appropriately challenged and included in the curriculum; teachers differentiate their teaching appropriately to respond to children's diverse needs; provision is made to overcome barriers to learning including special needs and the needs of second language learners; language is developed across the curriculum; and children have increasing opportunities to learn through the use of technology. Within these broad parameters, the NLS focused on raising standards of reading and writing; although we were at pains to stress the founding importance of oracy, speaking and listening were outside our remit.

A *Framework for Teaching*

The Framework's stated aim was to:

> … cover the statutory requirements for reading and writing in the National Curriculum for English and contribute substantially to the development of speaking and listening. It is also relevant to teaching across the whole of the National Curriculum. Skills, especially those that focus on reading and writing non-fiction texts, should be linked to and applied in every subject.
>
> (DfEE 1998b: 4)

It interpreted the National Curriculum English requirements in the form of a detailed planning guide for teachers, by means of a recommended programme of term-by-term teaching objectives. The concept of a common framework was axiomatic. Everything else we did in the Strategy would be driven by this and designed to deliver its objectives. It was essential, therefore, to get it right and to have it agreed – two challenging though not always compatible objectives. It was designed to serve a number of connected purposes to:

- explicate the National Curriculum in greater detail and do for schools a job that was challenging and difficult to undertake individually
- ensure children's entitlement through common teaching and learning objectives to secure breadth and progression, and significantly raise expectations
- improve achievement for all children and close the gap by levering standards of lower attainers up to age-related expectations
- promote objectives-led teaching and learning
- articulate *what* teachers should teach and redirect attention to the business of how to teach
- frame a common professional language and understanding about the teaching of literacy to create conditions for common training, continuity and consistency of practice
- provide structure for school leaders to manage school improvement.

Consultation on the Framework development

Political timetables are always short, especially for a newly elected government with high aspirations and specific manifesto pledges. We had eight months between May and December 1997 to complete an agreed draft, ready for publication, with distribution scheduled for April 1998 and implementation the following September. A major effort went into revising and developing the NLP Framework and the associated training materials to secure agreement, and get materials published on time. Apart from the sheer weight of the task and its logistics – we had to produce and agree the Framework before we could begin generating resources for training. Great attention had to be paid to the capacity and willingness of schools to take it on.

The process was not easy. Literacy debates generate strong, sometimes extreme views. Teachers, by and large, were willing to be flexible and would try whatever worked best, but others – teacher trainers, advisers, academics, those with programmes to promote, lobby groups – often disagreed strongly. In these heightened circumstances, however, the need for agreement was galvanized by the prospect of 200,000 teachers implementing the Framework in less than a year's time. Other practical constraints also governed the decision process, including:

- sustainability: getting it right enough to last for the next five years – a major curriculum document like this is not something that can easily be modified once it is in the system
- accessibility: the Framework was addressed directly to teachers, so its structure, scale, style and tone had to be attractive, practical and accessible
- school resources: teachers' skills and time, books, IT facilities, class sizes, school organization etc. were system factors which could make or break successful implementation
- capacity to change: teachers' practice needed to change and the Framework had to be designed to challenge but also to build on existing practice. It mattered that teachers recognized the objectives as relevant, helpful and aspirational.

The biggest area for negotiation was across the divide between the phonics and whole-language protagonists. We set out the rationale for the NLS approach in Chapter 2, and remain convinced that the searchlights metaphor, with its differentiated and special emphasis on word level work in the early years is right, and that subsequent research has strengthened rather than diminished this perspective. The difficulty, which has persisted throughout the life of the Strategy, is that some of the groups most fundamentally committed to the priority of phonics were intellectually intolerant of anything in the literacy curriculum that sounded like encouraging children to investigate, generalize or bring their own knowledge of language to bear on the business of reading and writing. Mostly, pressure on the Framework development came from this side, while those committed to a broader view of literacy worried, expressed concern, offered advice and warned that over-emphasis on phonics would be inappropriate and very hard to implement with teachers.

Time was the great discipline; failing to agree was not an option. In the end agreement was secured through a mixture of negotiation, compromise and the exercise of editorial authority. The Framework reflected a broad consensus and those not prepared to bury their hatchets became increasingly marginalized. It remained an uneasy peace however, which had to be continually managed with determination and tact. Arguments about the Framework were not about to go away. Nevertheless, it was a considerable achievement.

The design of the Framework

Structure and rationale

The Framework set out an agreed definition of literacy in the primary school based on the expectations described for level 4 attainment for 11-year-olds in the National Curriculum.

> Literate primary pupils should:
> - read and write with confidence, fluency and understanding;
> - be able to orchestrate a full range of reading cues (phonic, graphic, syntactic, contextual) to monitor their reading and correct their own mistakes;
> - understand the sound and spelling system and use this to read and spell accurately;
> - have fluent and legible handwriting;
> - have an interest in words and their meanings and a growing vocabulary;
> - know, understand and be able to write in a range of genres in fiction and poetry, and understand and be familiar with some of the ways in which narratives are structured through basic literacy ideas of setting, character and plot;
> - understand, use and be able to write a range of non-fiction texts;
> - plan, draft, revise and edit their own writing;
> - have a suitable technical vocabulary through which to understand and discuss their reading and writing;
> - be interested in books, read with enjoyment and evaluate and justify their preferences;
> - through reading and writing, develop their powers of imagination, inventiveness and critical awareness.
>
> (DfEE 1998b: 3)

It was designed to reflect hierarchical levels of sense and meaning that structure language, and was linked to the rationale for learning (Chapter 2). Rules and conventions govern:

- how we may and may not combine sounds in English, which combinations make meaningful words
- how these words are written down and spelt
- how words can be combined into sentences
- how grammar and language choices serve authors' differing styles and purposes
- how all these elements can be combined to create coherent, meaningful texts.

Many children starting school in England already have a substantial experience of language. They understand and use oral language intelligibly, automatically, intuitively and with considerable accuracy across a wide range of everyday purposes.

They may use language for a variety of purposes, for example to ask, assert, direct, describe, recount, greet, refuse, invite. They recognize when utterances do and do not make sense, play with sounds and words, imitate the language of others, use language imaginatively to suppose and pretend; and enjoy simple games and jokes based on bending or breaking language rules. Language experience of this kind is a foundation for successful literacy development. Children develop the capacity to focus attention on speakers' meanings while using other levels of language: grammar, word construction, pronunciation etc. automatically. Early oral language development is learned and used intuitively, without the need to reflect upon or describe it, and results from high levels of one-to-one interaction, correction and practice in contexts of closely shared activity and experience. A significant minority of children do not have this experience, sometimes through lack of opportunity and stimulus at home or because English is not their first language and, in some cases, because of specific disorders which inhibit normal language development. From the earliest stages, the *Framework for Teaching* recognized the importance of encouraging teachers to provide for and capitalize upon breadth and richness in children's early experiences at every level of language.

But for all children, while confidence and facility with oral language are of founding importance, learning to be literate demands a more reflective understanding about the workings of language. There are at least two reasons for this. Firstly, written language is visually encoded, which involves understanding how the letters of the English alphabet represent the sounds and structures of speech. Readers and writers need to learn how these sub-structures work in written language to an automatic level so that, as with oral language, they can go straight to the meaning of a text without obstruction. However, because alphabetic representation is built on publicly accepted conventions it is intrinsically hard to discover, with high potential for learners to make false generalizations. A second reason concerns differences in the styles and structures of spoken and written language. Written language has to carry all its meaning in the visual representation of words and sentences, and what these evoke in the reader. Oral language is embedded to varying degrees in the context in which it occurs. This enables listeners and speakers to draw on added situational information derived, for example, from their knowledge of the place, time, activity, awareness of the speaker's intentions and from a range of aural and visual cues, intonation, volume, stress, emphasis, the use of action, gesture and facial expressions.

Contextual information of this kind is much weaker for readers and virtually absent for writers: there are no non-verbal (aural, gestural etc.) clues and situational information is seldom available. Because written texts have to 'stand on their own feet' they require different structures from spoken language. Furthermore, written texts may have styles and constructions not used in everyday speech. Writing tends to be structured in complete sentences, whereas spoken language is commonly phrasal and elided, tending to greater 'completeness' only in relatively formal situations. Most importantly, written texts often contain underlying meanings which readers need to infer and writers need to construct. Reading with comprehension requires understanding of how language is used to convey these meanings – reading between and beyond the lines. Fluent writing is an even greater challenge. Composers of writing have to anticipate and manage readers' responses, lay clues, select and structure language for particular effects and organize the overall sequencing and cohesion of the text explicitly to achieve their purpose.

Because reading and writing require this explicit understanding, the Framework was designed to reflect the structure of language in a simplified but broadly accessible way. It was built up in three parallel strands labelled *word level*, *sentence level* and *text level* to plot a progression of teaching objectives over the seven years of primary schooling. This structure was also allied to the underlying rationale for learning in Chapter 2 and to the recommended approaches to teaching in the Literacy Hour (see Chapter 4). The overall structure of strands and sub-sections is given in Table 3.1.

In the consultation there was considerable debate about the order of presentation of the three levels: word, sentence and text. Understanding and composing text, i.e. the text level objectives, are the intended outcomes of reading and writing instruction and sentence and word level objectives serve these ends so it was argued that the text

Table 3.1 Outline structure of the NLS *Framework for Teaching*

	Word-level work	Sentence-level work	Text-level work
Reception Year Ages 4–5	• Phonological awareness, phonics and spelling • Word recognition, graphic knowledge and spelling • Vocabulary extension • Handwriting	• Grammatical awareness	• Understanding of print • Reading comprehension • Writing composition
Key Stage 1 Ages 5–7	• Phonological awareness, phonics and spelling • Word recognition and graphic knowledge • Vocabulary extension • Handwriting	• Grammatical awareness • Sentence construction and punctuation	• Fiction and Poetry: – Reading comprehension – Writing composition • Non-fiction: – Reading comprehension – Writing composition
Key Stage 2 Ages 7–11	• Revision from Key Stage 1 • Spelling strategies • Spelling conventions and rules • Vocabulary extension • Handwriting (up to age 9)	• Grammatical awareness • Sentence construction and punctuation	• Fiction and Poetry: – Reading comprehension – Writing composition • Non-fiction: – Reading comprehension – Writing composition

level objectives should appear first, on the left of the page. But overriding concerns that the word level objectives might continue to be considered unimportant if placed 'at the end' determined that word level objectives were presented first.

Objectives in each strand ran from a common stem *Pupils should be taught:* for example,

- to understand how story book language works … (Year R, 4–5-year-olds)
- to use commas in lists … (Year 2, 6–7-year-olds)
- to summarize in writing the key ideas from a paragraph or chapter … (Year 4, 8–9-year-olds)
- to recognize the features of balanced written arguments … (Year 6, 10–11-year-olds).

Although the objectives were primarily addressed to teachers as teaching objectives, they were worded so that they could equally serve as learning objectives for children, for instance reformulated into *I can …* statements. The objectives could also operate as assessment and improvement criteria and as a basis for explaining the school's expectations to parents and others.

The link between reading and writing

There is a tendency in debates about literacy to focus most of the attention on reading. To some extent, this is understandable. Research, particularly experimental research in psychology, has always had a stronger focus on reading than on writing, and writing is more complex to investigate. There are more data available for comparisons about reading and it is easier to measure. Also, there is a common assumption that, because competent writing almost always presupposes the ability to read, reading should be the first priority and, that with reasonable encouragement and opportunity for writing, children's reading experiences will carry across into their writing. This is not necessarily the case, as data on reading and writing attainment over the years has shown (see Chapter 9).

The Framework characterized the processes of reading and writing as the inverse of each other – complementary sides of the same coin (Figure 3.1). Although reading and writing are quite obviously different skills, they draw on the same core of linguistic knowledge. Effective comprehension (reading) and composition (writing) rely on well-developed oral language, knowledge of text and sentence structures and literary language, and the graphic conventions of print and screen. Effective decoding for reading and encoding for writing rely upon the reader–writer possessing a mental lexicon of words that can be recognized or retrieved almost automatically. Building and accessing this lexicon of words in alphabetic languages such as English is greatly facilitated by knowledge of the orthographic structure of words in relation to their phonological structure and the skills of blending for reading and segmentation for writing. Writing relies on the additional skill of text transcription by hand or keyboard.

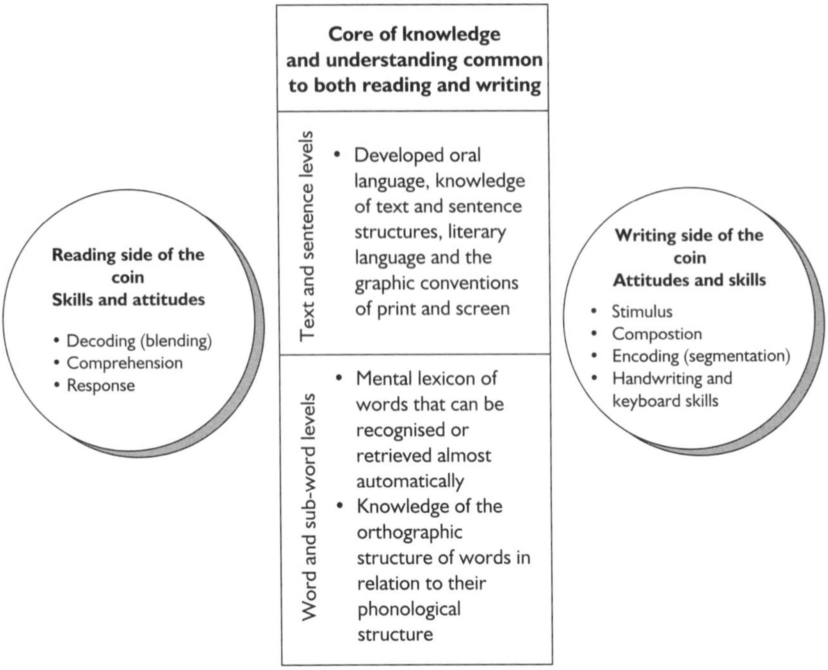

Core of knowledge and understanding common to both reading and writing

Text and sentence levels

- Developed oral language, knowledge of text and sentence structures, literary language and the graphic conventions of print and screen

Word and sub-word levels

- Mental lexicon of words that can be recognised or retrieved almost automatically
- Knowledge of the orthographic structure of words in relation to their phonological structure

Reading side of the coin
Skills and attitudes

- Decoding (blending)
- Comprehension
- Response

Writing side of the coin
Attitudes and skills

- Stimulus
- Compostion
- Encoding (segmentation)
- Handwriting and keyboard skills

Figure 3.1 The reading–writing coin

The parallel development of reading and writing provided systematic, mutually supportive opportunities for children to apply and consolidate skills in both directions. As children develop skills and strategies in reading, they are taught to reflect on these and apply them systematically in writing. Reciprocally, by drawing on the knowledge gained from composing and transcribing, writing contributes to better understanding of how authors organize texts and select language, and to a more extended and systematic awareness of words, word meanings and spelling. Just as observational drawing supports and develops the skills of observation and vice versa, so reading (i.e. decoding and comprehending texts) contributes to the development of writing (i.e. composing and transcribing texts) and vice versa. The principle is supported by evidence about the experience of young fluent readers who commonly learn reading and writing as related and mutually supportive aspects of the same process (Clarke 1984), and research by Clay and others connected with the pedagogies of *reading recovery*, where early literacy support programmes make extensive use of writing to support the development of phonological awareness, word recognition and spelling.

The structure of progression

The Framework defined a progression of reading and writing, aligned with the National Curriculum across the primary years across three broad phases:

- age 4–6 years, early reading and writing, distinguished by a rich experience of books and experimentation with writing. It focuses on the effort required in learning to decode and encode words, alongside the development of oral language and comprehension, and the acquisition of language, concepts and conventions particular to texts.
- age 7–9 years, consolidation, where decoding and spelling of a large number of words becomes automatic. The reader–writer achieves an internal lexicon of words to be drawn on at speed so that their conscious effort can be directed to comprehension or composition of the text. The phrase 'going subterranean' resonates well with teachers. It takes longer to gain automaticity in writing than reading because retrieving words from the lexicon with sufficient accuracy to write them is more demanding than word recognition for reading. There is also the additional physical demand of transcription attached to writing. In order to gain this fluency, children learn about the morphological structure of words, strategies for reading and spelling words and benefit from ample opportunity for practice. Their fluency is enhanced by an awareness of the organizational and navigational features in texts. During this period children gain a more sophisticated understanding and use of vocabulary within basic sentence construction.
- age 9–11 years, freeing up attention during reading and writing from concentrating on decoding and encoding to concentrating on comprehension and composition. Children make great strides in learning about text and sentence structure, and cohesion. They develop strategies such as inference, deduction, assumption, supposition, conjecture, implication, evaluation to help them read more sophisticated texts and also to begin to use in their writing.

These three phases of reading and writing are built into the structure of the Framework, summarized in Table 3.2. This pattern also had the benefit of corresponding with a common organizational structure in many of our smaller schools where children are taught in mixed year groups. Because the gradient of progression was shallower within than between the stages, the Framework was amenable to planning across a two-year cycle.

Everything in the Framework was designed to serve the aim of reading and writing for meaning. In practice it meant that the progression of word level objectives, across the three phases, while starting by focusing on early decoding skills became increasingly aligned with, and subservient to, broader expectations at the text level. Thus, as the word level objectives progressed, increasing emphasis was given to spelling, vocabulary extension and language choice in support of comprehension and composition. Interconnectedness was even stronger for the sentence level objectives. The teaching of grammar was not being promoted *per se*; this traditionally adopted a legislative approach to correctness, rules to be obeyed rather than tools with which to be creative. But, while it made little sense to learn about word classes or sentence structures in isolation, learning how grammar could be used and manipulated to

Table 3.2 Three phases of literacy acquisition

		Word recognition and spelling	Comprehension and composition: text and sentence levels
Reception year and KS1 Ages 4–7	Building skills and knowledge	• concept of word • visually recognised/ retrieved words • alphabetic code, segmentation and blending • transcription (by hand or keyboard)	• oral and literary language • development and concept of 'story' • concept and conventions of print • concept of sentence • response and purpose
Early KS2 Ages 7–9	Developing automaticity/ fluency	• morphemic construction of words • some etymological connections recognised between words • spelling strategies • practice for speed and fluency	• oral and literary vocabulary development • word modification and basic sentence and text cohesion • navigation of print and screen • response and purpose
Later KS2 Ages 9–11	Developing advanced comprehension and composition	• word recognition and spelling, generally automatized	• development of advanced comprehension strategies • text organisation and cohesion • complex sentence construction • response and purpose

influence the purpose, structure and style of written texts is central to the growth of comprehension and control in reading and writing.

There had been a resurgence of concern about the place of grammar in the curriculum in the 1970s (DES 1988) which was included in the National Curriculum in 1989. Research had consistently shown no positive effect of grammar teaching on quality of writing. But, as Roger Beard pointed out in his review of the research literature for the NLS,

> ... there has also been a growing feeling that grammar teaching has unfulfilled potential, particularly if it reflects contemporary English, rather than a Latin-based model of the language, and is authentically related to the purposes for which language and literacy are used.
>
> (Beard 1999: 49)

In the 1990s the practical value of genre theory in Australia and its related research in England by Maureen Lewis and David Wray (Lewis and Wray 1995) was beginning to impact on teacher training and literacy publishing. In the Framework the national curriculum was interpreted in the light of this work and incorporated six non-fiction distinct, yet overlapping, text types into the objectives in the Framework at text level. We also angled the work on grammar towards its function in creating effective sentences for specific purposes and genres.

Key areas of content in the Framework

The content for each term was arranged on a double-page spread, for ease of access, and contained a recommended text range closely linked to the word, sentence and text level objectives (Figure 3.2).

Text range

From the outset, the NLS set out to secure children's fluency and confidence in reading so that they established a lifelong enjoyment in books and the skills to interrogate a wide range of text-types – through reading, children would 'develop their powers of imagination, inventiveness and critical awareness' (DfEE 1998b: 3). Teaching objectives were designed around specific genres of literature, poetry and non-fiction texts for each term, for example:

> *Year 1 term 3 (5–6 year olds):* stories about fantasy worlds; poems with patterned and predictable structures; variety of poems on similar themes; information texts including recounts of observations, visits and events.
>
> (DfEE 1998b: 24)

> *Year 4 term 1 (8–9 year olds):* historical stories and short novels; play scripts; poems based on common themes, e.g. space, school, animals, families, feelings, viewpoints; a range of text non-fiction types from reports and articles in newspapers and magazines, e.g. instructions.
>
> (DfEE 1998b: 38)

Word level objectives

Reception and Key Stage 1 (4–7 years)

From the outset, the NLS took the view that a progression of word level work should be identified separately in the Framework and taught in focused ways through games and activities (see Chapter 4 and Huxford 2006). Early objectives focused on developing phonemic awareness, for example through recognizing and exploring rhyming patterns and extending patterns by analogy and invention. Further objectives for phonemic awareness and learning phoneme–grapheme correspondences led into a detailed progression for teaching phonics for spelling and reading: from the segmenting and blending of phonemes in consonant-vowel-consonant (CVC) words

YEAR TERM

4 2

Range

Fiction and poetry: Stories/novels about imagined worlds: sci-fi, fantasy adventures; stories in series; classic and modern poetry, including poems from different cultures and times.

Non-Fiction: (i) Information books on same or similar themes; (ii) explanation.

Word level work:
Phonics, spelling and vocabulary

Pupils should be taught:

Revision and consolidation from Year 3

1 to read and spell words through:
- identifying phonemes in speech and writing;
- blending phonemes for reading;
- segmenting words into phonemes for spelling;
- correct reading and spelling of high frequency words from KS1 and Y3;
- identifying syllabic patterns in multi-syllabic words;
- using phonic/spelling knowledge as a cue, together with graphic, grammatical and contextual knowledge, when reading unfamiliar texts;
- recalling the high frequency words learnt in KS1 and Y3;

Spelling strategies

2 to identify mis-spelt words in own writing; to keep individual lists (e.g. spelling logs) and learn to spell them;

3 to use independent spelling strategies, including:
- sounding out and spelling using phonemes;
- using visual skills, e.g. recognising common letter strings and checking critical features (i.e. does it look right, shape, length, etc?);
- building from other words with similar patterns and meanings, e.g. *medical, medicine*;
- spelling by analogy with other known words, e.g. *light, fright*;
- using word banks, dictionaries;

4 to practise new spellings regularly by 'look, say, cover, write, check' strategy;

Spelling conventions and rules

5 to investigate what happens to words ending in *'f'* when suffixes are added;

6 to spell words with the common endings: *-ight*, etc.;

Sentence level work:
Grammar and punctuation

Pupils should be taught:

Grammatical awareness

1 to revise and extend work on adjectives from Y3 term 2 and link to work on expressive and figurative language in stories and poetry:
- constructing adjectival phrases;
- examining comparative and superlative adjectives;
- comparing adjectives on a scale of intensity (e.g. *hot, warm, tepid, lukewarm, chilly, cold*);
- relating them to the suffixes which indicate degrees of intensity (e.g. *-ish, -er, -est*);
- relating them to adverbs which indicate degrees of intensity (e.g. *very, quite, more, most*) and through investigating words which can be intensified in these ways and words which cannot;

Sentence construction and punctuation

2 to use the apostrophe accurately to mark possession through:
- identifying possessive apostrophes in reading and to whom or what they refer;
- understanding basic rules for apostrophising singular nouns, e.g. *the man's hat*; for plural nouns ending in *'s'*, e.g. *the doctors' surgery* and for irregular plural nouns, e.g. *men's room, children's playground*;
- distinguishing between uses of the apostrophe for contraction and possession;
- beginning to use the apostrophe appropriately in their own writing;

3 to understand the significance of word order, e.g.: some re-orderings destroy meaning; some make sense but change meaning; sentences can be re-ordered to retain meaning (sometimes adding words); subsequent words are governed by preceding ones;

Text level work:
Comprehension and composition

Pupils should be taught:

Fiction and Poetry

Reading comprehension

1 to understand how writers create imaginary worlds, particularly where this is original or unfamiliar, such as a science fiction setting and to show how the writer has evoked it through detail;

2 to understand how settings influence events and incidents in stories and how they affect characters' behaviour;

3 to compare and contrast settings across a range of stories; to evaluate, form and justify preferences;

4 to understand how the use of expressive and descriptive language can, e.g. create moods, arouse expectations, build tension, describe attitudes or emotions;

5 to understand the use of figurative language in poetry and prose; compare poetic phrasing with narrative/descriptive examples; locate use of simile;

6 to identify clues which suggest poems are older, e.g. language use, vocabulary, archaic words;

7 to identify different patterns of rhyme and verse in poetry, e.g. choruses, rhyming couplets, alternate line rhymes and to read these aloud effectively;

8 to review a range of stories, identifying, e.g. authors, themes or treatments;

9 to recognise how certain types of texts are targeted at particular readers; to identify intended audience, e.g. junior horror stories;

Writing composition

10 to develop use of settings in own writing, making use of work on adjectives and figurative language to describe settings effectively;

11 to write poetry based on the structure and/or style of poems read, e.g. taking account of vocabulary, archaic expressions, patterns of rhyme, choruses, similes;

12 to collaborate with others to write stories in chapters, using plans with particular audiences in mind;

Figure 3.2 The National Literacy Strategy *Framework for Teaching* (Source: DfEE 1998b) through to the reading and spelling of common long vowels in single-syllable words and the syllabification of words.

Lists of the most common high frequency words were included alongside the phonics. Research on word frequency in reading shows that typically, about 50 per cent of words that occur in children's books are accounted for by approximately 100–150 common words (see Adams 1990: 160–2 for a brief discussion of this evidence), many of which are highly grammatical but low on intrinsic meaning e.g. verbs *go, are, have, should*, prepositions *as of, off, to*. Also, some of these words are phonemically irregular e.g. *come, was, water* and need to be explained. The lists proved quite controversial with some of our more 'purist' critics arguing that we were encouraging out-dated 'look-and-say' strategies. However, the guidance was clear:

> The high frequency words in the back of the Framework are not intended to be taught by rote. They are included because they represent a high proportion of the words children are likely to meet in the early stages of reading. Many of these words are phonically regular and thus perfectly decodable. A proportion, however, are irregular and will need to be taught as 'tricky words'. You should use this list as a checklist to ensure that all regular words can be decoded, as children learn the relevant phonic skills. You should teach children to recognize the other words as they encounter them in shared and guided reading.
>
> (DfEE 1999b: 7)

Word level objectives also included vocabulary extension, handwriting and presentation skills.

Early Key Stage 2 (7–9 years)

Earlier phonics learning was consolidated but the focus turned to spelling. Spelling teaching in England had been dominated by the 'Look, cover, write, check' procedure (Cripps and Peters 1990). A visuo-kinaesthetic approach, it was based on the conclusion that spelling rules were ineffectual as a way of recalling the spellings of words and that learning by writing groups of words which contained a common string of letters, regardless of phonemic or morphemic consistency, fixed spellings in memory. However, phonological research had shown a link between phonemic awareness and effective spelling (Brown and Ellis 1994) and Peter Bryant at Oxford University was leading research in the 1990s which was beginning to show the effect of morphemic knowledge on children's ability to spell words. The objectives in the Framework introduced a multi-strategy approach to spelling which reflected the predominantly consistent morphemic structure of words interfacing with the complex phonemic structure and the need for a developed capacity for visual recall.

Objectives ensured that phonic work was revised, consolidated and extended into a new and greater emphasis on spelling through learning to use a range of strategies to construct and check spellings, for example:

- sounding out and spelling using phonemes
- checking the visual features of spelt words – recognizing common letter strings, critical features
- building up words from known patterns e.g. *sign, signal*
- spelling by analogy e.g. *light, fright*
- using dictionaries in increasingly sophisticated ways.

Children tackled regular multi-syllabic words, investigated and used spelling conventions and rules and began to investigate the morphemic structure of words as an aid to vocabulary development and spelling. Spelling and vocabulary extension came together. For example, investigating how spellings change when *…s* and *…es* are added, what happens to words ending in *…f* when pluralized, the spellings of regular verb endings *…s, … ed, …ing*, recognizing and using prefixes *mis-, non-, ex-, co-, anti-*, to generate new words from root words.

Vocabulary was extended through continued collecting and re-using new words that arise through interest, reading and experience alongside more systematic explorations of synonyms, antonyms, homonyms, affixes and their effects on the meanings and grammatical functions of words, e.g. transformations of nouns and adjectives into verbs through the addition of suffixes such as *…ify, …ize*, or nouns and verbs into adjectives: *wash…able, hero…ic*. Attention was also given to selecting words and phrases for effect, accuracy and precision. The over-riding purpose is to explore, investigate, discover and apply word patterns under the guidance of the teacher, which extend vocabulary by mapping connections between words and codifying rules and conventions which work.

Later Key Stage 2 (9–11 years)

During the last two years of primary school there was increasing emphasis on independent strategies and use of reference sources for word investigation. Work on spelling conventions and rules was consolidated and extended with more attention to word roots and their connections to spelling e.g. *remit… permit… admit… progress… regress… digress… congress…* etc., pronunciation and spelling e.g. words with common letter strings but different pronunciations e.g. *ough, oo*, homophones. Objectives focused more on the origins and derivations of words, the effects of word choice and the stylistic features of words and phrases such as onomatopoeia, idioms, metaphors, figures of speech, slang, formal terminology.

Sentence level objectives

Sentence level objectives were aimed at understanding the uses of grammar and punctuation in shaping texts rather than the teaching of grammar per se – 'tools not rules'. With this in mind, three essential aspects of sentence level understanding were identified: sentence construction from simple to complex, language choice and modification for precision and effect, and cohesion to connect words, phrases and sentences purposefully and coherently. Control of each of these aspects is fundamental to critical reading and composing writing composition. These elements are woven through the sentence level objectives in each year to help children recognize and use structures and conventions to shape their own writing.

Reception and Key Stage 1 (4–7 years)

Sentence level consisted of two strands: grammatical awareness, and sentence construction and punctuation. Objectives ensured that children read for sense e.g. through re-telling or reading aloud with appropriate intonation taking account of syntax and punctuation. Learning from texts to inform writing started early at sentence level. There were objectives for observing and internalizing literary vocabulary and grammatical structures in their reading such as agreement between words, e.g. *I am, the children are* and word tenses, e.g. *see/saw, go/went,* to be used in speech and writing. Establishing the concept of a sentence was the all-pervading objective for young children so that by the age of 7 years they could construct a simple text with sentences punctuated with capital letters and full stops. In addition they were expected to recognize punctuation for questions and speech and begin to use question marks in their writing and to use commas to separate items in lists.

Early Key Stage 2

In the middle primary years, objectives to ensure appropriate intonation in reading and attention to grammatical agreement in speech and writing continued as sentence structures and punctuation became more complex. In addition, there was a focus on understanding, by classifying, the functions of words within sentences, considering options for modifying words and evaluating their effectiveness, for instance: 'identify the use of powerful verbs, e.g. "hobbled" instead of "went" ...' (DfEE 1998b: 38).

Sentence construction objectives led towards understanding the specific sentence level features that attended the various types of text, for example:

> ... understand the differences between verbs in the 1st, 2nd and 3rd person, e.g. I/we do, you/you do, he/she/they do/does, through:
> • collecting and categorising examples and noticing the differences between the singular and plural persons;
> • discussing the purposes for which each can be used;
> • relating to different types of text, e.g. 1st person for diaries, personal letters, 2nd person for instructions, directions, 3rd person for narrative, recounts;
> ...
>
> (DfEE 1998b: 34)

Also during this period, teachers were expected to develop children's awareness of complex sentences and how to begin composing them for writing.

Later Key Stage 2

In the last stage of primary schooling, objectives focused on using standard English and the structural features of impersonal and formal writing. Building on previous years, there was systematic attention to the use of complex sentences in writing for different purposes, linked to the genre and text-type characteristics encountered through reading. For example, they were expected to combine and relate ideas, select appropriate language, modify nouns and verbs for precision, order phrases and clauses for effect and use a range of connectives for cohesion. By the end of Key Stage 2, children were expected to use a full range of punctuation in their reading and all but the most complex in their writing, including speech punctuation and the apostrophe.

Text level objectives

Reception and Key Stage 1 (4–7 years)

Understanding of print was the priority for the youngest children: its distinction from drawings, constancy in meaning, direction (top to bottom, left to right), terminology (e.g. page, cover, author) and variety of purposes. The objectives required submersion in stories, poetry and information books and a growing familiarity with story language and structures, patterns in poems and the modes of language for notices and instructions. In parallel with the sentence level objectives were those that encouraged children to search for meaning when reading and not be content with simply decoding words. When reading books containing words that they were unable to decode, they were encouraged to use problem-solving strategies such as 're-read(ing) a text to provide context cues to help read unfamiliar words'. The objectives for writing encouraged experimentation particularly in role-play and the use of 'experience of stories, poems and simple recounts as a basis for independent writing, e.g. re-telling, substitution, extension, and through shared composition with adults' (DfEE 1998b: 18).

During Key Stage 1, alongside the word level objectives to provide a solid foundation for decoding, the text level objectives ensured that children were well grounded in oral and literary language to be able to comprehend and interpret texts. There were objectives in story telling and comparing told and written versions of stories; objectives which introduced children to narrative elements such as typical story structure, characters, dialogue, settings; and, by the end of the period, objectives to help children discuss and compare story themes handled by different authors. There were poetry objectives in each term through which children would read, recite, compare, contrast and collect their favourite poems. At the beginning, writing was still highly scaffolded through shared writing to compose with the teacher, using existing poems or stories as templates. Early attempts at creating characters as pictures and captions developed into objectives to write simple descriptions as 'wanted posters' or passports. By the end of the period children were expected to write a sustained story independently using appropriate language to sequence events, e.g. *after that.*

Foundations for non-fiction reading and writing were laid during this period through teaching children to read and act on information from captions, labels, lists and instructions. They were taught to gather information and present it in these formats and later to refer to written sources and write a simple description, report or recount of events. They would have a basic knowledge of how the alphabet is used to order indexes, dictionaries and glossaries. For example, by the end of the period they should be able to write:

- simple instructions using appropriate format and impersonal language
- a non-chronological report, 'using appropriate language to present, sequence and categorize ideas.

(DfEE 1998b: 31)

Early Key Stage 2 (7–9 years)

Objectives for older children continued to stress reading for meaning, enjoyment and responding to fiction, non-fiction texts, plays and poetry. The exploration of ideas, forming and justifying opinions and preferences and language play were all fundamental to reading development. But objectives also embodied an 'apprenticeship' approach: examining texts closely to discover how authors built stories, poems and plays, and using these as templates or frames for experimenting with and practising writing. Objectives for narrative focused on aspects of character, settings, openings and conclusions, with parallel writing objectives for crafting these elements. Reading objectives on paragraphing, dialogue, the uses of language for effect were reflected in writing objectives on story planning, dialogue writing and language choice. By age 9, children could be expected to write simple, continuous and coherent texts in narrative and non-narrative forms, sometimes containing short chapters and the additional features of a book, such as title page and contents.

Distinguishing fact from fiction, begun in the early years, progressed to distinguishing fact and opinion. Objectives took children further in their ability to read and write recounts, non-chronological reports and instructions and introduced two more text types: explanation and persuasion. But they were also expected to read and write texts which crossed these boundaries such as letters and newspaper articles and had a distinct form of their own. Children's earlier knowledge of alphabetically ordered texts was turned into an ability to interrogate these sources: they were taught to prepare for locating information by reviewing existing knowledge and finding the gaps; they were taught how to decide on the usefulness of a text through scanning the layout, pictures, headings, bullets, opening sentences and key words on screen and paper for pertinent subject matter and skim reading to ascertain the content of the text; they were taught how to extract information from the text through text marking, note-taking and summarizing. They then applied this knowledge to their own production of texts.

Later Key Stage 2 (9–11 years)

There was a step change in text level objectives from early to later Key Stage 2. By 9 years old, children were assumed to be competent readers, able to gain a basic understanding from text and ready to delve beneath the surface, infer meanings and understand metaphor, imagery, ambiguity and parody. Scaffolding of writing objectives was gradually removed so that by the end of primary school, children were expected to be confident in writing a well-structured narrative using techniques to vary pace and develop characters and settings. Reading objectives ranged widely, examining types of narrative structure, exploring and comparing stories in different media, working with older literature and texts from a variety of cultures. Earlier work on viewpoint was developed to distinguish between author and narrator, investigate and manipulate narrative viewpoint and analyse the treatment of different characters, e.g. minor characters, heroes, villains, and their perspectives on the action in stories, novels, plays and films. Other objectives focused on active reading strategies, attitudes, preferences and responses to texts. Poetry objectives formalized children's previous experiences using imagery by introducing ideas of simile, metaphor and personification. Children learned about and read and performed new forms such as ballad, narrative poem, sonnet and rap. Children were also given ample opportunity to write poetry, 'to convey feelings, reflections or moods in a poem through the careful choice of words and phrases' (DfEE 1998b: 45).

Work in non-fiction also shifted up a gear. Five of the typical text-types (recount, instruction, report, explanation, persuasion) had been introduced by this point and some were quite well developed but all now took on a new level of complexity. For instance, as an extension of recounts there were objectives for reading and writing biography and autobiography:

- to distinguish between biography and autobiography;
- recognising the effect on the reader of the choice between first and third person;
- distinguishing between fact, opinion and fiction;
- distinguishing between implicit and explicit points of view and how these can differ;

(DfEE 1998b: 51)

Discursive texts were introduced, giving children the opportunity to examine and construct both sides of an argument. Having established the typical format and language features for each text type, children were expected to select the appropriate style and form to suit a specific purpose and audience, drawing on their knowledge of different non-fiction text types. Other objectives continued the focus on locating and evaluating information, taking and making notes e.g. in preparation for a talk, debate or subsequent writing, and critically evaluating texts for bias.

Using the Framework

The breadth and progression of the literacy learning agenda reached well beyond the expectations of the school curriculum of 1997. Most of the objectives, although demanding, were within the reach of most children and having them defined enabled thousands of teachers and children to rise to the challenge. It also defined how far there was to go, especially in writing.

The Framework set out to create a bridge between the general requirements for English in the National Curriculum and the detailed day-to-day planning required of teachers. Although it was deliberately precise, those who accused it of being over-prescriptive and 'one-size-fits-all' often failed to recognize just how big a challenge it presented to schools. Not only were teachers now expected to teach to objectives, which was new for many, there were large and crucial gaps in teachers' subject knowledge across all of the strands, at word, sentence and text levels. There was no predetermined order for teaching the termly objectives which were presented as a connected and coherent set for each term. Detailed planning of which objectives to select, how to group and sequence them, when to teach them, which texts or other resources to work from, and which activities to work through, was left to schools. All this left a lot of very wide and challenging scope for schools to make choices and set priorities. 'The Framework provides the content. Medium-term planning should be used to distribute this content to achieve balance and coverage of the objectives over a term or half term' (DfEE 1998b: 15).

The introductory distance learning materials provided some general guidance on planning which was expected to get the majority of schools started, on the principle that the Framework should give teachers choice and generate diversity within coherent boundaries. Schools and local authority consultants brought a wealth of previous planning experiences and their own priorities to this task of planning to objectives. Some schools opted for maximum linkage between objectives in planning to teach all the sentence and word level objectives through the chosen text. This approach, in skilful hands, proved very successful in raising the standard of literacy in the class as well as being a stimulating and enjoyable experience for the children. But in other situations it resulted in tedious over-use of the text and inadequate teaching of the sentence and word level objectives. The opposite also occurred where teachers did not recognize the in-built cohesion between objectives in the Framework and chose unrelated word, sentence and text level objectives which were therefore not mutually supporting.

During the first year as teachers taught the objectives, there was a growing demand from schools for more detailed help with planning. Further guidance was produced, based on a thematic approach to planning derived from the text level objectives to show how objectives could be linked and managed, and illustrate tangible outcomes for children. Over the years guidance and exemplification of this kind has been multiplied by the NLS, for example through samples of medium-term plans for each term, along with planning criteria (DfES 2003a) and a planning guide (DfES 2004a). In 2000, to accommodate some of the structural terminology of the Framework, an overview for each Key Stage was provided and, subsequently, sets of yearly 'target statements' for reading and writing, which drew from and prioritized the objectives in the Framework, taking account of the criteria for marking the national tests (DfES 2000d; 2001b). Additionally a raft of other support was generated through local authority consultancy teams, teacher-based websites (e.g. the DfES teacher-net) and developments in the schools publishing sector to align books and materials with the NLS objectives.

Working with the Framework also helped to create a consensus that had not existed at the outset, that phonics and spelling would best be taught discretely and then applied in reading and writing. In line with this, the previously accepted structure of the Literacy Hour was changed to put the teaching of word level work at the start of the lesson – a significant signal to schools, and those who supported them, about the importance of these objectives.

Early concerns about the Framework diminished as schools became familiar with it. For example, the decision to provide termly rather than annual objectives had met with a mixed response. Some teachers suggested they would have preferred the flexibility of annual objectives particularly in relation to non-fiction objectives that needed to fit against other curriculum areas. Writers of the parallel mathematics Framework decided on annual objectives with some designated as 'key' objectives. However, within a year they had supplemented the mathematics framework with detailed unit plans setting out the within-year progression. On balance, providing a Framework of detailed term-by-term objectives was probably the right choice for literacy at the time, because:

- establishing a within-year progression in the literacy curriculum was paramount
- literacy is different from mathematics as a subject. The latter divides more neatly into topics, while literacy has greater emphasis on skills which need to be systematically recycled in varying contexts throughout the year. For this reason, it is harder to plan and, at the time, no tradition of progression planning existed in schools
- the objectives contained detail of subject knowledge, suggestions and outcomes for teaching that would not have been possible in higher order annual objectives
- the objectives at the termly level were instantly accessible and teachers were able to teach them immediately.

Other worries that the objectives might have been pitched too high dissipated as children showed they were capable of more than some of their teachers expected. The Framework had a knock-on effect into secondary schools as teachers were forced to revise their expectations of what children coming into year 7 could achieve. Evidence that the Framework had been well received was apparent from local authority professional development sessions, surveys of head teachers (CfBT 2000) and the external evaluation team (Earl *et al.* 2003). In their report on the National Literacy

Project which acted as a pilot for the National Strategy, the Ofsted evaluation concluded:

> The Framework has had a positive impact on the planning of work on reading and writing. Teachers have welcomed the clarity of content on what to teach in the Literacy Hour and the progression set out within and between lessons. In the vast majority of schools, the use of the Framework has produced a more consistent, whole-school approach to the planning and organization of the Hour and has raised teachers' expectations of what pupils can achieve.
>
> (Ofsted 1998: 9)

Again, at the end of the first year of NLS implementation, they reported:

> The Strategy has been adopted enthusiastically by the overwhelming majority of primary schools. Concerns expressed initially about an adverse reaction to the specific nature of the teaching objectives have proved largely unfounded. Teachers have found that these make good sense and provide a key to progression and continuity that schools have often striven in the past to achieve by themselves, not always successfully.
>
> (Ofsted 1999: 8)

The Framework underpinned the teaching of literacy in English primary schools from 1998 onwards. It triggered an extension and deepening of teachers' understanding of literacy and provided the basis for developing the subject and its pedagogy. When it was written, it was expected to have a life of about five years to provide a sufficiently stable foundation for implementation and professional development. In fact it remained unchanged for almost a decade. It was appropriate, therefore, in the light of new evidence and much improved practice, to review and revise it.

Revision of the Framework

In 2004 a nationwide consultation exercise was launched to take views on its renewal. The story about how these changes came about is told in Chapter 10. Speaking and listening objectives had been devised in a joint project by the NLS and QCA in 2003 which needed to be included (DfES 2003d). Information technology had advanced exponentially during the life of the Strategy, partly caused by the demands of the Strategy but substantially by high government spending on equipment and training; for example, by 2005, primary schools had overtaken secondary schools in their purchasing of interactive whiteboards. During the period since 1998 the increased availability of multimedia texts had created the need for an additional set of reading skills as well as augmenting the already rich array of textual genres. A renewed Framework needed to reflect these changes and to formalize the acceleration in phonics in the early years; since the publication of *Progression in Phonics* in 1999, the Framework had fallen out of step with the pace of phonics teaching that was being advocated. Not only was our understanding of phonics developing in this country but we had learned a lot more about the essentials of reading comprehension, writing and the connections between them.

The next iteration of the Framework (DfES 2006a) in 2006 is very differently conceived with a different role. In the new version, the language and literacy content is arranged under 12 new headings intended to reflect the foci of the revised National Curriculum assessments: speaking, listening, group discussion and interaction, drama, word reading, word structure and spelling, understanding and interpretation, engaging and responding, creating and shaping texts, text structure and organization, sentence structure and punctuation, presentation.

The changes are comprehensive. The new structure is radically different and bears little obvious resemblance to its predecessor. Much effort has been invested in the revision, which is intended to reinforce in practice the theoretical disjunction between decoding and comprehension in early reading development, set out in the Rose enquiry into the teaching of early reading (Rose 2006). More attention is given to speaking and listening on the grounds that good listening comprehension predicts reading comprehension when accompanied by a broad, enriching experience of reading. But while the new version covers territory similar to the original, the emphasis is clearly upon re-centering the whole Strategy from 4–11 years for reading *and* writing, on a specific psychological model of the early reading process. As well as driving a wedge between word recognition and comprehension, the reorganization of objectives also de-couples reading from writing, making these essential links less explicit and less evident to teachers. Recent position papers published to guide schools on the revised structure set the precepts out (DfES 2006b). References to developing reading strategies have been deleted along with the searchlights metaphor. Also the revised structure is no longer aligned with the secondary school Framework which retains the same overall structure as the original NLS document; this will make continuity harder to plan and may affect the prospects for transition and common discourse between primary and secondary schools.

We raised some questions about the implications of the 'simple model' in the previous chapter, but from the point of view of the Framework there is also a deeper issue, brought out in this critical observation by Stuart, that 'the treatment of reading comprehension in the NLS *Framework for Teaching* … could better be described as teaching literary criticism rather than facilitating reading comprehension' (Stuart 2003: 2).

The Framework, as we noted at the start of this chapter, is about the curriculum. The curriculum, in turn, is a public determination of what children should learn, based on agreed values. There are questions about what it is worthwhile for children to know and derivative, practical questions about how best they might learn it. The curriculum should take account of psychological theory but it cannot be determined by it. Clearly, the phonics objectives are vital. No one seriously contests this, and without doubt, psychology has contributed greatly to our understanding, justifying a priority for systematic and separate teaching. But comprehension is about understanding and understanding is about knowledge. Whatever processes of comprehension are postulated by psychologists they are logically contingent on prior value assumptions about what is to be understood. The comprehension objectives set out in the Framework thus stand outside 'simple' or any other psychological models of comprehension. Psychology may tell us that something is hard to learn or is best learned in one way rather than another. But the fundamental question for psychologists, if they choose to engage with education, is how far their models, simple or complex, are capable of delivering desired objectives, not whether the desired objectives can be derived from the psychologists' models.[1]

Nevertheless, the big message from the NLS experience is that the new Framework, whatever form it takes, needs to remain at the foundation of the Strategy. Its teaching objectives have been fundamental to securing standards, progression and major improvements in teaching quality. In the broader context of the central reform agenda, the principles underpinning the Framework are at least as important as its detailed structure. The first of these, in the NLS, was a clear and understandable rationale, derived from the basic structural features of language: word, sentence and text. The second was coherence: aligning the literacy curriculum with the generic teaching methodologies recommended in the Literacy Hour. The simplicity and consistency of these big messages were essential to its successful implementation. The third was its responsiveness to the needs and capacities of schools at the time, and a fourth was its power to challenge schools without being rejected.

The NLS Framework was, of course, a document of its time, and review and revision were overdue. A powerful saving grace for all central ambitions of this kind is the levelling effect of the teachers who have to interpret and implement it. We hope and expect that the consequences of these changes will be the retention of best practice from the NLS with a renewed emphasis, about which all are agreed, on teaching phonics to the youngest children. In time, we may also hope that attention will not be further diverted from the far greater challenge of teaching children to write effectively.

---

1   The latter commits what philosophers call the 'naturalistic fallacy' i.e. jumping from facts to values, by falsely deducing from the fact that something occurs, to the conclusion that it must be right. Psychology arrives at all sorts of conclusions about human behaviour. While this is informative, nothing follows from this evidence about the desirability or otherwise of its conclusions.

Chapter 4

The Literacy Hour

A new level of intervention

The development of the *Framework for Teaching* went hand in hand with the Literacy Hour – a clearly defined period of time, every day, with a distinct structure for teaching literacy. The Literacy Hour was the visible manifestation of the NLS in practice. The Government embarked on the Strategy determined to make a difference and it was clear from the research on school improvement and system change that the difference had to be one that affected practices and teaching behaviours in classrooms. The Literacy Task Force was convinced by the evidence that the most influential factor in school improvement was the quality of teaching, which was also the factor considered most immediately amenable to influence by Government. Other factors related to poverty, housing, opportunity and employment mattered greatly and were subject to other policy initiatives but improving teaching was the key to improving standards and educational opportunity and thus critical to Labour's longer term aims of social justice.

The Framework was axiomatic in setting expectations for schools but it was clearly not enough. The difference would be made by the much bolder step of intervening in the methodology of teaching. Hitherto, literacy, seen as a core skill (or set of core skills), had been subsumed into subjects with a more clearly defined knowledge content (e.g. history, science, geography) to save time in a crowded curriculum. In many schools literacy was not a clearly defined subject worthy of a time-allocation or therefore, specific pedagogy. The Framework defined the distinctive content and the Literacy Hour defined a time and a series of pedagogies.

The provenance of the Literacy Hour

Three sources of evidence were important. First, research into teaching approaches provided a theoretical basis for constructing the Literacy Hour and the elements within the Hour. This included work by academics such as Margaret Donaldson, Andrew Pollard, Paul Black and Dylan Williams, Ted Wragg, Barbara Tizard, David Hopkins and David Reynolds, and more specifically in literacy, Margaret Clarke, Marie Clay, Roger Beard, David Wray and Maureen Lewis, Bob Slavin and Peter Hannon. Material by Michael Fullan, Michael Barber and Bruce Joyce and their colleagues on implementing professional development provided a powerful steer. In the early stages, Roger Beard was commissioned to review evidence of the provenance and effects of the various teaching methodologies being proposed. These were later summarized in a publication, *National Literacy Strategy: review of research and other related evidence* (Beard 1999). His advice to the task force and national Strategy provided a valuable evidence base on which the principle and practices in the Literacy Hour were established.

Secondly, school inspection evidence from the previous ten years defined the picture, setting out the weaknesses and obstacles to improvement along with a broad agenda for what needed to be improved. We noted in Chapter 1 how Ofsted's report *The Teaching of Reading in 45 Inner London Primary Schools* (Ofsted 1996b) had assumed political significance pointing to serious shortcomings in the teaching of reading, focusing attention on the importance of clear curriculum content, progression and the values of direct and large-group teaching.

Third, careful account was taken of what worked: the proven and successful practices that had credibility and transfer value for teachers. Influential practices in England included the work of the Centre for Language in Primary Education and the University of Reading, Centre for Language and Literacy both of which, over many years, made major contributions to teachers' understanding of literature, reading for meaning, the development of reading strategies, early and later writing development and literacy assessment. The *Literacy Initiative from Teachers* (LIFT) project which introduced an early version of a Literacy Hour, based on best practice in New Zealand schools, was proving highly successful in the London borough of Westminster (Sainsbury *et al.* 1998). While, in a very different way, *Best Practice Phonics* by Ruth Miskin, a head teacher in another borough, Tower Hamlets, was having notable success in promoting early reading skills. Successful literacy projects in other countries were also reviewed. From Australia, these included the Children's Literacy Success Strategy (CLaSS) in Victoria by Carmel Crévola and Peter Hill (1996), shared and guided reading by Don Holdaway (1979) and developing practices in the teaching of non-fiction and genre theory through *First Steps* by a team led by Alison Dewsbury (Education Department, Western Australia 1994).

From New Zealand, Reading Recovery was already established with a strong research and evidence base and a network of significant expertise. It had three important lessons for the Strategy. First, it had a proven pedagogy which was understood by, and acceptable to, teachers. It provided a detailed and codified version of high quality mainstream practices for slower readers. Second, it was predicated on the assumption that schools could and should put consistent and high quality first teaching in place to reduce the number of children who would need additional help, and to support them adequately as they came through the programme. A major problem at the time was the failure of schools to provide sufficient mainstream classroom support for children who had benefited from this expensive programme. Third, alongside other pressures for change, Reading Recovery was pressing schools to develop more instruction-based and consistent practices. Its approach demonstrated that generic practices could be specified, integrated into a common lesson format and, with high quality professional development, be delivered by teachers consistently in a wide variety of contexts. It had to be possible to create a common pedagogy for all primary teachers which would have a sufficiently strong generic core to allow for adaptation and differentiation in the wide variety of settings while creating a common language of primary literacy teaching.

By 1997, the principle of a Literacy Hour was not new to schools. The idea had found its way into staffrooms and existed in a variety of forms in various parts of England, and abroad. The greatest influence was, of course the National Literacy Project, where:

> … head teachers regarded the introduction of the Literacy Hour overwhelmingly positively, whilst pointing out that it had major implications in terms of management and resourcing.
>
> (Literacy Task Force 1997: §4)

But the idea of a commonly structured literacy lesson was also central to other projects, for example the LIFT project in London, the successful *First Steps* project from Western Australia and the *Success for All* programme from the United States, which were being trialled in England at the time. Following publication of the first Literacy Task Force report in February 1997, the National Foundation for Educational Research undertook its own survey of Literacy Hour practices in England (NFER 1998). To some extent, this survey was overtaken by events since it was not published until May 1998 when schools were already preparing for the NLS. However, it did indicate a considerable variety of approaches that had been in place prior to the NLS and its predecessor the NLP.

Underlying the introduction of the Literacy Hour was the principle of a common generic teaching structure for all teachers as the foundation of an ambitious, nationwide professional development programme. Evidence pointed to the conclusion that improvement required changed practices. Changing practice in turn required common structures, a shared language for professional discourse and training, common objectives and expectations, universal implementation and, most importantly, fidelity to the plan. The change had to be practical, well justified and evidently likely to succeed but it was doomed from the outset if schools were allowed to cherry-pick the bits they liked and implement it or not, as they chose. Scope for choice and flexibility were built in but the main parameters were negotiable only if a school could demonstrate that they had a more efficacious approach.

The Literacy Hour was constructed to deliver what came to be called *quality first teaching*. The principle was foreshadowed in the preliminary Task Force reports which took account of evidence from Australia and New Zealand where consistent, high quality class teaching was expected to lift around 80 per cent of children to the expected levels in literacy by age 11. These children were referred to as the 'first wave'. Approximately a further 15 per cent of children, whose progress might be inhibited for a variety of reasons, would require additional support to catch up, while around 5 per cent or less would be likely to have specific learning difficulties of some kind that might require specialized support. These two groups were referred to as *waves 2 and 3* respectively. The Literacy Hour was conceived on the 80 per cent assumption, as a structure from which group-based *wave 2* support could be generated and which would provide the appropriate supportive framework to underpin the additional support programmes coherently. It was part of a drive to raise expectations substantially among teachers and to challenge widespread and damaging assumptions that children with reading difficulties were children with 'special educational needs', requiring specialist support. These ideas will be explored in detail in the next chapter.

Principles of learning and teaching

In his advice to the NLS, Roger Beard identified a range of core principles, derived from research evidence on effective teaching. These included high expectations, defined goals, structured lessons, instructional variety, pace and time management, high levels of student time on task, high success rates for students and varied interactive teaching strategies. These general principles formed the background for developing the rationale and structure of the Literacy Hour. With these in mind, the Literacy Hour was founded on five principles.

Secure subject knowledge

Effective teaching requires teachers to have very secure subject knowledge. When learning new material, children can exhibit partial understanding and confusion. They may provide incorrect but feasible responses or examples, for instance of a classification. A teacher who is aware of common misconceptions and their reasons is able, by careful questioning and prompting, to lead children towards real understanding. The Framework and the professional development provided through the NLS were designed to update teachers in their subject knowledge on the basis that this knowledge would be secured though the process of using, teaching and accommodating it.

Teaching to objectives

A fundamental objective-setting philosophy ran though the whole Strategy, connecting national quantitative targets right through to qualitative learning objectives for children. It was all about having clear objectives and high expectations, and making these *visible* – to teachers, parents, governors and the wider community but, above all, to children. A fundamental lesson from the NLP and from the research on effective teaching is that children succeed when they are clear about what they are expected to learn. It was a principle that children were taught skills, concepts and strategies *and* were taught to reflect on them to gain understanding and control. This 'meta-cognitive' theme pervaded the Framework with its emphasis on reflection, control and the use of appropriate technical language. The theme was borne out in the structure of the Literacy Hour itself which encouraged teachers to let children in on what they were expected to learn, to teach them to discuss and think about what they were learning and, through the plenary session at the end of each lesson, to reflect on and describe what they had learned. Throughout the early training and as a continuing theme of the broader primary strategy, schools have been encouraged to translate their quantitative targets into 'curricular' targets relevant to specific groups of children e.g. classes, year groups, ability groups, gender groups, summer-born children and so on.

Together, the Framework and the Literacy Hour served to re-focus teachers' attention from planning *what* to teach, to a new focus on *how* to teach. Hitherto, lack of clarity at school and national level about the literacy curriculum had left many teachers stranded. School policies were often vague, detailed schemes of work seldom existed and teachers either had to reinvent the literacy curriculum for themselves or fall back on the structure provided through limited commercial programmes – which, understandably, most did. In setting out the range and progression of expected learning, the NLS set a new challenge. Instead of merely following or selecting from programmes, teachers had to choose materials and devise activities to meet given objectives. It placed a new responsibility on them not only to teach but to ensure to the best of their ability that children learned.

The Literacy Hour was built on the expectation that children should take joint responsibility with the teacher for their learning, and the guidance made this clear. This approach, 'assessment for learning', originating from work by Paul Black and Dylan Wiliam (Black and Wiliam 1998) at Kings College, London, gained momentum through the work of Shirley Clarke (1998, 2001) and became a cornerstone of the Primary National Strategy learning and teaching materials (DfES 2004c). In a successful classroom, children should:

- be clear about what is to be achieved – objectives, purpose, outcomes
- plan and manage their own work, and know what to do if they are stuck or when they have finished
- ask when they do not understand
- monitor and self-correct as they work
- initiate and extend learning activities
- use evidence and information sources independently
- give information and opinions confidently, knowing their views will be valued
- access resources independently as required
- have a repertoire of skills for using tools and materials, including ICT
- evaluate and reflect on their own learning and achievement.

High quality interactive teaching

In Chapter 1 we noted that, with the exceptions of reading literature to classes and class introductions to creative writing lessons, whole-class teaching was rare in the literacy curriculum a decade ago. A national debate had been launched about teaching methods but most primary teachers needed to be convinced about the value of whole-class work and to develop a range of workable strategies, e.g. for observing and assessing, directing, demonstrating, modelling, questioning and explaining, listening and responding to children. Teaching was expected to be:

- discursive – characterized by high quality oral work;
- interactive – pupils' contributions are encouraged, expected and extended;
- well-paced – there is a sense of urgency, driven by the need to make progress and succeed;
- confident – teachers have a clear understanding of the objectives;
- ambitious – there is optimism about and high expectations of success.

(DfEE 1998b: 8)

Professional development for teachers addressed the practicalities of allowing children time to think out and contribute individual responses, methods for handling misconceptions, differentiating questions and ensuring that the pace was suitable to keep all children involved and include the children less able to cope in a large group situation. Teachers readily adopted the use of peer discussion as a teaching tool but quality dialogue between the teachers and children was slow to get off the ground (Mroz *et al.* 2000; English *et al.* 2002; Burns and Myhill 2004). The work of Robin Alexander (2000) spurred the NLS to revisit the use of dialogue in the Literacy Hour and some of the best examples can be seen in the joint publication with the Qualifications and Curriculum Authority (QCA), *Speaking, Listening, Learning* (DfES 2003d).

Teaching to promote active learning

The principle of teaching for active learning is aligned with the arguments presented in Chapter 2 that literacy skills must be taught but the successful integration of reading and writing skills has to be driven by the actions of learners themselves. The principle of active learning was implicit in the wording of many of the teaching objectives using phrases such as 'collect and categorize', 'investigate and learn', 'experiment with', 'explore and discuss', 'research', 'collect and explain', 'compare'. Illustrations of active learning: interacting and responding, investigating, exploring, problem-solving, were woven through the professional development and guidance on the premise that learning of this kind helps motivates children, helps them to make sense of and thus retain knowledge, as well as cultivating wider competence to reason and think reflectively. Teachers were expected to teach children to:

- link new learning to what they already know
- make connections, generalizations and construct rules
- generate and test hypotheses
- express and clarify their ideas and opinions

- have strategies for problem-solving
- use a range of writing strategies such as talking aloud, using representations e.g. actions, drawings, maps, notes, diagrams
- imagine and empathize
- use inference and analogy to aid learning
- analyse actions, ideas, processes and texts to understand and explain how they work
- critically respond and evaluate.

Scaffolding

The concept of scaffolding as a teaching device grew from the work of Vygotsky (1978) and Bruner (1986). In a teaching context 'scaffolding' applies where a teacher performs part of a complex process while the learner carries out the other part, and is suggestive of an apprenticeship model. The term scaffold implies the gradual withdrawal of support as the learner becomes proficient. Bruner describes a teacher scaffolding a child as he learns how to build a pyramid out of a set of interlocking wooden blocks:

> She was the one with the monopoly on foresight. She kept the segments of the task on which the child worked to a size and complexity appropriate to the child's powers. She set things up in a way that the child could recognize a solution and perform it later even though the child could neither do it on his own nor follow the solution when it was simply told to him. In this respect, she made capital out of the 'zone' that exists between what people can recognize or comprehend when present before them, and what they can generate on their own – and that is the Zone of Proximal Development, or ZPD. In general what the tutor did was what the child could not do. For the rest, she made things such that the child could do with her what he plainly could not do without her. And as the tutoring proceeded, the child took over from her parts of the task that he was not able to do at first but, with mastery, became consciously able to do under his own control.
>
> (Bruner 1986: 75–6)

The Literacy Hour is a form of scaffolding. Children read or write with maximum support from the teacher during shared text work, with focused and gradually decreasing support during guided work and none during independent work.

Scaffolding occurs in shared reading through strategies for teaching young children about reading through modelling and demonstrating reading behaviours, and enabling children to participate in structured and semi-independent ways. Guided reading, where children read for themselves with support from the teacher is a carefully scaffolded step towards independence. The choice of reading material in independent reading is a form of scaffold. For instance, patterned texts have repeated phrases and rhymes which enable children to read more quickly without struggling to decode every unfamiliar word.

Scaffolding is also essential to the teaching of writing. Teachers can support the learning of a large group by controlling the process of either the transcription or the composition of writing to enable the children to concentrate on one or other process. Using these techniques children can learn to compose texts without the inhibiting problems of simultaneously transcribing it, and vice versa. Over time, support can be incrementally reduced to enable children to manage and integrate both processes. The introduction to the NLS *Grammar for Writing* (DfEE 2000a) guidance describes the approach. A common form of more structured scaffolding, pioneered in England by Maureen Lewis and David Wray (1995) and promoted in the NLS was the writing frame. A writing frame can provide a scaffold of the textual structure by, for instance, suggesting connectives to open each sentence: first, next, then, later … so that the child need only concentrate on the remaining construction of the sentence and its transcription on to page or screen.

The structure of the Literacy Hour

> The Literacy Hour is designed to provide a practical structure of time and class management which reflects the structure of teaching objectives in the NLS Framework. While the Framework provides details of what should be taught, the Literacy Hour is the means of teaching it.
>
> (DfEE 1998b: 8)

The Literacy Hour was designed as a basic default model, for schools to adopt and adapt. It was intended to guarantee one hour of daily continuous teaching time for classes of 30 or more children with no additional support. The basic lesson structure was represented in the form of a clock (Figure 4.1).

The structure of the Hour was compatible with common practice in primary school lessons i.e. class work followed by group and independent work, followed by a whole-class plenary session, although the class work was a lot more challenging and there was a new emphasis on guided and collaborative group work. Time allocations were for guidance, to ensure that each of the components occurred in a reasonable balance and with good pace, and time management. Teachers were also expected to work to a balance of connected reading and writing objectives over the course of a week and to plan Literacy Hour lessons in sequences, to provide continuity and development.

The decision to recommend one hour per day was based on the working assumptions underpinning the balance of subject time for English in the National Curriculum. For English (speaking and listening, reading and writing), this amounted to 180 hours per year over a 36-week year for Key Stage 1 and slightly less for Key Stage 2, equivalent to about one hour per day overall. It was significantly less than allocations in most other countries. For example, in Australia and the United States it

4 *KS1 and KS2*
Reviewing, reflecting, consolidating teaching points, and presenting work covered in the lesson.

1 *KS1 and KS2*
Shared text work (a balance of reading and writing).

Whole class
approx
10
mins

Whole class
approx
15
mins

Group and independent work
approx
20
mins

Whole class
approx
15
mins

3 *KS1*
Independent reading, writing or word work, while the teacher works with at least two ability groups each day on guided text work (reading or writing).

KS2
Independent reading, writing or word and sentence work, while the teacher works with at least one ability group each day on guided text work (reading or writing).

2 *KS1*
Focused word work

KS2
A balance over the term of focused word work or sentence work.

Figure 4.1 Structure of the Literacy Hour (Source: DfEE 1998b)

was not unusual to find a two-hour minimum. An hour per day was also significantly less than the average time actually devoted to literacy spread across a day prior to the NLS – estimated by the Schools Curriculum and Assessment Authority to be between 22 and 25 per cent per week. We could not exceed a discrete hour without risking the accusation of squeezing the statutory curriculum and stealing time from other subjects. The structure and organization of the Literacy Hour was also based on the assumption that most teachers worked with mixed ability classes of about 30 pupils with no additional adult support. These conditions have changed significantly since 1998. Today there are thousands more classroom assistants actively supporting teachers in their classrooms and teacher–pupil ratios have improved. Working from these basic assumption, the Literacy Hour was designed around a number of principles to:

Provide a minimum entitlement: ensuring that *all* children had full access to literacy teaching in line with the requirements and guidance for English in the National Curriculum. With additional support, a central objective was to include and provide for all children in the same lesson through a combination of strategies to 'level up' and 'hold in' lower achievers while challenging the more able.

Cover objectives under each main strand in the Framework: the lesson structure was designed to reflect the structure of the Framework quite explicitly. Text level work was expected to occur in every Literacy Hour with word and sentence level work, the ratio depending on the specific objectives being covered and the age and stage of the children.

Increase instructional time for children: through a series of linked teaching episodes, each child was directly taught in classes or groups for about 75 per cent of the time and worked independently for about 25 per cent – every child would be taught at least once a week in a small group for reading or writing. This new pattern contrasted sharply with previous individualized patterns of teaching where teachers taught for about 75 per cent of the literacy time but typically, each child was getting direct instruction for only about five minutes per week.

Embody a repertoire of successful teaching methods: well-paced shared reading and writing, focused, systematic teaching of phonics and spelling, guided reading and writing, purposeful independent and collaborative work, and plenary time for reflection on, and assessment of, learning.

Guide the balance of teaching and learning: the first half of each lesson was roughly divided between 'shared text work' (reading or writing) and focused word or sentence work. Then, while the children worked independently, the teacher would work with a small group on guided reading or writing for about 20 minutes. Each lesson would close with a short plenary session. Initially, Literacy Hours were conceived as a series of five lessons over a week with a common text or texts and a balance of emphasis around 60/40 for reading and writing, respectively.

Differentiate for a range of abilities: through appropriately levelled tasks and the judicious challenging, questioning, feedback and acknowledgement, teachers would 'level children up' and 'hold them in' to age-related expectations set out in the Framework. These were to become the ground rules for the concept of 'quality first teaching'.

Provide for the direct and separate teaching of phonics and other word level skills: this was a common and repeated message to schools and those who supported them. John Stannard summarized it in an address to the Publishers' Association in the Autumn of 1998:

> … there are basic necessary skills of phonics, spelling and handwriting which can be taught in enjoyable and active ways but which are essentially arbitrary conventions. For this reason, the rules governing these skills are hard for children to discover and it is as easy for them to make wrong generalizations or none at all. In this sense, the teaching of phonics is akin to the teaching of handwriting – mis-learned or unlearned skills quickly become counter-productive habits which are difficult to remedy. Many KS2 teachers recognize this to their cost in children who carry reading and spelling difficulties with them through the school. These skills cannot just be taught contingently as children meet them

in context. They need systematic and regular attention to get them established early. This too is reflected in the Framework and in the structure of the Literacy Hour.

(Address by John Stannard to the Publishers' Association, Autumn 1998)

The daily Literacy Hour was designed to harness and promote all these principles in a practical, manageable structure for teachers. Its strength lay in its common concepts and common generic structure. The title 'Literacy Hour' generated considerable initial impetus by creating a concept in a sound-bite, in need of explanation, that drew the attention of teachers, children, parents and the media.

Chapter 6 describes the implementation of the Literacy Hour by schools, from September 1998, through a combination of distance learning materials including detailed guidance and video illustrations, sent to each school in six units covering the key aspects of literacy teaching and learning, along with more intensive support for a significant proportion of lower performing schools.

Teaching the components of the Literacy Hour

The two components in the first half of the Literacy Hour, shared text work, sentence or word work were whole-class sessions to teach the three levels of objectives in the Framework. The guided and independent sessions which followed were for practising and applying the learning from the first half hour. The final whole-class 'plenary' session was for reviewing, assessing and consolidating the learning. Parameters had been formulated around each component but in effect each had a broad remit to accommodate the age of the class and the objectives to be taught. Guided reading, for instance, in a class of 5-year-olds, looked very different from that in a class of 8-year-olds. As the literacy strategy got underway, schools modified and developed these components, shared their experiences with each other, with their literacy consultants and other professionals. Over time the components and their relationship to each other evolved.

Word work

Word work had a discrete place in the Literacy Hour to ensure regular and systematic coverage of the word level objectives in the Framework. In the reception year and Key Stage 1 (4–7 years of age) this time was allotted primarily to phonics with a limited time for learning phonemically irregular words, and in Key Stage 2 (7–11 years of age) to spelling. It was expected that the vocabulary objectives would be covered contextually within shared reading and the handwriting objectives would be taught outside the Literacy Hour, though obviously applied within it.

Phonics teaching in the Strategy evolved in a number of ways. As discussed in the previous chapter, the pace of the content accelerated by about a year but approaches to teaching also developed. Essentially a pragmatic decision was made at the beginning of the Strategy to suggest teaching approaches that would be acceptable to the widest number of teachers and later, through publishing more detailed and structured guidance, to move teachers towards more effective approaches. For example, there were staging posts to arrive at:

- discrete teaching of phonics
- through-the-word segmentation
- phonemic blending.

At the beginning, the distance learning materials illustrated teaching phonics from texts. A year later, by suggesting a range of games, *Progression in Phonics* (DfEE 1999b) recommended a discrete approach to phonic teaching, unrelated to texts with a lively, enjoyable and fast pace for 4–6-year-olds. This approach continued in a supplementary folder *Playing with Sounds* (DfES 2004b) which presented a different approach to teaching segmentation from that suggested in *Progression in Phonics* because teachers were by then comfortable with teaching segmentation of vowel sounds quickly. Letter-by-letter or phonemic blending was a potential sticking point; for many teachers it epitomized what they perceived as wrong with phonics – 'barking at print'. At the beginning the problem was circumvented by suggesting blending through a process of analogy though rime. In *Progression in Phonics,* phonemic blending was introduced as the inverse of phonemic segmentation and in *Playing with Sounds*, oral phonemic blending and practice material for blending for reading were included.

By 1998, the place and importance of phonics and other word level work had become more strongly established, supported by *Progression in Phonics* and a national training programme for all schools, together with a clear recommendation to teachers of younger children that they should put word level work at the start of the Literacy Hour as a regular active daily occurrence for the whole class. This rapidly became the established and preferred pattern in most schools.

Perhaps because of the deep-rooted resistance to using phonics for reading, teachers were much more willing to apply phonics to spelling than reading. The concept of searchlights (see Chapter 2) tended to be misapplied in reading unfamiliar words. Even when children knew the letters and could blend it was common practice for teachers to encourage them to use context and grammar as the first port of call in figuring out a word and if this did not help, only then to suggest they look at the letters. The term 'over-phonicked' was disparagingly applied to children who unsuccessfully attempted to use phonics to read words they did not recognize. A closer examination revealed that although these children had mastered the skill of blending, they still did not possess sufficient knowledge of the alphabetic 'code' so would, for example, attempt to read words by pronouncing a phoneme for each individual letter (e.g. *l-i-g-h-t*) because they did not recognize a digraph (e.g. *igh*) as a phoneme. In a publication for years 2 and 3 on guided reading (DfES 2003a), this issue was highlighted using the video analysis of a child's reading.

Beyond phonics, investigation, hypothesis testing and problem solving were central to the development of spelling. The Strategy had moved away from the common perception that English spelling was irregular and haphazard and advocated a teaching approach that would involve curiosity and challenge in the learner and hopefully the teacher. Great stress was laid on investigating and understanding spelling patterns and conventions, morphological and etymological connections and playing with words. A book by Melvyn Ramsden (1996) was an inspiration in which he describes his delight as a teacher when he discovers something new about how words are spelled alongside his class of children. Spelling investigations were introduced in the distance learning materials and the following year the NLS published further support for teachers, the *Spelling Bank* (DfEE 1999c) for 8–11-year-olds. This provided lists of words through which to initiate investigations, modus operandi for conducting investigations and details of the convention each investigation was designed to reveal.

Vocabulary extension objectives were an equally important section of each term's word level objectives but, because extending vocabulary beyond common high and medium frequency words is so context dependent, little could be specified. This was possibly an under-rated aspect of the work in schools but it was never seriously evaluated in practice by the NLS or Ofsted, so it remains an area of great importance but considerable vagueness. The new emphasis on vocabulary recommended by the recent Rose review (2006) of early reading is a welcome re-emphasis, though similarly vague in what is recommended.

Shared reading

Shared reading was popularized by Don Holdaway (1979). The term literally means reading from the same ('shared') text. The point about the 'same text' was, first, to contrast with the common practice of individualized reading; in shared reading all the children were engaged in the same learning activity. Additionally, the teacher and all the children could see and refer to the same enlarged version of the text. This was usually a 'big book' or a text projected onto a screen or interactive whiteboard which made it easier for the teacher or child to indicate a precise part of the page (screen), word or sentence. In the Literacy Hour, shared reading was the generic strategy for teaching the text level reading objectives (comprehension and response) to the whole class. The texts were chosen on the basis of the range of narrative and non-narrative texts, poetry and plays recommended in the Framework for the term. For instance, the text range in one term (about three months) for a class of 8- and 9-year-old children was 'historical stories and short novels; play scripts, poems based on common themes; a range of text-types from reports and articles in newspapers and magazines; instructions' (DfEE 1998b: 38). For shared reading, it was recommended that the texts should be more challenging than the majority of children would be comfortable reading independently because the teacher was supporting their reading. 'This is particularly valuable for less able readers who gain access to texts of greater richness and complexity than they would otherwise be able to read' (DfEE 1998b: 11).

There was no set formula for a shared reading session. It took a variety of forms depending on the objectives being addressed, the only features in common being the teaching unit of a large group, usually the whole class, and the shared text. Shared reading was a vehicle for teaching a wide range of skills and knowledge and engendering understanding and dispositions. The teacher could demonstrate, model, assess, explain and lead discussion with the children in analysis and investigation – because everyone could see the text. Using large books in the early stages of reading, teachers could demonstrate 'the ways texts work', for instance, page turning and orientation from left to right and top to bottom and the common features of texts such as title, author, illustrator, contents and index. Enlarging the page or screen facilitated teaching layout, punctuation and other devices to assist meaning. It also made navigating reference material much easier to teach.

Shared reading provided the context for modelling and practising reading skills. As the children acquired phonics skills, the teacher could model decoding unfamiliar words, could give the children some practice at this in the context of the shared text and could model and explain strategies to build fluency. Similarly teachers could demonstrate to older children the skills of skim reading, summarizing the main points and scanning the page for specific content, explaining the processes as they did them. Shared reading made the comprehension process that was invisible and inaudible in silent reading, visible and audible. Teachers (and children) could model the process of comprehension by explaining their deductive and inferential thinking processes as they were reading. They could also demonstrate, using the enlarged text, how to impose an organization on a chapter or paragraph to aid comprehension by using coloured pens to annotate main and subsidiary points. When the children were discussing the text they could point out salient features and justify a point they were making with direct reference to the text. Analysing the structure of texts to inform writing was also facilitated by using an enlarged version.

Shared writing

In the early development of the NLS, the main focus was on reading for three reasons. First, because raising reading standards was the clearest and most pressing priority, second, because it was widely assumed that improvement in reading would bring writing improvement in its wake and lastly, the challenges it would present to teachers and children were underestimated. As a result, relatively little Literacy Hour time was being devoted to writing and many schools, anxious about the erosion of the creative writing lesson, took to suspending the Literacy Hour one day per week to provide time for more extended writing. However, there was little evidence that these practices, which we described in Chapter 1, were having much impact on improving standards.

As awareness of the writing challenge grew, the NLS responded with some formative guidance on teaching writing, *Grammar for Writing* (DfEE 2000b, 2000c) and *Developing Early Writing* (DfES 2001b). These two publications focused on the teaching of writing composition. This was formative work at the time and drew on evidence from psychology, linguistics, genre theory and educational research into effective teaching of writing. The guidance stressed the systematic linking of comprehension and text analysis in reading to text construction in writing. It re-asserted the point and purpose of learning grammar and promoted an understanding of grammar teaching as 'tools' rather than 'rules'. Three major aspects of language knowledge – language choice, sentence construction and cohesion – were identified to help teachers structure their work and provide a Framework of progression based on the sentence level objectives in the NLS *Framework for Teaching*. Most importantly, they addressed the practicalities of teaching, presenting a common approach to teaching with 'shared writing' as the foundation and detailed guidance on lesson planning, progression and the use of specific objectives. This writing initiative was introduced through a national professional development programme, first for trainers to improve their knowledge of grammar, and then on to teachers, to disseminate the materials. Since that time, concern that writing is still seriously lagging behind reading in quality of teaching as well as test results resulted in a steady stream of guidance including some targeted at boys' writing (DfES 2005).

The process of shared writing was derived from shared reading and fulfilled a similar function by making the processes involved in writing very explicit. All aspects of writing – planning, drafting, revising, editing and proofreading – were directly taught and scaffolded so that the children were not expected to write without careful preparation. The linking of reading and writing objectives meant that in shared reading the class would analyse texts in anticipation of writing in the same style or genre (see Chapter 3). This gave the children a clear model of the form of the text and its language features. There were then three stages of teaching before they were expected to write independently – demonstration writing, teacher scribing and supported composition – exemplified in *Grammar for Writing* (DfEE 2000a).

First, in a brief demonstration phase, teachers planned or wrote, explaining what they were doing and why. They could model overall planning of the text or the shape of a paragraph, thinking aloud as they made choices and moved sections around. They might model the drafting of two or three sentences, explaining why they started the sentence in a particular way or decided on a particular choice of vocabulary. Most importantly they would demonstrate the process of revising and refining the writing, explaining their reasons for changes. This short period of demonstration might be followed or interspersed with a process that was known as 'teacher scribing' during which they would ask for suggestions from the children. This was an opportunity for trying out different suggestions and discussing the merits of each. It could also be used to assess children's explicit knowledge of effective writing techniques.

Supported composition was an important buffer between whole-class composition of a shared text written by the teacher with the collaboration of the children, and each child composing his or her own text. Generally, children worked in pairs to plan or draft some writing. In drafting, they might compose the next sentence, verse or paragraph in the sequence that had been started and demonstrated by the teacher. Typically, the children would write on hand-held dry-wipe boards and the teacher would circulate amongst the children as they wrote, giving on-the-spot support. They would then display them so the teacher could review the general and specific level of learning and teach accordingly. Working in this way under the direct supervision of the teacher paved the way for the more demanding task of independent writing.

With the considerable investment in computers and broadband access in primary (elementary) schools in England, the source of texts expanded to include electronic texts. Whiteboard technology greatly enhanced shared reading and writing. It became easier to annotate texts, to save and recall various drafts of the same text, display two texts side by side for comparison, make and store generalizations about text types, create a template and much more. The whiteboard could display digital texts and the navigation and reading of digital texts could be modelled. Writing expanded into creating multimedia texts.

Sentence level work

The sentence level objectives were also taught in a whole-class setting either discretely in the allotted 15-minute slot in the Literacy Hour but, more commonly, within the context of shared reading and writing. This was uncharted territory for many teachers and an area of some uncertainty for the Strategy at the outset. The early distance learning materials exemplified practical approaches to teaching the sentence level objectives through which teachers could build up their own knowledge of grammatical functions and terminology. But a year later with the development and publication of *Grammar for Writing*, all of the sentence level objectives were assimilated into the teaching of writing. The title of this book contained the clear message that knowledge of grammar was functional – to enhance writing. A constructivist approach similar to that for spelling was recommended for teaching sentence level knowledge. Children investigated data – examples of the word class or sentence construction in the teaching objective – generated lists of its features and conventions for its use, investigated uses of grammar in shaping texts to serve the author's purposes and applied these through the process of shared-to-independent writing outlined above.

Gradually emerging during the first year of the Strategy was a coherent teaching sequence that started with shared reading: the comprehension and interpretation of text and response to it. The focus in shared reading then shifted over to text analysis to explore how authors constructed texts for particular purposes. Part of this analysis was a scrutiny of the text for sentence level language features such as apt choice of vocabulary, deliberate placing of a clause or adverbial phrase at the beginning of a sentence to create an effect or use of punctuation. This led seamlessly into planning and executing a piece of writing. Particularly with the older children, the distinction in the Literacy Hour between shared text work and sentence level work became blurred.

However, there are and remain serious challenges in the teaching of writing in relation to the level of teachers' knowledge about language and the effective use of the shared-to-independent reading pedagogy. Ofsted picked the point up in their final report in pointing out that some teachers' knowledge was still not sufficiently consolidated to teach sentence level objectives appropriately:

Recent guidance and training on the teaching of writing – Grammar for writing and Developing early writing – have included helpful descriptions of shared writing. … Few teachers, however, know enough about when to use these to best effect or, crucially, how to teach the important sentence level objectives within the context of shared writing … Although the training updated teachers' subject knowledge about grammar and, in the case of younger teachers, added substantial new knowledge, teachers whose grammatical knowledge was uncertain are not yet sufficiently confident with it to be able to use it intuitively and responsively in teaching writing.

(Ofsted 2002a: §60)

Guided reading and writing

For about 20 minutes in the second half of the Literacy Hour teachers worked with a small group of five or six children of similar reading ability on guided reading or writing. The form of guided reading adopted in the Literacy Hour was based on procedures used in the Reading Recovery programme with individual children (Clay 1979), adapted for a group (Fountas and Pinnell 1996). The overall objective of guided reading was to secure children's effective use of word reading and comprehension strategies and to build fluency so the procedure for younger and older children differed. With younger children, teachers provided a scaffold by introducing the text, relating it to the children's previous reading experience and then they listened, assessing and supporting, as the children read aloud individually and simultaneously at their own pace. Teachers then drew out some learning points such as working out the pronunciation of a word or how to deduce the meaning of new vocabulary and led a discussion to reveal the children's comprehension. Older children might be expected to arrive at a guided reading session having read the text, prepared to take part in a discussion to deepen their understanding and assimilate comprehension strategies for future use.

Working in a group was considered a more efficient use of the teacher's time and a more propitious learning experience for each child than the traditional approach of hearing children read individually. Resources of books for group guided reading were scarce at the outset of the Strategy but publishers were quick to produce sets of books and accompanying teaching suggestions specifically for guided reading. In 1998 the Reading Recovery National Network (2000 revised edition) published *Book Bands for Guided Reading*, a reference text for reception and Key Stage 1 teachers, grading about 4,000 books into ten levels of difficulty and providing helpful examples at each of the band levels. Subsequently they produced a handbook on guided reading for Key Stage 2 teachers (Institute of Education 2002).

The distance learning materials provided an introduction to guided reading which for many schools was new. Some schools had previously used a 'round robin' approach to group reading in which each child read aloud in turn. At first, many teachers found the suggested process of all the children reading aloud quietly but simultaneously while they monitored and supported, inconceivable. Video material that was produced in the second year of the Strategy was found to be very helpful but inspectors reported that guided reading was slow to take off and after four years wrote:

> Guided reading remains probably the most effective and efficient way of teaching reading, provided it is done well. This report draws attention, however, to the persistent weaknesses in its teaching at both key stages, as well as difficulties with timetabling it...
>
> Teachers need support to strike the fine balance between, on the one hand, teaching guided reading effectively so that pupils benefit from the direct teaching and assessment and, on the other, providing the rest of the class with work at the right level of challenge which the pupils can manage independently. This has never been easy. Further training, together with guidance on how to deal with the rest of the class, is essential.
>
> (Ofsted 2002a: 18)

Organizationally, guided reading remains a challenge for teachers who have to manage productive independent work for the remainder of the class at the same time. But it is an essential step from shared into independent reading, for younger children, by enabling the teacher to support and hear readers in manageable groups. The alternative is to fall back on the practices of individualized reading, which were failing too many children before.

Guided writing was introduced on the back of guided reading. It was used in varying ways in the early stages of the Strategy, for example to support collaborative and independent writing; to share, review and redraft writing. However, there was some doubt about the efficiency of the teacher's time in guided writing, especially in the younger age groups, where much of the session was spent tutoring spelling. It also competed for time with guided reading, which is the greater priority. There were other practical problems: guided reading used different texts from shared reading and was therefore a discrete session with a clearly defined methodology not thematically connected with the rest of the literacy lesson. But the subject for the guided writing sessions had to be drawn from the shared class-work. This meant that for each piece of writing, only one or at best two groups would have a guided writing session so it was essential that the writing could be achieved without this support. As the approach to teaching writing developed, it became clear that much of the journey towards independence in writing could be accomplished through class-work without the intervening guided group work. Because writing is a visible process, whereas reading is not, it is possible for children to work independently or in pairs on composing and sharing writing as part of a class lesson. In the guidance, *Grammar for Writing*, shared writing was strengthened and some of the process of guided writing was incorporated into supported composition.

Group work remains a vital part of the Literacy Hour for both reading and writing but the pattern has evolved. Guided reading remains a key element for all younger children and, in a more differentiated way according to need, for older children, whereas for writing, teachers take a much more flexible approach to working with groups which they judge according to the opportunities and demands of the task at hand.

Independent work

The term 'independent' in this component referred to the children's independence from the teacher, not 'individual' work. Children might work individually or in groups in this session and were expected to do so independently, without recourse to the teacher who would be focused on working with a group in guided reading or writing. This was the moment of minimal scaffolding. Having been supported in reading or writing through the shared and then guided work, children were expected to be well placed to read or write independently and should have the opportunity to do so. This could be reading for pleasure, researching a topic, practising letter–sound correspondences, carrying out a spelling or grammar investigation, writing notes, planning, drafting, revising, editing.

Because independent work occurred at the same time as guided group work it served two purposes which should have been compatible though, in practice, this was not always the case. Independence is an essential part of the literacy development process embedded in the structure of the Hour. Children need to be able read and write independently and to have increasingly effective strategies that enable them to do so. While children work independently, the teacher should be free to work effectively with a guided group for a short uninterrupted time. In the early training materials, there were practical suggestions about classroom organization and management to identify appropriate activities, help children access the materials and equipment they required and to be clear about tasks and what to do when finished, to ensure that the teacher remained undisturbed. These were welcomed by teachers who, in the main, were unused to teaching a group while the rest of the class worked independently.

However, teachers found this difficult and often provided low-level activities to keep children occupied or abandoned the guided work so that could ensure children remained on task. For the first three years of the Strategy, Ofsted reported that the independent period was the weakest part of the Literacy Hour. But in 2002, they reported improvements with around 85 per cent of lessons having satisfactory or better independent work, and that:

- more lessons give pupils opportunities to work on group and independent writing tasks which build on earlier shared work
- the level of challenge of these tasks has increased
- teachers have become more skilful in organising the independent and group tasks.

(Ofsted 2002a: 13)

The plenary session

The final ten minutes of the Literacy Hour which came to be known as the plenary, was an opportunity for the teacher and the children to consolidate the work carried out during the hour: rectify misperceptions, draw out generalizations and rules, restate procedures, articulate and summarize learning and flag up the direction of the following day's work. The overarching aim was to help children reflect and think about their own learning and to use the time to promote meta-cognitive learning which was more secure and transferable. It was also an opportunity for the teacher and pupils to gauge the level of learning achieved during the hour.

The big idea behind the plenary session was linked to the emerging research on assessment for learning. Teachers were expected to make learning literacy objectives clear to children and to use the final few minutes of the lesson to remind them about these expectations and discuss progress towards achieving them and what might be needed next. By and large, goals would be set for the whole class though progress towards them would be differentiated. Some children might have more specific goals to meet their needs which could also be monitored and picked up from time to time in the plenary session. This approach to setting pupil targets was entirely new when the Strategy began and it was not surprising that many plenary sessions were devoted more to sharing and celebrating achievements, and housekeeping than reflection and self-assessment. Over the years, however, as increasing emphasis has been given to the practices of pupil targets and self-assessment the use of this plenary has evolved and it is common now to find learning targets set for every child and for these to be a focus of discussion in the classroom.

The inspectors commented that 'Effective closing plenary sessions occur where the teacher has made the learning objectives precise and had given the pupils tasks that relate to the main theme of the lesson' (Ofsted 2002a: 14).

Flexibility and the evolution of the Literacy Hour

The Literacy Hour was designed to create a common framework for practice and has proved to be a powerful idea. It was conceived as the practical manifestation of the *Framework for Teaching* and presented to schools as a 'default' model: a benchmark and a baseline for practice. It has been the vehicle for establishing common practices and the foundation of the national training and support programme. For many schools, it has provided structure and authority for school leadership of literacy and became an important tool for local authorities in the business of school improvement. Equally, it has been very influential in shaping public perceptions of primary school literacy.

The Literacy Hour was never a static idea. One of the guiding principles, strongly advocated by Michael Barber, was that the everyone in the Strategy should 'learn as they go'. The Literacy Hour was a big idea and has remained a constant feature but its structure and balance have changed over time alongside teachers' developing understanding of literacy and how it should be taught. The 'learn as you go' principle was linked to a second big strategic idea that there must be 'flexibility within a common framework': flexibility to learn and enable schools to adapt the structure, but a common framework of shared language, understanding and practice. In their final report, the external evaluation team noted that:

> One of the most striking features of the implementation of the NLS and the NNS is the way in which Strategy leaders have modified elements of the Strategies (or messages about those elements) in response to information about progress and challenge. The overall vision set out through the Frameworks has remained constant but specific priorities and emphases have shifted somewhat in response to data about pupils' strengths and weaknesses and to feedback from LEAs.
>
> (Earl *et al.* 2000: 128)

We described how the various components of the Literacy Hour evolved in the previous section, in relation to emerging evidence about its effectiveness. These changes included:

- evolving and explicating advice on the teaching of phonics
- reordering the sequence of the first two parts of the Literacy Hour to give phonics greater prominence and reinforce the message that it should be taught discretely and begun earlier than in the original advice
- developing support and resources for guided reading and underlining its prominence in the Literacy Hour
- developing explicit shared writing practices through the *Grammar for Writing* and *Developing Early Writing* initiatives, in response to outcomes in the national tests
- embedding the teaching of sentence level objectives into the teaching of writing
- absorbing the earlier guided writing practices into shared writing to make more time and priority for group guided reading
- developing resources to help teachers improve the plenary sessions at the end of the Literacy Hour
- more recently, with changes to the Framework following the enquiry into the teaching of early reading, the phonics element of the Literacy Hour will be revised again. In some schools this is already taught as a separate element away from the Literacy Hour and this may become a more widespread practice in the early years.

One of the strengths of English primary education is its tradition of professional independence; teachers have their own classes and tend to do things their own way. If required to change they are usually cooperative. They take on new ideas but then adapt them to fit their circumstances. In 1998 the Literacy Hour offered a stable idea at a time of public criticism and professional uncertainty about literacy teaching. Though many of the detailed practices were new and challenging, its structure and approach resembled a form of classroom and lesson organization that was already familiar. It was designed to ease implementation but also to have development potential. For example, almost all teachers knew about shared reading and could launch this without much difficulty, even teachers of older children for whom it had not been a common practice. The Strategy provided training, guidance and pump-priming money to get this started. Similarly guided reading, though a great challenge, could get started at an organizational level while more detailed training and support to schools was provided. Word level work was always going to be a challenge which is why it was not placed first in the original form of the Literacy Hour.

As we shall note in Chapter 6, the Strategy reversed the traditional approach to professional development. Instead of moving from theory into practice it set out to change practices first. The Literacy Hour has been uniquely successful in bringing this about. But the practices, assuming they are well founded and effective, should then lead to enhanced understanding which secures and extends them. The downside, as critics have often pointed out, is that this might simply encourage compliance and dependency. The specific model of organization, its tight focus on practices and its presentation in the image of a clock were communicated and perceived prescriptively and the Strategy did not shirk from this. There was a good deal of scepticism but remarkably little resistance from schools. Most teachers accepted that things had to change and got on with the job because they had to. But because the Literacy Hour never was, or could be, a simple prescription to be slavishly followed, it engaged more and more teachers in having to think about and plan what they would do and seek help and support to do it. It was impossible to teach it without careful planning and some degree of understanding. Dependency varies in proportion to teacher's understanding and confidence and this remains an important challenge for the Strategy and particularly for those engaged in initial teacher training. Looking at the NLS in the context of other large-scale reforms, the final evaluation report from the external evaluation team makes the point:

> Most teachers indicated that they believe they have the knowledge and skill to implement the strategies well … However, some may feel they have fully implemented the strategies but may lack awareness of the underlying principles (perhaps partly due to the early emphasis on the structure of lessons, e.g. the 'clock' in the Literacy Hour). Or some may lack subject knowledge that will limit their further improvements. Not knowing that they don't know, these teachers will have made the easier changes required by the strategy and may not recognize that many changes and more knowledge are still required. Other studies corroborate these conclusions, finding that teachers often failed to realize what was involved in sophisticated teaching or curriculum reforms. Missing the underlying principles, they tended to implement the changes in superficial ways, without an awareness of what would be needed for a profound change in practice.
>
> (Earl *et al.* 2000: 94)

The Literacy Hour in its varied forms is the practical outcome of the Strategy in the classroom. Evaluation evidence shows that, despite the difficulties of implementation, it has had a profound impact on teachers' practice and a measurable impact on children's achievement (see Chapter 9). What is less clear is how far it has increased teachers' deeper understanding. Nevertheless, the changed practices have evolved and been sustained, backed by continuing professional development in every area of the country. When it began, the Literacy Hour was expected to launch the Strategy and run its course in two or three years but, nearly ten years on, the concept has proved remarkably resilient and is still at the core of literacy practice in primary schools across England.

Chapter 5

Differentiating the Strategy

Flexibility within a common framework

The principle of flexibility within a common framework is one to which we return in subsequent chapters. The common frameworks of targets, rationale, teaching objectives, pedagogies and the Literacy Hour provided the foundation of shared ideas and practices that drove the Strategy. These ideas needed to be relatively simple and powerful and were designed in the first instance to change teachers' practices. Fidelity to the principles was essential for rapid and successful implementation. But it was also fundamental for the Strategy to exploit this common framework in differentiated ways. The principle of differentiation was driven by the needs of the children and, in particular, by the imperative to tackle the problem of 'the long tail of under-achievement' that had been identified in the two reports from the Literacy Task Force (see Chapter 1). This involved differentiation at every level of implementation – local authority, schools and the classroom; major refinements in data analysis and data literacy to better target support; and a detailed programme of development to generate training and resources for use with children.

Three levels of differentiation

In Chapter 4 we described the Literacy Hour and the associated concept of 'quality first teaching'. Differentiation was designed around the first priority of ensuring Literacy Hour 'quality first teaching' across the system. The aspiration of the government was that eventually 'first' teaching would reach a sufficient level of quality to guarantee 80 per cent of the children in the country the standard expected for their age; a further 18 per cent might reach the same standard for their age with additional support. These figures were derived from the Children's Literacy Success Strategy (CLaSS), the literacy strategy in the state of Victoria in Australia jointly run with Peter Hill and Carmel Crévola in the University of Melbourne.

> Within CLaSS, schools will be expected to adopt a set of targets derived from those of Clay and Tuck (1991) in their 'three waves of teaching.' They argue that with good teaching in the first year of schooling … one can expect 80 per cent of students to have reading and writing under way.

During the second year of schooling … with appropriate one-to-one intervention using Reading Recovery, one can expect to have a further 18 per cent under way. This leaves approximately two per cent for further referral and special support will be necessary during their third year of schooling …These targets may be expressed as follows:

First Wave – Good first teaching (80 per cent of students under way)

Second Wave – Intervention: Reading Recovery (98 per cent of students under way)

Third Wave – Further referral/Special assistance (remaining 2 per cent of students).

(Crévola and Hill 1996: 11)

Referring to the Victoria literacy strategy the incoming government wrote in 1997:

In New Zealand … the 80 per cent who learn to read first time are referred to as the first wave and those who catch up through Reading recovery as the second wave. This still leaves in the region of five per cent of pupils who are known as the third wave. It would be disastrous to write off this group by excluding them from the target. Many of them, although they will have identified special educational needs, can nevertheless learn to read well. Each of them needs an individual learning plan and we recommend that under the present Code of Practice … arrangements are made to meet their literacy needs.

(Literacy Task Force 1997: §105)

Working within a figure of around 20 per cent provision of additional support for children's learning needs was already established in local government planning. The Warnock report (DES 1978) had estimated that, overall, as many as 20 per cent of children might experience, at some time during their schooling, educational needs for which additional provision might be necessary. At the time, however, the challenges of writing were underestimated. The main priority for the NLS at the start was reading and it was assumed, somewhat naively as it turned out, that writing standards would develop in concert with rising standards of reading. This appeared to be the case for children at 7 years old and has proved to be a reasonable assumption. In 2006 there was only a three-point difference between national reading and writing outcomes (reading 84 per cent, writing 81 per cent). However, the NLS was extrapolating from patterns of attainment for younger children to ambitions for 11-year-olds, and here the emerging picture was very different. The Literacy Task Force was advised by the School Curriculum and Assessment Authority that it would be safe to assume a close correlation between reading and writing achievement but it rapidly transpired that this was not the case (see Chapter 6). While the assumption held for reading, it did not hold for writing, which is a very different challenge for teachers and children. In practice, however, the assumptions were reasonable since, although the wave 2 programmes had a reading and writing input, the greater emphasis overall was on targeting reading failure to create conditions for greater success in writing.

To achieve the target, the Strategy would need to differentiate carefully and precisely for each wave, but still within the common framework. The Strategy saw its relationship to this three-wave structure as increasingly devolved. It would be strategically and operationally responsible for the delivery of quality first teaching through the implementation of the Literacy Hour. Quality first teaching was an entitlement for all children and a foundation for children who had additional wave 2 support, consistent with the Literacy Hour. The NLS developed the programmes and trained teachers and teaching assistants to deliver wave 2 support but the decisions about how and to whom it would be provided were the business of the schools, with advice from their local authority if needed. Wave 3 children who, by definition, had a range of identified special educational needs, would be catered for entirely by local means because of the highly individual nature of the provision required; it would not be appropriate for the NLS to attempt any form of universal provision. This devolved approach changed under the Primary National Strategy in 2002, when guidance was produced nationally to support the estimated 5 per cent or less of SEN children.

Differentiation for wave I

The first priority was to ensure quality first teaching and this required placing resources where the need was greatest and recognizing that differentiation was an important feature of quality first teaching and did not simply kick in when children had failed to thrive first time around. Differentiation was driven from the centre: differentiated targets for local authorities and schools; differentiated support for schools; differentiated support to pupils.

Differentiated targets

The national 80 per cent target was disaggregated to take account of the varied contexts and histories of local authorities. Each of the 150 authorities was expected to make a proportionate contribution to the national target. This implied that some, already performing above the target, were set higher expectations while others were expected to meet lower targets. From the start, there was a floor target of 70 per cent for the lowest performing authorities below which no one was expected to fall. (This target was increased to 78 per cent in 2003 on the basis of improving performance at the lower end of the range.) At the time, this was a significant challenge to some. In the first year, these differentiated targets were simply 'handed down' to local authorities on what came to be known as 'brown envelope day'. It was not one of the Strategy's more auspicious moments. In subsequent years, there was negotiation between local authorities and central government on where to set targets within an indicative range based on the arithmetic of the LEA's performance in relation to the national expectation.

Local authorities, in turn, went through a similar process with each of their schools to ensure that schools, too, would make a proportionate contribution to the national target. The process became more sophisticated and, as the NLS developed, schools have become increasingly able to use data to target pupils individually or in groups for additional support and monitoring. The *Framework for Teaching* together with detailed supplementary guidance on identifying and setting individual pupil targets, and quite detailed feedback from the national tests, increased the precision and sophistication with which individual schools could pinpoint children's needs and identify the important things they needed to learn or re-learn in order to progress. Thus, the national 80 per cent could be unpacked right down the line to actions for teachers in support of individuals. Schools' ability to translate numerical targets into 'curricular targets' remains at the heart of the improvement process. The more recently developed *Intensive Support Programme* (ISP) is a highly successful manifestation of this principle, designed to support under-performing schools through detailed pupil-level needs analysis, intervention and monitoring (see Chapter 8).

Differentiated support to schools

The principle on which schools were supported to implement the NLS was 'intervention in inverse proportion to success'. More resources and support were allocated to schools facing the greatest challenges. All schools were entitled to a two-day conference to introduce the NLS, four days of professional development for all staff using distance learning materials and some additional school funding to buy books. It was estimated that between 40 and 50 per cent of schools nationally would require more intensive support to raise their standard in literacy. 'These will be schools either serving areas of social disadvantage where attainment is significantly low, or those where performance is relatively poor' (DfEE 1997a: 24).

In the first year of implementation, 10 per cent of schools received 'intensive' help from their local authorities which comprised a programme of support from literacy consultants and five days of professional development for two key teachers from each school. The professional development was to enhance the subject knowledge of the two teachers and prepare them for running the professional development using the distance learning materials in their schools. Each school in this programme was entitled to a number of days' visits from a literacy consultant to advise the head teacher and literacy coordinator on analysing their pupil data, organization of literacy in the school, teach demonstration Literacy Hours and support teachers as they started teaching the components of the Hour. In subsequent years, the intensive support principle continued but with greater flexibility, allowing local authorities to deploy support to more schools on more of a sliding scale, according to need.

Schools in greatest need were also allocated central funding and materials for running summer schools and booster classes. But a large number of local authorities chose to supplement the central government funding for the Strategy and created additional consultants, directly supported a greater number of schools and provided additional summer schools and funding for booster classes for older children to raise attainment in readiness for the national tests. Similarly, when in 2002 the ISP was launched in local authorities with schools in particularly challenging circumstances, other local authorities chose to join the scheme as associate members without external funding but with access to related professional development.

ISP built on lessons learned from work across the literacy and the numeracy strategies. It was designed as a whole-school programme. Those taking part agreed to achieve a set of non-negotiable base-line conditions within a specified time, and held school professional development sessions from which they devised whole-school curricular targets layered for each year. They were supported by a link adviser and one consultant who drew on the expertise of numeracy or literacy consultants as required. This programme was very successful in galvanizing schools into an organization which raised standards faster than the average in their local authorities.

Although the success of the NLS was measured by its capacity to increase the proportion of 11-year-olds achieving level 4 in English, schools were emphatic that they expected the Strategy to improve standards for all children. Special schools attended the initial two-day conferences to launch the Strategy and most subsequently took it on. Schools which catered for children with emotional and behavioural difficulties generally found that they could use the Framework objectives with the year group for which they were intended. Schools for children with moderate learning difficulties (MLD) were also able to use the objectives, perhaps with some modification, some months or a year or more later. Those with severe and profound and multiple learning difficulties could work on similar objectives even though at an age which might be considerably below their age-related peers. Supplementary guidance on children with special educational needs (DfEE 1998c), produced in the autumn of 1998, was addressed to teachers in mainstream schools, attached special classes and special schools. The HMI report summarizing the implementation of the NLS in special schools two years later was very positive, suggesting that '… many of the schools in the survey were able to teach the NLS successfully without making many significant adaptations' (Ofsted 2000a: 4). An additional advantage of special schools taking on the Strategy was the opportunity for integration with mainstream provision:

> … many local authorities sought to increase the opportunities for pupils from special schools to work alongside their peers in mainstream schools as part of their inclusion policy. That schools had adopted a common approach to teaching literacy was of considerable benefit to those MLD pupils who attended their neighbouring primary schools on several mornings each week, as they were able to participate in the familiar Literacy Hour with some degree of success.
>
> (Ofsted 2000a: 5)

In 2000, comprehensive professional development was provided for special schools (DfEE 2000f). The two modules, 'The management of literacy at school level' and 'Teaching and learning strategies', provided the incentive and the resources for schools to be aspirational for their pupils and to realize those aspirations.

Differentiated support was also provided within schools. Head teachers and their leadership teams were the initial conduits for the Strategy in each school. Thereafter, the focus moved to the literacy coordinators who had regular contact with their local authority consultant and attended professional development sessions on interpreting and using data, monitoring and supporting staff and on specific areas of the literacy curriculum. Concern that head teachers were not as well informed as their staff prompted a round of conferences specifically for them in 2000. These and corresponding National Numeracy Strategy conferences the following year highlighted the need for further support for the head teacher and leadership team and for three years 25 per cent of schools each year were invited to join the primary leadership programme.

Defined cohorts of teachers received focused curriculum support: reception and Key Stage 1 teachers received phonics and writing; Key Stage 2, spelling and grammar; there was support for year 2 and 3 teachers in the transition between Key Stage 1 and 2; each year there was considerable support for year 6 teachers, those who had ultimate responsibility for ensuring that 11-year-olds achieved a level 4. Specific guidance was produced for reception teachers on using the Literacy Hour in a play-based curriculum. A programme of professional development was produced specifically for classroom assistants. Guidance was written for the growing number of expert or leading teachers and they also received tailor-made professional development to support them in their role and to extend their subject and pedagogic knowledge.

Guidance was also produced for teachers who had classes containing children from more than one age-group as they were working from objectives from two or more years and needed to consider how to adapt the Literacy Hour to accommodate some multilevel teaching. This guidance suggested the following options for adapting the Literacy Hour:

- following the Literary Hour, but reducing the amount of whole-class time to allow for more group time;
- increasing the time to allow for more group teaching while retaining the same level of whole-class work – this takes more curricular time and may affect the balance of teaching time for other subjects;
- making use of an additional adult to provide simultaneous teaching or support during the Literacy Hour; and
- setting across a number of classes – this is possible in some circumstances, but it is important to take care to ensure that setting does not lower the expectations of what low attainers and children with other special needs can achieve.

(DfEE 1998c : 100)

Differentiated support to pupils in wave 1

Support for pupils in different year groups was differentiated within wave 1. From the beginning, year 6 children received particular support. These were the children who, in the first year of the Strategy, had not received Literacy Hour teaching in their schooling and had just one year to ensure their literacy skills were sufficient to access the secondary school curriculum. Summer schools were provided for children within three months of the election of the new government, and booster classes were provided the following year. The test at the end of year 6 was becoming increasingly 'high stakes'. As well as measuring each child's capacity to access the secondary curriculum, it represented the school's, LEA's and government's success in reaching their interim targets. A resulting tendency to replace much of the teaching in year 6 with repeated test practice prompted the Strategy to provide detailed planning and teaching resources specifically for year 6, including an exemplar 'bridging unit' to support children between the primary and secondary phases of their education, on the assumption that falling grades reported in the first year of secondary school were partly caused by lack of continuity over the transition period.

Analysis of national test results in year 6 and results from internal school testing in other years revealed deficit areas of the curriculum and the Strategy supported these by producing materials on specific subjects for each year, for example, general guidance and phonics in years R and 1, spelling in years 2 and 3, guided reading in year 3, example bridging unit for middle school between years 4 and 5, comprehension in year 5. Booster and summer schools were also extended to year 5. Guidance was offered for organizing the literacy curriculum for children in mixed age classes.

'Quality first teaching'

Quality first teaching was underwritten by the combined structures of the *Framework for Teaching* and the Literacy Hour. The characteristics of quality first teaching are described in the previous chapter. Quality first teaching is not, however, 'one size fits all'. It is essential that children's individual needs are met and teachers in primary schools aspire to provide instruction that can be accessed by all the children in a mixed ability and often multi-ethnic class. They employ devices to support children with sensory impairment, a carefully considered format to support children with behavioural difficulties, alternative and extension activities to stretch the most able and scaffolding to support the less able.

Differentiation was needed in some content areas more than others. Generally the text level reading objectives were sufficiently broad to be appropriate to all the children in most mainstream classes. While the writing objective might need to be modified for some children, they could still share the same writing purpose and audience with the others in the class. Content at word level was where greatest differentiation was needed and children could be working on objectives a term or a year or more behind their peers. However, wave 2 programmes were created so that children would, wherever possible, be 'held in' with the rest of the class so that they could benefit from the teaching and learning in the Literacy Hour. Educational psychologists regarded the Framework of objectives as a valuable starting point for deciding targets for the individual education plans (IEPs) of children with special educational needs. The government subsequently published 'P' scales to cater for children working towards National Curriculum level 1 so that the children, their teachers and parents could measure small steps of progress. The Strategy produced extensive guidance and ran professional development for schools to enable them to decide how the objectives could be differentiated and modified for children with special educational needs (DfEE 1998c, 2000f), children learning English as an additional language (DfEE 1998c, DfES 2002a) and gifted and talented children (DfEE 1998c, 2000e).

A basic principle of the Literacy Hour was inclusion. All children were entitled to quality first teaching. It was argued that the pedagogies suggested within the components of the hour were highly suitable for all children. Indeed, successful special needs methods were recommended as suitable pedagogies such as modelling reading and writing strategies, scaffolding learning, systematic phonics, organization of work, understanding how texts are created, writing frames and the uses of specific learning objectives for self-monitoring and assessment. However, to accommodate children with particular needs resulting from, for instance, a sensory impairment, giftedness, attention or language deficit, a partial knowledge of English, teachers needed to adopt measures to ensure that these children were able to take full advantage of their teaching.

The principle that all children were entitled to quality first teaching in the Literacy Hour was endorsed by an NFER literature review commissioned by the DfEE.

> Teachers should assume that all pupils can be included within the normal structure of the Literacy Hour unless there is evidence … that the particular difficulties of certain pupils warrant a different approach. However, at the same time, teachers need to be aware that classroom approaches will have to be differentiated in order to accommodate what is often an abnormal profile of skills in pupils with identified special educational needs, particularly those with severe needs. This will probably involve all the well-established strategies for differentiation.
>
> (Fletcher-Campbell 2000: 83)

Differentiation within the elements of the Literacy Hour

Within the Literacy Hour, guided reading and writing were, by definition, differentiated by ability, allowing the teacher to work with a group of children on objectives specific to them. Where there was an additional adult available, they might also support an ability group. During independent time there was ample opportunity for differentiation and in Fletcher-Campbell's words, it involved 'all the well-established strategies'. Children may be working on the same task but with different expected outcomes. For example, they might be concentrating on varied sentence construction in a piece of writing. Whilst most of the class would be expected to frame some complex sentences, the teacher would be looking for added panache from the most able and would be delighted if the less able produced their argument in a coherent sequence of correctly punctuated simple and compound sentences. Alternatively a writing task may be scaffolded in various ways such as using writing frames or being given a list of possible vocabulary or the opening paragraphs or plot. Independent work was also an opportunity to give individuals or groups of children tasks to consolidate a specific skill or body of knowledge to catch up with their peers. Increasingly, as teachers became comfortable with teaching to objectives, they used individual or group curriculum targets as short-term goals for children to achieve. These would often be expressed as 'I can … ' statements such as 'I can write a sentence using a capital letter and a full stop.'

It was within the whole-class sessions in the Literacy Hour that concerns about appropriate differentiation were most keenly expressed and accusations of one-size-fits-all directed. In fact, as discussed in Chapter 4, the medium of whole-class instruction offers enhanced opportunities to children with particular needs such as those with dyslexia, those who are coming to grips with learning the English language and those who are behind their age-related peers in deductive and inferential reasoning. In shared reading, children who have difficulty decoding text can discuss on equal terms with their peers, themes, motives and literary effect; children learning to speak English are immersed in a contextual experience particularly if the teacher explains terminology, verbally or pictorially; children who tend to understand only the literal aspects of text can learn to infer through observing inferential thinking being modelled.

The guidance offered to teachers in the annex to the Framework in autumn 1998 detailed approaches with the whole class that were generally good teaching but added specific suggestions for ensuring that children with additional needs such as those with sensory and language impairment, those learning English as an additional language, those with behavioural or learning difficulties, could fully access the lessons. The NLS at this point became a welcome conduit for special needs and language professionals to introduce approaches and organizational ideas which had been the exclusive province of the few for too long. The NLS with its immense infrastructure of specialist consultants and its written guidance became a vehicle for messages about good inclusive teaching. Some of these important messages were new to some teachers, for example, facing children with hearing difficulties when speaking to them, enlarging material for the visually impaired, using objects and pictures to explain vocabulary and idioms for the benefit of children learning English as an additional language, differentiating questions to accommodate the range of abilities, limiting the number of oral instructions to help children with a receptive language impairment and for children with expressive language difficulties 'echoing back' their answers in expanded form. The professional development *Supporting Children with Special Educational Needs in the Literacy Hour* (DfES 2000f) was an excellent vehicle for purveying good practice in managing behaviour so that everyone benefits from the maximum time available for learning.

However, this professional development was an opportunity to convey the principles as well as the practices of inclusion. It projected the ideology that all children have the right to the very best education and that the dispositions and actions of their teachers are central to their progress. Again literacy teaching was an opportunity for values and messages about good teaching to be promulgated. As the national inclusion policy was taking effect and special school places reduced, more children with difficulties likely to affect their learning were attending mainstream schools and most teachers were encountering children with sensory, language, cognitive, emotional and physical disabilities. So this material also provided specific knowledge about teaching children with various difficulties which many teachers would not have known from their initial training (preparation). Likewise the numbers of children learning English as an additional language grew exponentially during and since the introduction of the NLS. The 1998 guidance was followed by professional development in 1999, revised in 2002, which furnished teachers with a new body of pedagogic knowledge about the specific problems of children learning to speak, read and write English. It tackled cultural issues and the specific needs of new arrivals and isolated learners.

In addition to teaching suggestions during the whole-class sessions in the Literacy Hour, the 1998 guidance discussed organizational options for other adults to support some children in the Literacy Hour:

> The Literacy Hour has been designed to be taught by a teacher working without support from an additional adult. Where this support is available, however, it should be used to maximum advantage. … It is important that these additional adults receive training about the National Literacy Strategy so that they can work alongside the teacher during the Literacy Hour. If they work with the class regularly, they should be involved in planning the literacy work with the teacher.
>
> (DfEE 1998c: 99)

The guidance suggested a number of appropriate ways that assistants could support the teaching in the class; for instance, during a 'whole class' part of the lesson, sitting near a child or group of children who had attention or cognitive difficulties and providing an additional explanation or encouraging them to formulate and make a verbal contribution to the lesson. Where two groups needed different teaching, an assistant might work with half the class while the teacher worked with the rest. During group work the assistant might work with a group or, depending on the activity, might provide support for the class while the teacher worked with a group. A particularly important suggestion was that children who would find the reading or concepts difficult in the shared text should work with the text the day before the shared reading session. Even though smooth running of the Literacy Hour was not dependent on a classroom assistant, the benefits were quickly realized and a government initiative to increase the number of assistants nationally was matched by the demand from schools.

The perceived gender issue in the years prior to the start of the NLS was that of girls not fulfilling their potential. Although still an issue in some quarters, it has been overtaken by extensive concern over the low standard of boys' literacy, particularly writing. It was argued with some degree of evidence from the pilot that the elements of the Literacy Hour favoured boys: they liked the discussion in the whole-class text sessions, they benefited from structured phonics teaching, they were motivated by problem solving in investigational work and they responded particularly well to the clarity of objectives and the expectation of measuring up to the criteria for successful working. Boys' standards rose; so did girls'. Therefore the gap between the boys and the girls barely narrowed. The Strategy continued to invest in research, materials and professional development to help teachers motivate boys to write, and write well (DfES 2005). But while some local authorities are reporting improvements there is still a considerable amount to do and we argue in Chapter 10 that this may require a renewed national effort.

Differentiation for wave 2

The main characteristic of 'wave 2' learners was that they needed to catch up with essential learning on which, for one reason or another, they had missed out. Reasons typically centred on limitations in support and experience for children beyond the school correlated with predictable social and economic factors – poverty, housing, employment, health, family disruption. Such disadvantage carried further problems of disaffection, behaviour and adjustment in their wake. This principle, that the great majority of lower achieving children had missed out on essential learning and needed support to 'catch up', was endorsed for children with special educational needs by the NFER literature review commissioned by the DfEE.

> There is no cogent evidence that, as a broad group, pupils with special educational needs which interfere with literacy acquisition require teaching approaches that are qualitatively or significantly different from those used for all pupils. However, there is evidence that pupils' effective learning in literacy depends on appropriate differentiation which will, in itself, often mean that the actual structure of the literacy teaching either has to be more explicit or composed/ balanced differently.
>
> (Fletcher-Campbell 2000: 78)

The first investment of wave 2 teaching was made in year 3. These children had not had the benefit of the NLS during their first three years of schooling, so a programme of additional literacy support (ALS) was created and funded, as a matter of urgency, for those children who had moved into Key Stage 2 (aged 7–8) below the expected level for their age. This programme had a reading element of guided and supported reading, substantial phonics and a sentence level writing component (DfEE 1999a). It was designed to be carried out three times a week by a teaching assistant under guidance from the classroom teacher with a group of not more than five children during the 20-minute group/independent session in the Literacy Hour. Its elements of content and organization were based on well-researched methodologies (Clay 1979; Hatcher 1994).

This was followed by a programme for those 5- and 6-year-olds, recognized by Marie Clay and subsequently by Hill and Crévola in the Australian strategy in Victoria, who after one year in school and receiving quality teaching did not yet have 'reading and writing under way'. Children were screened at the end of the first term in year 1 (their second year in school). Sessions began in the following term, three times a week, but unlike ALS this was outside the Literacy Hour (DfES 2001c).

A third intervention programme was also considered necessary for the older children. Quality teaching may be offered and teachers are very resourceful in enabling children to access it but for various reasons already pointed out children can fall behind. Further Literacy Support (FLS) was designed for children in year 5 (aged 9–10) who lacked confidence in reading and writing. As many of these children were boys, the programme was designed to appeal to them in particular. Its main thrust was to oblige them to take responsibility for their own learning and assuage the feelings of resentment and lack of self-esteem that beleaguer underachieving children at this age (DfES 2002b).

The necessity for three programmes was in no way considered a failure of the Framework objectives and the Literacy Hour to provide quality first teaching. The point of the 'Warnock 20 per cent' was that for a number of reasons in order to keep up with the considerable standard our society expects of children, some need periodic additional help. Other children may fall behind through absence, illness or an emotional upheaval and may only need additional support once in their schooling. A number of children, once off the ground in year 1, may not require further support. Others who coped quite well in their early education may find aspects of comprehension difficult and a number of boys need additional support in writing. The extra and differently designed wave 2 provision at Key Stage 3 (age 11–14) recognized the same issues.

There were common principles underpinning all three primary programmes:

- The programmes were not an alternative to quality first teaching but based on the premise that despite quality first teaching some children needed additional support in order to be held in to the same level of achievement as their peers.
- They were designed to be taught by a teaching assistant, additional to the class teacher.
- Participants were selected against clear criteria.
- The sessions in each module were cumulative with learning being revisited and revised.
- The programmes contained three sessions a week and were intended for a small group, over a time-limited period.
- Sessions were brisk, lively and interactive.
- All the materials required for teaching the modules were provided.

- Interaction was built in between teaching assistant and classroom teacher to keep the teacher informed and maintain continuity.
- Professional development for both the classroom teachers and the teaching assistants was designed to ensure involvement from the classroom teacher and continuity for the children.
- There was staged professional development over a series of sessions to ensure that participants could deepen their understanding and seek support from colleagues and experts.
- Each programme had a homework element so that parents were directly involved in their children's learning.
- Assessment and progress checks ensured that children's learning was monitored.

Managing interventions across the school in terms of continuity and coherence for children as well as organizing staff, teaching spaces and equipment was an area that was closely examined and best practice was collated and disseminated. As we stated in Chapter 1, no stone was left unturned in relation to managing, as well as teaching, literacy. The work in this area contributed to the examination of working practice across the system in workforce reform.

Wave 3 support

The NLS created no specific programmes for wave 3 on the basis that the small percentage of children who needed this support was a disparate group and that those involved in their support should tailor their teaching to the individual child, making use of resources as they considered appropriate. The DfES commissioned Greg Brooks to update his review of effective programmes which was issued to local authorities and schools so that teachers had the best available evidence to guide them in their choice of materials (Brooks 2002). However, the Strategy did provide a coordinated effort to mobilize local agencies to ensure that children's literacy needs were systematically supported in line with appropriate adjustments to the age-related expectations in the Framework. Regional conferences brought together those responsible for literacy and those responsible for special educational needs in each local authority. The first meeting revealed issues of coherence, and a certain suspicion between these two groups, both responsible for children's literacy development. This antagonism might have largely dissipated if they had forged better communications and the special needs services would have found that teachers using the NLS Framework were more in tune with their approaches to teaching than before. In response, the Strategy appointed regional directors and additional funding to support local authorities in coordinating their services to devise appropriate wave 3 provision.

We discuss the effectiveness of the Strategy in meeting the learning needs of most children and in reducing the long tail of underachievement in Chapter 9. But its effectiveness in providing differentiated and focused support was clear from early on. Compared with any previous government curriculum initiative it was very well-funded and resourced. If schools or local authorities raised an issue, the Strategy sought and published a response in the form of guidance or materials. The demands grew from all quarters: feedback from Ofsted, communications to the DfES, feedback from consultants in local authorities and initial teacher trainers. In fact in a short space of time both the literacy and numeracy strategies became publishing outfits. As explained in Chapter 4, the NLS resisted demands to produce full-blown lesson planning but a great deal of material was made available and with hindsight we feel that we fell into the trap of attempting to answer every differentiation query when we should have consolidated and made clearer the basic principles upon which teachers could base their own decisions.

Nevertheless, differentiation has been a core principle throughout the evolution of the Strategy. The wave 1–3 assumptions were mirrored in similar provision made by the numeracy strategy and have helped schools and local authorities to deploy support with increasing precision. While the Strategy was anxious to avoid the one-size-fits-all perception that it inevitably attracted at the outset, it also needed to maintain a constant and common coherent vision. Differentiation deteriorates into undisciplined diversity without the common vision to set the benchmarks, standards and expectations against which variations in practice and achievement can be planned and evaluated. The external evaluation team drew attention to this principle of 'adaptation within a coherent vision', and we shall return to it in later chapters.

> From the beginning, NLNS have been concerned with balancing entitlement for all pupils with recognition of individual differences. … teachers are encourage to take account of pupils' differences, but in a managed way within the common structures of the Literacy Hour.
>
> (Earl *et al.* 2000: 13)

Chapter 6

Implementation

The National Literacy Strategy can be described in three broad phases, which were planned but which also evolved in response to changing needs, opportunities and constraints:

- implementation – development and introduction, 1997–98
- securing the Strategy for sustainability and greater devolution, 1999–end of 2001
- devolving the Strategy to schools through the evolution of a broader Primary National Strategy, 2002–present.

The three phases also need to be viewed against the background of developing research and theory about the management of large-scale reform in education. Three key figures in this field were Michael Barber, who carried overall responsibility for the Strategy and was accountable to the Minister for its implementation and success; Michael Fullan, who led the external evaluation team and had an established international reputation as leading researcher in the field; and David Hopkins, also a significant contributor to research on leadership and school improvement, who replaced Michael Barber at the DfES in 2001 as Chief Adviser to the Secretary of State on School Standards. As the NLS evolved, it became a major source of evidence for researchers and, to some extent, a test-bed for new ideas. In this chapter, we describe the first phase of the Strategy, depicted by Michael Barber as a phase of 'informed prescription' (Barber 2002), during which the expectations were set and content and training were agreed and developed. This phase included the first year of implementation in LEAs and schools. It was a time of rapid concentrated effort to get all schools to embrace a common literacy agenda.

In Chapter 1, we described the state of literacy teaching in primary schools prior to the introduction of the NLS. It was clear that, despite many pockets of successful practice, there was little widespread agreement about literacy teaching beyond the generally accepted practices of individualized work from reading programmes and the stimulation and facilitation of extended, creative writing in classrooms. Schools were universally concerned about the need to improve standards; they did not need convincing about the moral argument but this created its own frustrations. Most teachers worked hard at literacy support, within and often well beyond curriculum time. There was no shortage of effort. As well as a moral imperative, the government was convinced of the long-term social and economic potential of literacy improvement. For all these reasons, the state of literacy in England as elsewhere in the world had become a matter of increasing public concern and frustration for more than a decade. This combination of concern and frustration was also propitious and provided a rare political opportunity for change.

The approach taken in the Strategy drew extensively on current research and practice so, in a sense, none of it was new. What was new, however, was the way in which the elements were assembled and presented into a comprehensive and practical approach, driven by the need to implement change urgently, on a system-wide scale over a defined political timetable. The NLS had to be shaped by the interdependent constraints of literacy as a 'subject', balanced with the strategic and more pragmatic disciplines of implementation. These challenges, in turn, had to be balanced against other policy priorities, not least the developing National Numeracy Strategy due to be rolled out in the following year alongside literacy.

When the Literacy Task Force published its interim report in February 1997, they took the long view:

> We recognize that our target is ambitious. We ... believe that our evidence – both national and international – suggests that (our target) is achievable. Bringing about a national strategy is therefore possible but only if there is a consistent national strategic approach over five to 10 years.
>
> (Literacy Task Force 1997: 15)

This timescale seemed appropriate and proved to be so. Successful implementation depends on clarity and stability. Principles and practices must be explicit and stable enough to enable a generation of children to progress through the changed system and to build sufficient capacity to sustain the change. The outline strategy was to become a practical commitment underpinning the Labour manifesto and Tony Blair's well-known statement of his three priorities: 'education, education and education'.

Everything moved rapidly. Over the period February to May, much of the preliminary practical thinking had taken place so that, in Michael Barber's words, we could 'hit the ground running'. Labour was elected in May 1997. Over the next two months the shape of the Strategy was agreed. By August of the same year the final report of the Literacy Task Force was published, committing the government to a five-year national strategy and the resources to support it, together with a further commitment in principle to continue the Strategy into a second term of Government. This degree of stability and support marked a changed and much more ambitious political climate for primary schools who responded positively but with predictable uncertainty. It sounded revolutionary and would prove to be so. The final report also redefined the target, taking account of feedback from consultation on the earlier report, to include writing as well as reading in the target. This was widely seen as a logical and proper extension of the target but has proved to be by far the greatest challenge over the lifetime of the Strategy.

The imperative to implement generates pragmatic questions about what can and should be done, for example:

- What evidently worked in raising literacy standards in schools and how transferable was it?
- What would teachers and head teachers recognize, assimilate and commit to, that would improve practice and outcomes, and in what form is this best presented?
- What was deliverable given the available support and training resources?
- What are likely to be the most effective incentives and levers for change?
- How could the Strategy deliver the short-term successes necessary to sustain resources and commitment from the Government and the public, while investing in longer term more sustainable change?

We already had evidence-based answers to these questions. The decision to create the *Framework for Teaching* and introduce the Literacy Hour were based on brief but extensive piloting through the National Literacy Project (see Chapters 2 and 3). The elements of the Literacy Hour combined and legitimated a variety of complementary practices, already familiar to large numbers of teachers. The Framework was already known to teachers and being adopted by schools in local authorities outside the project. There were grounds to expect that many teachers would recognize and be predisposed to adopt it. The NLP was monitored and evaluated by the National Foundation for Educational Research from 1996 to 1998 who reported:

- significant and substantial improvement in children's test scores in the course of the project. Pupils in participating schools had scores below the national average at the outset. Final test scores had improved by approximately six standardized score points, so that they were still below, but significantly closer to, the national average
- head teachers regarded the introduction of the Literacy Hour overwhelmingly positively, whilst pointing out that it had major implications in terms of management and resourcing
- children gained in reading confidence in the course of the project, saying that they needed less help with their reading at the end than they had initially; their levels of reading enjoyment were high
- the project schools offer a valuable model for schools currently implementing the National Literacy Strategy.

(Sainsbury *et al.* 1998)

The NLP had demonstrated what could be implemented on a large scale. There was evidence of change at work from other small-scale projects such as *LIFT*, *First Steps* and *Success for All*, and experience of this work fed into the NLP. But big changes on the scale envisaged have to be economic and easily transferable. The NLP had captured in a few simple ideas that everyone could grasp, e.g. a target, a Literacy Hour, a Framework of objectives, a universal training programme. It was capable of transfer without corrupting its core practices, and viable in terms of available capacity i.e. teachers' existing skills and potential, and the available resources – human, material and financial. In other successful projects the intensity, detail and costs of training required to deliver them were either too costly or too unreliable to scale up to the level needed. The NLP provided a formula, and evidence that it could work on a large scale.

Setting a target

 The original target proposed by the Literacy Task Force was for raising standards of reading. However, there was some feedback arguing that it should be set for reading and writing jointly. At the time, the School Curriculum and Assessment Authority (SCAA) tested reading and writing but did not report writing results separately, so there was no information on whether the inclusion of writing would make a difference to the prospects of attaining the target. At the time, SCAA advised that it should make little or no difference:

> SCAA suggests that there is a very close correlation between the reading component of the Key Stage 2 tests and English as a whole (correlation 0.84) and that 58 percent of pupils achieved level 4 in the reading component of English in 1996 compared to 57 percent in English as a whole.
>
> (Literacy Task Force 1997: 14)

As a result, a target was set for English as an aggregated score for reading and writing. In retrospect this was bad advice and an unfortunate decision. By the time the NLS was launched, reading and writing were separately tested and immediately began to reveal big differences in the levels achieved by children. Chapter 9 looks at this data in more detail but, in essence it shows that, had this been known, it would have made sense, educationally and politically, to set separate targets for reading and writing.

Aggregation of the two tends to obscure the scale of reading achievement in primary schools. While the headline figure is always for English, press and public commonly construe it as a measure of reading. Ambiguity in the public mind also creates opportunities for those in opposition to beat the Government with its own stick. Even the 2005 Parliamentary Select Committee enquiry into the teaching of reading used the ambiguity to under-rate progress in reading, suggesting that 'around 20 per cent of children do not achieve the standard for reading (and writing) expected of their age' (House of Commons Education and Skills Committee 2005: 3). At the time, national attainment in English was 79 per cent while reading results were almost 85 per cent (i.e. 81 per cent for boys and 89 per cent for girls, averaged but rounded down to 84 per cent).

In retrospect, although the English target has been politically difficult, it was probably a good thing because it helped to shape the Strategy and provided a very high degree of challenge at every level. Nevertheless, it is ironic to reflect that, had the target been confined to reading, as originally planned, the 2002 80 per cent would have been exceeded by 2000 and sustained, while schools would have been within only a point or two of the more ambitious 85 per cent set by 2005. Despite this, the 80 per cent level 4+ target for 11-year-olds in English was announced, defining the improvement trajectory and setting expectations and commitments for schools.

Principles of implementation

All-at-once or bit-by-bit?

The target was the driver but a further key decision centred on how the proposed changes would be managed. In essence there were two big options: all-at-once or bit-by-bit. Should a change of this kind be managed in a gradual way or should it happen all at once with a 'big bang'? The case for gradual introduction centred on the need for careful capacity building and investment in the early stages. It took numerous forms, for example implementing the Strategy upwards through each school over a number of years; or starting with only the weaker schools in the first year. This approach was fed by concerns that implementation for everyone at once might simply be unmanageable and unsustainable. It also appeared to be lower risk because it looked less aggressive.

Notwithstanding the risks, the Task Force resolved to take a 'big bang' approach. A slow process would have too little momentum. Effective change requires the rapid accumulation of critical mass to reach a 'tipping point' and become institutionalized. Also slow changes can have negative impact because they generate uncertainty, and create scope for the unwilling to resist involvement. They also compromise the authority of managers and leaders in implementing change and the accountability process itself. The overriding constraint, of course, was the political timetable and the public promises on standards made by Government. These and other considerations led to the conclusion that the NLS would be inclusive, highly pro-active, and timed to begin for everyone from the start of the term in September 1998. Schools would be expected to implement the Strategy in all classes in the course of the first term. This was a key decision which cleared the air and left no one in any doubt about what would be expected. It set a Herculean challenge to have a revised NLP Framework, all the training and guidance, together with a national infra-structure competent to deliver the Strategy to 18,500 schools and about 200,000 teachers, in place and on time.

We needed change at every level if the targets were to be met. This meant challenging schools in advantaged as well as disadvantaged areas. If the NLS came to be seen as a remedial strategy, directed only at schools or local areas where standards were low, it would achieve only modest gains nationally. Hitting an ambitious national target necessarily requires improvements well in excess of the target for a significant proportion of schools. Every school had a part to play. This meant differentiating the national target first to local authorities so that each made a proportionate contribution to the national target and then, via local authorities, to each school to ensure that their contribution was also proportionate. What seemed obvious to us at the time was less obvious in practice. Many schools and some local authorities had gone unchallenged for years. They were complacent about improvement because school performance was generally in line with, or above, national averages, and they had received 'satisfactory' inspection reports. This large group of average schools proved hard to convince at the time and have presented the Strategy with one of its most persistent challenges over the years.

Pressure and support

We described in Chapter 1 how the previous conservative government had left a strong legacy of school improvement established on three foundations:

- national standards to set expectations and frame assessment criteria, through the statutory National Curriculum
- an evolving school inspection service, Ofsted, with an increasingly clear focus on the public reporting of institutional performance, and intolerance of school failure
- increasing financial autonomy and self-management by individual schools with differentiated funding to support weaker schools, and monitoring over defined improvement timescales on the principle of 'intervention in inverse proportion to success'.

This general approach had notable success in tackling the problems of very weak schools. But despite significant gains in school improvement, there had been too little impact on overall standards of achievement, for two reasons. First, although inspection told schools about their strengths and weaknesses, it was almost a truism that weaker schools would lack the professional capacity to improve themselves without outside support – in particular, as Ofsted frequently reminded us, most of these weaknesses centred on school leadership and the quality of teaching. Second, while improving weak schools is obviously necessary and cannot be ignored, it does little to contribute to the improvement of average schools where many of the lower performing children tend to be. In average schools the added value in terms of children's progress is, by definition, average and, by the law of averages, much of it is also below average. As indicated above, many of these schools went unchallenged while still, collectively, failing thousands of children.

The pressure/support framework was essential to improvement but would be rebalanced. Pressure and challenge would be strengthened to provide more focused leverage. National assessments for 7- and 11-year-olds were refined and grew in status to be perceived by teachers, parents and children as increasingly important measures of educational performance. Similarly, school inspections, league tables, performance management and career development were all, over time, connected to the national standards-raising agenda. But, while pressure played a key part in driving implementation, the major preoccupation for the Strategy was to provide the missing support dimension. The prospect of practical support was broadly welcomed in schools as a new and more helpful emphasis on how they might improve in place of the repeated mantra that they should do so. The prospect of entitlement to professional development by all teachers was part of a new deal to engage them in raising standards and encourage the profession, which had become unduly passive and compliant under the previous regime. 'Instead of finding themselves the beleaguered targets of public criticism, we hope primary teachers will come to see themselves as playing a leading part in a major social transformation' (Literacy Task Force 1997: 36).

The strategy was to be launched with a huge professional development programme for every teacher comprising school-based distance learning and intensive training courses, guidance, resources, a new nationwide team of literacy consultants to advise and support schools, support and professional training for all head teachers, training in leading and managing literacy in schools, and training for local authority personnel. The National Year of Reading provided a further background of support to parents and the community, raising public awareness, enhancing teachers' status and providing additional authority for schools in the task of engaging parents.

Changing behaviour to change minds

Until the advent of the NLP, the Government had been content to prescribe the broad requirements of a national curriculum but stood well back from any interventions in classroom practice. In 1991, the Secretary of State, Kenneth Clarke, set out his position, in response to publication of a discussion paper on curriculum organization and classroom practice:

> ... I want to make it absolutely clear that I see teachers taking the lead. The Secretary of State should encourage debate to cause teachers to question their current practice ... not ... tell ... [them] how to teach or organize their classes. Change in Primary schools is for teachers themselves to take on.
>
> (Clarke 1991)

A revolutionary feature of the NLP was its focus on intervening at the level of classroom instruction. It was designed not just to promote debate but to change practice. Experience of implementing the project, as well as evidence about change management outside education, led to the conclusion that while change must be rooted in evidence and justifiable theory, explaining the theory to everyone was not the most practical first step in securing change. A more effective approach was to help teachers change what they do in classrooms, in the expectation that changing teaching behaviours will lead to changes in professional attitudes, knowledge and understanding. This was the only practical basis on which to move forward; the changes needed to be common, palpable and effective. The big caveat of course is that everything teachers were asked to do had to be grounded in evidence of effective practice and robust theory. This general principle was formulated as 'changing teaching behaviours in order to change minds' and discussed widely with local authorities and schools in the run-up to implementation. The principle that behaviours tend to shape beliefs was already established in change and reform processes in industry but was new to education where practice in teacher training and professional development traditionally ran in the opposite direction – first convince teachers about the reasons for change and only then desired changes will happen. Michael Barber, reflecting on the experience of the NLS, later argued that

> ... this popular conception is wrong. Winning hearts and minds is not the best first step in any process of urgent change. Beliefs do not necessarily drive behaviour. More usually, it is the other way round – behaviours shape beliefs. ... Only when people have experienced a change do they revise their beliefs accordingly. And often they must experience change over a period of time for such beliefs to change permanently. ... Successful strategies for change require the leadership to establish and maintain an emotional and professional environment in which others can explore new experiences with a sense of purpose and a feeling of some security.
>
> (Barber and Phillips 2000: 9)

The concept of the Literacy Hour had grown from this principle. It was designed to change teaching behaviours through practical and transferable teaching methods, in the expectation that this would lead to changed attitudes and beliefs. The process of practice into theory, as a way of delivering complex system-wide change, was manageable, clear and practical. Although it was not necessarily comfortable, it did make sense to teachers. The strength of the Literacy Hour, with all its associated teaching methodology, was that it encapsulated this principle in a simple phrase. It looked and sounded like change, attracted attention from the media and gave parents and the community a concept; like it or not, the Literacy Hour was perceived as an idea that had come to stay.

Prescription and flexibility

As well as balancing pressure and support, a similar balance needs to be struck between prescription and flexibility for schools. The Canadian evaluation team drew attention to this in their first evaluation report on the literacy and numeracy strategies:

> The perception of prescriptiveness remains an ongoing challenge ... Providing too much flexibility, however, always carries with it the risk of a return to past practices. Establishing a workable balance is difficult. The Strategies must consistently demonstrate how individual pupil's differences can be accommodated within the NLNS.
>
> (Earl *et al.* 2000)

Education policy is, of course, bound to be prescriptive. It is by its nature about what schools *ought* to do, but the balance of prescription needs to be carefully managed and justified. Government needs to secure equity and rights for children but, equally, diminishing the autonomy of schools can reduce accountability, create unhelpful dependencies, and limit teachers' capacity to think and learn for themselves. The NLS was built on the justified assumption that much was already known about what worked in literacy teaching, based on the evidence of research and school inspection, and that this knowledge could be defined and justified. There was an overwhelming moral case, in the interests of children, for disseminating this pedagogical knowledge more systematically to schools.

The approach discomfited some teacher trainers and researchers who saw the prescriptive elements as a threat to professional and academic autonomy and, in some cases, a direct challenge to cherished theories and ideals about learning and teaching literacy. By and large, teachers, head teachers and professional associations were less exercised about intellectual autonomy and more concerned about the potential of the NLS for increasing workloads and accountability. Despite these objections, the majority of schools saw the Strategy as a constructive effort to clear a way through confusing and often competing recommendations from academic experts and commercial interests. There was also an opposite pressure for increasing prescription from Ofsted who wanted to retain the precision of term-by-term objectives from the pilot NLP Framework, and from teachers themselves: 'just tell us what to do and we'll do it' was a common message, symptomatic of the frustration expressed by many schools who felt over-criticized and under-supported in a system where messages about literacy teaching were often confused and conflicting.

In fact, none of the recommendations on the use of the *Framework for Teaching*, the implementation of the Literacy Hour or involvement in the training, was mandated. They were given 'default' status. Schools understood that the NLS guidance would be used to benchmark practice and that, while they were expected to adapt and use it flexibly, if they rejected the NLS, their alternative approach should be demonstrably as good or better.

> Our presumption will be that the approach to teaching we set out, based on the NLP, will be adopted by every school unless a school can demonstrate, through its literacy action plan and schemes of work and its performance in NC Key Stage tests, that the approach it has adopted is at least as effective.
>
> (Literacy Task Force 1997: 23)

Predictably, the effect of this was that the majority of schools regarded the advice as 'all but' statutory and almost all schools complied. In practice, however, there was to be a good deal of flexibility, because the teaching objectives in the Framework were just that. There was no specified sequence, no prescription about what emphasis schools should give them or how they might be selected or grouped in the curriculum and, of course, no specified texts or topics. The NLS provided a framework for planning and teaching but was far from being a syllabus or programme. Some schools did take the 'default' advice creatively and continued with their existing approaches. These tended to be successful schools often exemplifying NLS principles in different ways, and the Strategy learned from them. Ofsted also noted this. While commenting on the additional workload involved in planning to the Framework's objectives, they also observed that:

> …the translation of these teaching objectives into concrete ideas for what pupils and teachers will actually do during the Literacy Hour, though time consuming, provides teachers with the scope to use imaginative and innovative ideas to personalize their lessons and make them lively and enjoyable.
>
> (Ofsted 1999: §26)

As the NLS moved forward over the next few years, this more flexible attitude to implementation was increasingly to become the theme, and the paradigm, for good literacy practice (see Chapter 8).

Core messages

Consistency and fidelity to the plan had to be underwritten by a few clear central messages that everyone could understand. In these early stages strong leadership from the centre was essential. From the Prime Minister, through the Secretary of State, the Head of the Standards and Effectiveness Unit in the Department for Education, to the Director of the Strategy and the national and regional teams, there had to be confidence and determination. None of this would have been possible without a clear agenda. The common messages had to be promoted without equivocation. The common messages were all about teaching and learning, and focused on the needs of classroom teachers. They had to be few in number, credible, memorable and manageable for teachers. At the point of implementation, predictably, the three big messages to all schools were:

1   Use the NLS Framework for planning and assessment.
2   Adopt the Literacy Hour or a suitable form of it throughout the school.
3   Everyone should engage in the training.

What lay behind these messages, of course, was detailed and challenging but the fact that the essence of the Strategy was able to be conveyed in this way gave it shape and momentum, and captured the attention of the profession, parents and the media.

To be effective, support needed not just to improve the skills of individuals; it had to generate systemic change that would rapidly become institutionalized within and across schools. For this reason, the support and training were pervaded by a common language about objectives and methodologies. This made it possible to share and transact ideas and practices on a system-wide scale. Although the speed of development and implementation left the Strategy with imperfections, its form and content were highly effective, and its power lay in the rapid introduction of a shared language and practices that most teachers recognized and were prepared to adopt. The parameters set out by the Framework and the Literacy Hour meant that, in less than half a term, almost all schools were talking a common language. This was immensely powerful. In schools across the country it was possible to see common features of teaching and learning, with clear and recognizable objectives. This raised the quality of debate and created a climate of common purpose and professional learning.

Contrary to the expectations of some, it generated a lot of diversity as teachers adapted and customized the recommendations to suit their needs. Many schools saw this as an opportunity and exploited it creatively. Of course, there were others who did not exploit the opportunity but tried to follow the NLS slavishly as though it were a programme. There were examples of teachers timing the segments of the Literacy Hour with a stopwatch or trivializing the Framework by treating it as a tick-list – an approach reinforced by some educational publishers who saw it as an opportunity to sell ring-binders full of 'quick-fix' worksheets for teachers. These schools tended to be the ones who were most at sea with the curriculum before the Strategy and who were ready to fall into a dependency relationship with it. Though this was a completely inappropriate response it did, at least, have the merit of getting weaker schools on board and creating the conditions for improvement. A constructive balance between central prescription and flexibility needs always to be counter-balanced with carefully judged compliance and creativity by school leaders and teachers. In the event, very few schools ignored or rejected the Strategy.

An infrastructure for support

The NLP already had a growing infrastructure through a national team of consultants, who trained and supported the project teachers. This team was led by the National Director but employed and deployed by each local authority. As an established national project, initiated and scrutinized by Ofsted, and well publicized in the national press, it was already known to a wider professional public. The key elements of the NLP created a sufficiently common Framework, already on the test-bed with readily transferable knowledge and capable of being scaled up.

Scaling up support from a project in 18 local authorities to match the needs of every primary school in the country presented a challenge. Primary schools in England vary in size and many are relatively small. They cater for children from pre-5 to age 11+ (equivalent to Grades K–6 in the US and Canada) and commonly have around two forms of entry i.e. between 15 and 20 teachers plus a deputy head and head teacher (principal). Class sizes are typically in the region of 1:30 and most teachers teach the whole curriculum. There is no tradition of specialist teaching. Almost all primary schools have coordinators for language and literacy, with responsibility for supporting colleagues, developing the school's policies and managing resources but, in 1997, they had very limited time to exercise these responsibilities. Primary school management structures tend to be flat with head teachers carrying high levels of accountability for supporting and quality assuring the work of each teacher, as well as managing the school's buildings, budget, personnel and resources. In contrast to secondary schools with their much larger subject specialist organization and devolved structures, there was no effective dissemination structure at the primary school level. An implementation structure was needed that would reach 200,000 individual teachers in 18,500 institutions, and enable us to communicate more or less directly with them.

At the time, there was little capacity to do this. Over previous years, local authority advisory services had been depleted. Those jobs that remained tended to be more generic than specialist. Largely because of Ofsted's attention to school improvement the roles had increasingly focused on general monitoring of school performance and preparing schools for inspection, rather than school improvement of the kind envisaged by the Strategy. A national support team had to be created urgently but there was much debate and concern about the risks of pulling so many good teachers out of schools, just when they would be most needed in the classrooms. In the face of some opposition, the Government went ahead and funded posts for 200 literacy consultants and asked local authorities to recruit them, to a nationally determined job specification, while the national team of regional directors quality-assured the process. The response was very positive and attracted large numbers of able teachers and trainers to the national team.

The implementation chain consisted of a team of regional directors who worked to the National Director and were responsible for promoting and directing the Strategy in regions, each of which comprised a number of local authorities (Figure 6.1). LEAs were the logical building blocks in the implementation chain, accountable, monitored and inspected on the performance of schools. Each local authority employed one or more advisor/inspector(s) on their education team, responsible for school improvement. These were almost all credible professionals with experience in primary school leadership, one of whom was identified as a Literacy Strategy Manager for the authority. Strategy managers had dual accountability to the local authority and to the NLS regional director. The 200 nationally funded consultants were supplemented in many authorities, bringing the total to around 300. These were to be the key resource. Consultants had high quality direct classroom experience, were credible language specialists and good trainers. This team worked under the direction of the national team of Regional Directors but were employed and deployed by the local authorities and responsible to the local Strategy manager.

Cascade training is always hazardous, especially on this scale, so the implementation structure was designed with as few layers as possible. The dual management of literacy consultants was important because it gave the national team a direct line to the classroom and underpinned relationships and accountabilities with the local Strategy managers.

Head teachers were the key change agents and the success of the implementation depended crucially on their willingness and capacity to take the Strategy forward in their schools. Every head teacher had the opportunity to attend a two-day conference with their language coordinator prior to implementation to explain the Strategy and to introduce the training materials. Schools were asked to complete an audit of their provision prior to the training. At the time, the principle of using self-assessment as part of a school-based improvement cycle was new to many and the response was mixed.

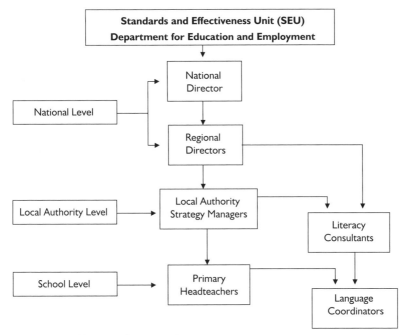

Figure 6.1 National Literacy Strategy infrastructure

It directed the attention of school leaders squarely on the management of the school curriculum and quality of learning and teaching in classrooms. At the time many head teachers were preoccupied with other management responsibilities such as buildings, finances, parental relations, personnel, behaviour and pastoral care, and spent little time in classes leading, supporting and disseminating quality teaching. Some, who had been away from the classroom for several years, lacked confidence as professional leaders and did not see it as their role to intervene in the work of their teachers. The underlying purpose was to use the literacy strategy, with the numeracy strategy implemented in the following year, as a basis for wider school improvement. The NLS provided a structure for moving primary school leadership forward, which has persisted and been refined over the years. As well as identifying a continuing need to improve leadership, Ofsted recognized the Strategy's potential in its report on the first year of the Strategy:

> In a relatively short space of time, the strategy has begun to influence every aspect of primary school provision. Like its predecessor, the National Literacy Project, the National Literacy strategy has been a catalyst for improvement in the quality of teaching and for raising standards of literacy in primary schools.
>
> (Ofsted 1999: §24)

Although the Strategy was to involve everyone and to be introduced at a stroke, the change could not possibly be managed at the same level for all. There was not enough skilled capacity. Though resources were generous, they were finite and, of course, schools' contexts and needs varied greatly. The Strategy had to differentiate and did so by providing something for everyone without exception, while giving more support where needs were greater. Every school had a 'lunchbox'[1] of distance learning materials covering all the key aspects of the Strategy. In addition, intensive face-to-face training combined with school-based consultancy was to be provided for the 10 per cent or so of schools that had furthest to go to reach their target, with further schools added each year up to 2002 so that about 50 per cent of schools would have received this training by then. This plan was adopted in the first year but by the second year gave way to a much more responsive and flexible system to enable local authorities to differentiate support in a more graduated way and expand access to training much more rapidly (DfEE 1997a). Local authorities were also able to deploy any additional consultancy support to other schools on a lighter touch basis to support implementation, demonstrate planning and ensure that schools were using the training materials appropriately.

It was resolved, as a matter of policy, to create the highest quality training and support materials possible. Other worthwhile initiatives had floundered as a consequence of poor materials which turned teachers against them or failed to give practical help at the appropriate level. Fullan (1999), commenting on the implementation of the NLS, drew attention to the importance of investing in quality materials:

> To achieve large-scale reform, you cannot depend on people's capacity to bring about substantial change in the short run, so you need to propel the process with high quality teaching and training materials ... there is still the problem of superficial implementation when new materials are in use, and even new practices in evidence, without the deeper understanding required for substantial and sustained implementation. But you get farther, faster by producing quality materials and establishing a highly interactive infra-structure ... of pressure and support.
>
> (Fullan 1999: 18)

In the first year of implementation, additional support was provided in a variety of ways to move the Strategy on. An additional £22 million was provided for schools to supplement book provision (averaging £1,000 per school), additional funds were allocated to increase the number of classroom assistants in schools, an extra school closure day was provided for every school to make a start on the training programme and commitments were declared, to be fulfilled over the coming years, to provide more classroom assistants and reduce teachers' workloads. Summer literacy schools

---

1   A large plastic container of six distance training units complete with overhead transparencies and videos of relevant teaching strategies was created and distributed to all schools. This was before most schools had DVD and PowerPoint technology. It acquired the 'lunchbox' epithet because one head teacher recommended colleagues to discard the materials and use the container for carrying their sandwiches – this got into the press and acquired the name thereafter. The joke became an asset because, like the idea of the Literacy Hour, it made the training pack memorable.

and 'booster' classes were introduced for older primary children to accelerate and 'catch-up' lower achievers, and revision guidance for teachers to support children about to take the national tests.

A total commitment

Securing 'buy-in'

Alongside the internal negotiations around the Framework and associated training materials, the public face of the NLS was being strengthened. Interest was growing in the NLP, as the shape of things to come was creating a professional appetite to know more about it. We found ourselves in the novel position of having to refuse schools access to drafts of the Framework and restrict circulation of the existing NLP materials to avoid later confusion. NLP pilot authorities found themselves increasingly interrogated about how it worked. Dissemination of the NLP principles and practices was well under way by the start of the school year in 1997 and many schools across the country were experimenting with forms of a Literacy Hour. The NLS capitalized on this, building up expectations, emphasizing messages about the prospects of practical support for teachers and encouraging schools, through their development planning, to be aware that they needed to prioritize professional development in literacy throughout 1998.

As well as these indirect influences, the NLS was explicitly promoted through public announcements, press releases, news items, addresses to teachers' conferences and publicity about successes in the NLP. There were detailed discussions with professional associations to reach agreement about the implementation process and the expectations that would be placed on schools. Such negotiations are never easy but were greatly facilitated by the prospects of big increases in support. The NLS was clearly not going to be something for nothing but it was a big improvement on the pressure-led approach to which schools had become accustomed. The expectation that the profession would take greater responsibility and earn greater status and reward as a consequence was welcome and attractive. Publishers were carefully briefed and convinced that the NLS would be here to stay. There would be a market for more tailored resources aligned with the Framework and the Literacy Hour and a secure financial basis for school purchasing over several years to make the commercial investment worthwhile. Further negotiations about amending copyright restrictions with the Publishers Association also oiled the wheels.

At central government level there were briefings and negotiations across departments within and beyond the Department for Education to ensure that the NLS had priority and other policy initiatives were aligned and, if necessary, subservient to this key initiative. Nothing was left to chance. The Prime Minister and Secretary of State took a strong, personal and committed interest – vocabulary like 'focus', 'persistence' and 'relentlessness' was common in political discussions about the Strategy. Everything was staked on success; the NLS was to be a precursor of further reform and it had to work.

Responsiveness

Prescription also carries reciprocal responsibilities. In the early stages, clarity, persistence and leadership were everything, but so too was responsiveness. What was centrally prescribed had to work in schools, whatever their circumstances. Michael Barber insisted on the precept that we should 'learn as we go' and be seen to do so. If prescription is to work, it needs to solve every problem and meet every objection constructively. This thinking was aligned with research into 'high reliability systems' and its applications in school improvement i.e. systems, like air traffic control, designed not to fail. Such systems have clear goals, high expectations and high degrees of stability and consistency but they are also alert to problems by anticipating and responding to them early, before they cascade into major difficulties (Reynolds *et al.* 2003).

As the launch of the NLS was in preparation, there was wide stakeholder consultation which raised practical problems in need of rapid solutions. How could a year-by-year Framework work in small schools and those with mixed year classes? How would it meet the needs of children with special educational needs or those with English as an additional language? How would it cater for the most able? How could teachers organize large classes and cope with behaviour problems? What provision would it make for pre-schoolers? How should it be implemented in special schools? Should children be set or ability grouped? How should the Strategy be implemented in reception classes for the youngest children when the National Curriculum and the Framework begin at year 1? How can the NLS be sustained in schools with high staff turnover and temporary teachers? How do I balance demands of the NLS against other competing priorities?

The Strategy team anticipated questions, and responded to others as they were raised, with additional guidance or resources, showing how the NLS could be applied and adapted to fit every need and circumstance. There was a commitment to cover every angle, so there could be no excuses. In those early stages, there was a rule that if anyone called or wrote in, they should have a personal response within 48 hours, preferably by telephone. Regional directors went out to meetings and conferences to invite critical feedback. This approach not only helped to stay focused on the practical needs of schools, it began to demonstrate a learning approach to improvement. The principle was to stay firm and not to cave in on the big ideas but listen to criticism, in an effort to learn, refine and keep everyone engaged. It was by no means a perfect fail-safe approach but overall it was effective in securing rapid and near-universal implementation, raising expectations and building confidence about the capacity to improve.

Fidelity to the plan

The effort to secure agreement and buy-in, and to respond to meet every concern or objection, laid the foundations for universal implementation. The operational principle was to create flexibility within defined boundaries; common practices adapted to meet differing needs and contexts. Fidelity to the plan was essential. Without it, there was a risk of diminishing the challenge because schools would 'cherry-pick' the bits they liked; large-scale professional development would be impossible and there could be no systematic evaluation from which to learn. In their final report in 2003, the external evaluation team reflected on the success of this principle:

> ... the overall vision, as set out in the Framework, has remained constant, although specific priorities and emphases have shifted in response to data about pupil strengths and weaknesses and to feedback from schools and LEAs. Strategy leaders have sought out, in a variety of ways, information about the progress and challenges of implementation and have adapted elements of the strategies to address problems that arose. Achieving a sense of common purpose that persists through such adaptation is no small accomplishment and is a significant contribution to the sustained effort required for large-scale reform.
>
> (Earl *et al.* 2003: 4)

Launching the Strategy

During the school year 1997–8, there was a massive investment in preparation to maximize the prospects of success. Everyone understood that the NLS had to be fit for purpose, straightforward to implement, practical and workable, and bring rapid success – whatever the circumstances of particular schools. We were acutely aware that we only had one shot at it and that the risks of failure were too dire to contemplate. By the start of the new school year, training materials were sent to every school; they were designed to cover six training days or equivalent and to be covered in the course of the school year. To strengthen and encourage fast implementation, a number of additional measures were taken:

- the National Year of Reading was launched
- the Government relaxed some of the statutory requirements in the National Curriculum, creating more time to focus on literacy
- three of the existing five school closure days were designated for literacy training, and an additional day, exceptionally, was permitted
- an intensive week of training with additional coaching and mentoring support was provided for the weaker schools
- national conferences for head teachers and local authorities were run to induct them into leadership, management and monitoring of the NLS
- special conferences were held for LEAs facing particular difficulties or likely to be at risk.

Following the launch in September 1998, everyone became intensely nervous about what might happen. We were completely in the hands of the schools and had been prescriptive to a level beyond anything they had previously experienced. We were relieved to find that almost all schools began implementing the Strategy from the start of September. By the end of the Autumn term 1998 the four components of the Literacy Hour were in place in the vast majority of schools (Ofsted 1999). There was sufficient positive feedback to be confident that the Strategy was on the right track. Schools reacted in a variety of ways. Many said it was constructive and helpful; they liked the common approaches and the much sharper focus on clear objectives to mark out progression. Almost immediately, it revealed a pervasive lack of basic knowledge about language and literacy by teachers and many of those who supported, advised and inspected them. There are many reasons for this initial success but, on reflection, the following were probably the most influential:

The quality of personal leadership: the strong sense of political will from Prime Minister Tony Blair and Secretary of State David Blunkett and Michael Barber, whose role was crucial. Michael stood at the head of the whole enterprise, took the political risks, insisted on fidelity to the plan with no excuses but, above all, generated an infectious and informed optimism among those who worked with him and more widely in the profession.

The skilful exploitation of a 'political moment' for a profession which had undergone years of demoralizing criticism. The combination of a rigorous, prescriptive but also more sympathetic approach created a receptive professional climate. Most thought the NLS was over-prescriptive but most also thought it worth trying. The combination of early success in classrooms and a recognition by heads that here was a tool with potential to support leadership, management and school improvement, gave it impetus and produced enough early wins to get it established.

A clear, unequivocal model for change: the Framework and Literacy Hour provided practical and well-grounded models which could be readily adapted to provide schools flexibility within the common framework, removing potential grounds for objection and exception.

Preparedness and expectations: most schools already knew about the Government's intentions; many were already aware of the NLP, its structure and practices, and a significant minority were already involved. The NLS was no great surprise for most; while it was a big step up from previous practice, it was, for many, a smaller psychological step.

Advocacy: despite the many nervous and critical responses from the profession about the speed of implementation and its prescriptiveness, there also existed a strong core of advocacy from those already involved in the NLP, supported by the emerging evidence of success, saying from within the profession that schools should engage with it and that it was likely to bring improvement.

The quality and comprehensiveness of the initial materials: training, guidance and expert professional support which went to all schools in the form of distance learning materials with further direct training for a smaller proportion of schools.

Ofsted: the perceived authority and leverage from school inspections by Ofsted of local authorities and schools which rendered the NLS 'all but' mandatory.

By the end of the first year, the general verdict on implementation was that the NLS had been successful. There was a guarded, 'so far, so good' from Ofsted

(1999). Almost all schools had implemented the Literacy Hour and there were encouraging improvements in literacy standards, the quality of teaching and school leadership. The press reported it as positively as one could expect. Although there was no room for complacency, there was enough success to sustain confidence, and a clear improvement agenda on which to press ahead. The first year had to be intensely proactive and this, inevitably, put schools and local authorities in a highly accommodative role. This balance of central control and local autonomy would need to be re-dressed if the initiatives were to be sustained. Michael Fullan captured the essence of the strategic problem, drawing attention to the need to balance 'downward investment' with 'upward identity' (Fullan 1999). There had been a focus on the former but after a year, more needed to be done to create a reciprocal identification with the principles and practices of the Strategy by those who were implementing it. Ofsted's evaluation of the first year commented on the impact of the Framework. Despite the considerable demands it was making on teachers:

> The dividends of careful preparation are already apparent. The Framework for teaching has already raised teachers' expectations, increased the pace to their teaching – particularly reading – and brought about a substantial improvement in teachers' subject knowledge.
>
> (Ofsted 1999)

The greatest challenge overall was the expectation for teachers to plan from, and teach to, objectives. Planning and teaching to objectives were the logical counterparts of the broader target culture. To make sense of numerical targets they need to be translated into curricular targets for teaching and learning. For example, if 25 per cent of children in year 5 were at level 3, what exactly should they be learning to reach level 4 by the end of year 6? Increasing precision at translating numbers into objectives was essential to securing progression and a crucial first step on a longer road towards tighter and more effective literacy leadership and management at every level. Most importantly, objective-led teaching was to be the foundation for systematically engaging children in their own learning through *assessment for learning*, which would become a core element of effective teaching and school improvement in a wider primary strategy during the next term of government.

By the end of the first year, the NLS was established but was far from secure. Although the longer term aim was to reduce the extent of central prescription and support so that schools would take increasing responsibility and 'ownership', it would have been disastrous to attempt such a change at this stage of implementation. It was expected, on the basis of research and the feedback from Ofsted and the external evaluation team, that the Strategy should move schools increasingly towards taking it on for themselves over roughly a five-year period, although these expectations were not strategically worked out at this stage. What was now needed was to embed the changes, deepen understanding and commitment, evaluate carefully over a number of years and learn, refine and improve as we went forward. Chapter 7 discusses this second phase of securing the Strategy.

Chapter 7

Securing the Strategy

The second phase of the Strategy ran from about the middle of 1999 up to the period just beyond the general election in May 2001, shortly before the 80 per cent target was due to be met. 1999 also marked the introduction of the National Numeracy Strategy. This was shaped in a similar way to the NLS with targets, introductory training, a parallel support infra-structure and a National Numeracy Year to reach the wider community. Schools were expected to give priority to establishing the new 'daily mathematics lesson' alongside the Literacy Hour. Maintaining momentum in the literacy strategy without generating conflicting demands and a perception of competition was paramount. If schools saw the strategies pulling against each other, all would be lost. It meant continuing and developing the literacy support, jointly managing the two distinct subjects in ways that emphasized coherence and multiplied benefits. Increased demands also required careful management at the local level, bearing in mind that increasing central support still needed to be addressed to each school and that schools had a finite capacity to respond. Inevitably, there were more demands on schools and some loss of priority for literacy. In practice, these demands were managed reasonably well by most schools, mainly because they were perceived as helpful and worthwhile and partly because the inputs were aligned with care. Parallel lesson structures helped and, wherever possible, similar language about teaching and learning was used, bearing in mind differences between the two subjects. Efforts were made at every level to emphasize the complementary nature of the two subjects and the potential for beneficial impact in both directions.

The second strategic phase was designed to consolidate but also extend the achievements of the early implementation. Strong persistent leadership from the centre continued throughout this period in an effort to embed effective practices, ensure a high degree of consistent professional development for teachers and school leaders, and develop knowledge and understanding about language and literacy on a broad front.

By now the honeymoon period was over and the work of embedding the Strategy was under way in earnest. The first year of implementation had brought significant success but it was fragile. The Strategy, largely through the Literacy Hour, had brought about the intended changes in teaching practices, achieved the critical mass needed to move forward and produced encouraging gains in teaching quality and attainment (see Chapter 9 for a detailed analysis of results). But for many, the changes were still only skin-deep. The Strategy now had to manage a rapid second level shift from simply following the practices of the Literacy Hour to a deeper level of understanding and belief by most teachers, if improvements were to be embedded and sustained. In their first annual report on the Strategy, the international team identified the issue:

> …we suggest that short term gains in literacy and numeracy can be accomplished through a greater focus on certain teaching procedures but that deeper and sustainable gains can only be made through more radical changes in teaching practices and beliefs – changes that require more active engagement of teachers in considering alterations in teaching…
>
> (Earl *et al.* 2000: 29)

This challenge was magnified by the fact that while large numbers of teachers had taken to familiar elements like shared reading and independent writing, the learning curve was likely to be steep. Word and sentence level knowledge was still generally weak and knowledge about text-types and genres for reading and writing was also new to many. There was an atmosphere of reasonable optimism and a much more secure belief than at the start of the previous year in the capacity of everyone in the system to improve. Predictably, things were set to become increasingly complex.

Much had been achieved; at the end of the first year Ofsted (1999) reported that:

- almost all schools, including special schools, had adopted the Strategy and made the necessary modifications to ensure that the activities were appropriate for their pupils
- the quality of teaching in the Literacy Hour improved throughout the year, though text level work was better than word level work
- teachers were more confident in teaching reading and moved away from the practice of 'hearing readers' to one in which they taught children to read directly
- phonics was receiving much greater priority in most schools with improved teaching but there are still too many lessons, around 20 per cent overall, where it was not taught well
- the best teaching was in years 5 and 6 (9–11-year-olds) but was weakest in years 3 and 4
- the leadership of the Strategy by head teachers was good in about 50 per cent of schools and weak in about 20 per cent, and the work of literacy coordinators had been satisfactory or better in more than 80 per cent of schools.

Further and more direct evidence came from the professional associations, broadly confirming Ofsted's observations. A survey by the National Union of Teachers confirmed the scale of the implementation and the need for further training, adding that about half the teachers surveyed said the Strategy had improved their knowledge of teaching literacy (NUT 1999). A similar survey of head teachers by their professional association confirmed that:

> The introduction of the Strategy has developed teachers' skills and knowledge and had a positive effect on the level of development of pupils' literacy. The content of the Framework has been positively received but teachers would prefer to use their professional judgement to implement the Strategy in a way that would best meet the needs of individual situations within the schools. There are major concerns regarding the development of pupils' extended writing ... there remain issues in relation to funding ... the desirability of maintaining workload at this level must be seriously considered.
>
> (NAHT 1999)

We also used qualitative analyses of national assessment data to identify more specific weaknesses in the literacy skills of 7- and 11-year-olds. Every year, the Qualifications and Curriculum Authority sampled test papers, drawing implications for teaching and learning. These analyses were increasingly aligned with the expectations of the NLS to give us valuable formative information. Particular attention was paid to the high proportion of children who achieved just below the expected level. If this group could be shifted upwards, the national target would be met and exceeded. For example, the 1998 test analysis largely reflected Ofsted's commentary but added helpful precision.

> Across all key stages, teachers should focus on raising the expectations of boys ...

7-year-olds achieving levels 1 or 2c need to:

Reading
- extend their knowledge of sound–symbol relations to read whole words and self-correct while reading aloud;
- vary ... reading strategies to find answers to simple questions;
- look beyond word-matching to answer questions whose phrasing differs from the wording of the text;
- identify main themes, characters and ideas in stories.

Writing
- improve their spelling through more work on discriminating phonemes within words and developing understanding of the way words are structured;
- make their meaning clearer by marking grammatical sentences with full stops and capital letters;
- learn more about how to select and organize subject matter when writing different kinds of texts (e.g. stories, letters, lists).

11-year-olds achieving level 3:

Reading:
- can retrieve direct information and evidence from a text but not explain its relevance;

Writing:
- can use commas in lists but not to mark sentence structure;
- need systematic teaching of spelling rules and conventions so that they use more than simple sound–letter correspondences and knowledge of familiar words when writing;
- do not use speech marks confidently;
- do not use paragraphs; their sequencing of narrative is not secure, as they have moved beyond simple plots, but they do not have a clear grasp of what the structure of their narrative or non-narrative piece might be.

(QCA 1998, p. 21)

Using this evidence alongside evaluations from the Strategy team revealed a range of subject knowledge, teaching and learning priorities which would define the training and support agendas over the next three years:

Whole-class teaching and differentiation: almost all primary teachers worked with mixed ability classes and the Strategy's emphasis on whole-class teaching raised questions about how to meet the needs of all children through techniques for sharing, interaction and questioning. This kind of teaching was already improving, particularly through the techniques of shared reading. Teachers were receptive to training and support which was developing their strategies. This emphasized the importance of working to objectives, using the plenary sessions in the Literacy Hour effectively for reflection and assessment of what had been learned, and laid firm foundations for the increasingly explicit use of 'assessment for learning' across both literacy and numeracy strategies.

Word level work: despite improvements, there was insufficient focus on systematic phonics teaching for the majority of 5- to 7-year-olds. Teachers' knowledge about the alphabetic system and how to teach it was too limited and there remained a widespread perception that because phonics required memorization and practice, learning had to be passive and dull. This conflicted with widespread, and proper, perceptions about the importance of motivation and active learning. The continuing critical debate about phonics added further uncertainty for teachers – who should they believe when there was so much disagreement between protagonists, some of whom were overtly hostile to the broad-based approach of the Strategy? In addition, children (and many teachers, as well) knew too little about spelling conventions and rules. The Framework laid considerable emphasis on progression of spelling knowledge by extending the foundations of phonics into understanding of spelling patterns, morphemic knowledge, pronunciation and vocabulary development.

Independent reading fluency: many teachers had difficulty organizing guided reading effectively. It was a considerable challenge which required them not just to understand how to support independent reading in a group but also to organize the rest of the class for useful independent working while they focused on tutoring the reading group. The teaching and application of strategies for error recognition, the use of reading cues and information redundancy, self-monitoring and self-correction (see Chapters 2 and 3) were also new to many teachers.

Comprehension: reading assessment results for older children also revealed a pattern. Too many children were reaching a level of reading fluency by 11-years-old but they were not meeting the level 4 criteria because they had insufficient understanding of texts and how to interpret them. For the great majority of children this was not in any way symptomatic of reading failure, it was simply a matter of knowledge – for teachers and children. Many children were failing to achieve level 4 because they had not been taught 'to show understanding of significant ideas, themes, events and characters, to use inference and deduction, or to refer to the text when explaining their views' (DfEE/QCA 1999: 57). The Framework contained a progression of text level objectives across a systematic range of text-types from year to year. Much of this was also new to teachers and needed to be grounded in a better understanding of authors' language choices and the organization of texts, related to purpose and audience, through using shared reading as the main vehicle. Building this understanding explicitly for teachers was to prove vital, not only to improve reading comprehension but also to provide the foundations for progression in writing.

Writing: by the end of the first year, it was clear that many teachers were abandoning the Literacy Hour for one day per week, to make time for extended writing. There was great concern about improving writing but only limited understanding about how to teach it. Time for extended writing was very important, though the effect of this 'Friday armistice', as it came to be known, was to simply practice and consolidate writing difficulties that already existed, most prominently for boys.

Other practical, organizational problems also needed attention including: detailed guidance on text selection, particularly for guided reading; practical support on how to use the Framework for planning and setting learning targets for children; the use of classroom assistants who were increasingly being employed to work alongside teachers as a result of additional funding through the literacy and numeracy strategies. Careful evaluation generated practical expectations and set priorities. To be effective, change on this scale must be driven by a few clear, simple messages about teaching and learning. In the first year, core messages centred on three general precepts:

- use the NLS Framework for planning and assessment
- adopt the Literacy Hour or a suitable form of it throughout the school
- everyone should engage in the training.

Now, based on evidence of the first year's evaluation, the Strategy could define more sharply what was likely to make the difference in raising standards, and support was centred on four key messages, negotiated and agreed with partners organizations (DfES, Ofsted, QCA) to improve:

- word level work, particularly phonics and spelling
- writing composition at every stage
- fluent and accelerated independent reading, through the guided reading process
- inferential comprehension across a range of text-types for reading and writing.

These deceptively simple priorities set big challenges. System-wide change requires system-wide learning to build capacity at every level, not only by teachers but also by those who lead, inspect and support them. Much of the learning to date had been reasonably comfortable for teachers. Initial support had been structured to achieve a smooth transition, taking account of existing beliefs and practices, for example recommending that the Literacy Hour should start with a shared reading experience, which would be attractive and relatively unthreatening to implement. But to continue raising standards, teachers had to move beyond this comfort zone. Unlike mathematics, the state of knowledge about literacy was imprecise. Some areas, particularly phonics, were heavily disputed; others, such as genre theory and grammar, were potentially useful but unfamiliar to many, while the teaching of writing was under-researched and needed to be developed. Almost all our resources were invested in developing knowledge and human potential to grow teachers' practical expertise and deepen their understanding. The Strategy's common language about literacy teaching became a powerful tool. It engaged people in a common enterprise, enabled them to learn and share experience and contributed to the wider aim of securing sustainable, institutional change at school level.

Recognizing the pivotal role of head teachers and in pursuit of Government's aim to devolve the Strategy to schools, literacy leadership was strengthened in two ways: first by ensuring that head teachers had up-to-date knowledge about literacy priorities and what they should expect of their teachers and children; second, through improving data systems and data literacy to help schools differentiate support more precisely to meet the needs of particular groups such as boys, children with learning difficulties, particular age groups, children with English as an additional language. Leadership was the key to successful implementation and after the first year it became evident that the focus on training teachers was beginning to leave many head teachers behind. In 2000, a national round of head teacher conferences was initiated to disseminate the characteristics of 'quality first' teaching which were embedded in the Literacy Hour and to focus particularly on the challenges of teaching writing, which had urgently to be improved. The approach was intended to complement and supplement other more generic leadership training that was available at the time by focusing on teaching, learning and the curriculum and was increased over subsequent years to focus on the leadership of learning and teaching across the whole curriculum.

Those working on the Strategies were keenly aware that the time for being proactive with primary schools was likely to be finite. Both literacy and numeracy strategies were part of a wider education reform programme set out in the originating White Paper *Excellence in Schools* (DfEE 1997b). Reforms were already afoot in pre-school, secondary, further and higher education. Through strategic planning and coordination the literacy and numeracy strategies tried to ensure that messages to schools were managed and aligned. At the same time, there was a concerted effort to ensure wider policy coherence. In any large department of state, there will be competing priorities and territorial interests but, to everyone's credit, these interests were mostly subsumed into the wider strategic policy plan. There was a clear political intention to create coherence between the literacy and numeracy strategies and other policies, for example: changes to school funding regimes, reduction in class sizes, special educational needs, standards for professional development, reforms in initial teacher training, new professional qualification for head teachers, the establishment of a General Teaching Council, the National Grid for Learning, the evolving workforce reform agenda, priorities for health, physical education and sport, Education Action Zones and a rapid growth of early years provision and training.

The literacy and numeracy strategies were designed to be the leading edge of school improvement and responsibility for these key teaching and learning agendas gave the NLS some political advantage. But coherence had to be worked at. The NLS had to be alive to policy developments across the board and ready to negotiate, persuade and accommodate other initiatives so that literacy remained an undiminished priority and schools continued to give it their full attention. Also, it rapidly became apparent that the existence of the Strategy's field force gave it a special position of influence. Alongside numeracy, the NLS was the only group in the Department with a direct line to schools and, across the system, the only field force of any kind dedicated to support rather than accountability. Through its structure, the NLS could develop and deliver support directly to schools in ways that others could not and, in policy terms, those who control the delivery chain tend to control the agenda. But success can be a problem as well as an asset. The literacy and numeracy delivery chain looked appealing to others with initiatives to promote and other priorities had to be 'piggy-backed' to avoid duplicating structures and thus pressures on the schools.

This position of strength was not destined to last for ever. Priorities change, policies become subsumed in wider agendas and centrally directed policies of this kind necessarily have a finite lifespan. It was realized that these four years were a unique opportunity which needed to be exploited. The evaluation team commented in their first report:

> To an extent that has rarely been achieved in other jurisdictions, other educational policies have been aligned with the NLNS (National Literacy and Numeracy Strategies). That the NLNS are a coherent and well-integrated set of practices and programmes is a considerable accomplishment. The coherence is not yet being experienced by all those in LEAs and schools but the central alignment of policies, resources and actions is very clear.
>
> (Earl *et al.* 2000: 18)

Strategically, everything had to be timed and prioritized in relation to the achievement of the 80 per cent target in 2002. The rate at which support could be generated and teachers trained was constrained by internal capacity and the capacity of primary schools to absorb and respond to rapid change. The large number of individual schools, their relatively small size, 'flat' responsibility structures and non-specialist teaching organization meant that, in practice, individual teachers and head teachers would need to absorb multiple inputs. Strategically this was a significant risk which needed to be managed with care. New initiatives had to be prioritized and 'layered' over time, to challenge schools, increase their commitment and motivation, but avoid overloading them. By 1999, a major effort was under way to develop new training, guidance and resources which would deliver the three core messages set out in the previous chapter, and remain carefully aligned with objectives in the *Framework for Teaching* (see Chapter 3). A broad strategic plan for professional development was generated – see Table 7.1.

Right across the strategic plan, the focus was on teaching and learning. The whole thrust of the work was to help schools translate numerical data derived from national assessments and targets into curricular objectives with workable strategies for achieving them. Alongside these big priorities designed for everyone, was developed a range of more detailed customized guidance for particular ages and groups of children: able pupils, those with English as additional language, pupils with special needs, children in reception classes:

> During 2000 both materials and training associated with the strategies became more purposeful and differentiated, often in response to feedback from schools and LEAs. With specific attention to the diversity of pupils in schools, training and support have been extended to include not only practices for use in most classrooms, and under typical conditions, but also adaptations for specific situations or particular groups of children.
>
> (Earl *et al.* 2001: 13)

Deployment of support was reviewed in the light of these priorities. Most elements in the plan would require a detailed training programme with teaching resources, an explicit and well-structured training course which could be delivered by each of the 300 consultants to about 50,000 teachers across the country in each target group (see Table 7.2), together with high quality, very consistent trainer-training for the NLS consultants who would deliver the courses.

The implementation chain was proving effective. Regional directors trained consultants and directed their priorities. Since the Strategy was funding all these posts, regional directors had strong, accountable relationships with consultants and a direct line to teachers. It was clear that consultants were having a beneficial effect in the schools where they worked, and that demand for their support outstripped supply. But by the start of the new school year in 1999, consultants had directly influenced only about 20 per cent of schools. It was necessary to expand support and get to more teachers in order to keep up momentum. The deployment strategy from

Table 7.1 Outline Strategic priorities 1999–2002

Priority	Means	Target Groups
Improve reading comprehension	Extend support for shared reading: • fiction and non-fiction text level objectives from Framework • extending teachers' knowledge of text features and purposes	Teachers of 7–11-year-olds
Phonics	• develop, introduce and train on new programme Progression in Phonics (PiPs)	Teachers of 5–11-year-olds
Spelling	• develop Spelling Bank guidance and training on rules and conventions with focus on active word level investigations and spelling strategies	Teachers of 7–11-year-olds
Teaching writing composition	• Grammar for Writing: resources and national training	Teachers of 7–11-year-olds
Teaching writing composition	• Developing Early Writing: guidance, resources and national training	Teachers and classroom assistants working with 5–7-year-olds
Introduce wave 2 support for lower achieving children	• Additional Literacy Support programme (ALS): guidance, resources and national training	Teachers and classroom assistants working with 7–9-year-olds
Develop wave 2 support for younger children	• Early Literacy Support programme (ELS): guidance, resources and national training	Teachers and classroom assistants working with 5–6-year-olds
Develop wave 2 support for older children	• Further Literacy Support programme (FLS): guidance, resources and national training	Teachers and classroom assistants working with 10–11-year-olds
Headteacher conferences	Second round focused on: • overview of NLS resources; defining Quality First Teaching; underlining priority of writing; improving uses of data	All primary headteachers

the first year simply could not be repeated; the rate of impact would be too slow and managing it all from the centre, too complex. Thus, as a first move towards devolving the Strategy, the national consultants' team was supplemented and local authorities were given flexibility to deploy consultancy in more differentiated ways to expand training and significantly increase access by schools. Additionally, consultants' roles were strengthened, giving them greater responsibility to balance different aspects of the job and encourage the development of 'expert teachers' who demonstrated lessons and supported colleagues mainly through being visited by others to see them at work.

Intensive effort was required by schools and the Strategy over this period to develop and deliver all the commitments in the strategic plan. Earl *et al.* (2000: 19) predicted in their first annual report on the Strategy that 'changing practice would be hard work – emotionally and practically'. They were right. By 2002 all the planned elements were in place. Most schools welcomed the support with mixed feelings. They were pleased to share in the growth of knowledge and could see obvious benefits for teaching and learning but the learning curve could be stressful and very demanding. The layering of support over time, addressing teachers and head teachers at different stages, close coordination with numeracy and the injection of additional resources for classroom assistants all helped to smooth the way.

Consistency and fidelity to the core principles were a discipline. If schools were to move towards sustainability, everyone in the delivery chain had to keep 'on message'. The great strength of the Strategy over its first four years was the persistent and uncompromising priority it received from Tony Blair, and the Secretary of State for Education, David Blunkett, which provided confidence, clarity and authority. Without this support, the Strategy would probably have gone nowhere. Even so, managing a large team of regional directors, trainers and support staff, while giving them scope to be responsive and professional, risks too much variety and a loss of clarity from the centre. Over the years, there was bound to be significant staff turnover in schools, and in some, staff turbulence was a major issue. The Strategy could not rely on the initial push to sustain capacity and needed continuously to re-run and repeat the core messages and training from the first year. Consultants, by and large, were thoughtful, creative people who needed to develop their own professional knowledge; some became frustrated by the need to repeat training and stick to the common agenda. Careful monitoring and performance management were needed to ensure everyone in the implementation chain stayed on course. But motivation was the biggest driver. The pressing agenda of new developments in the strategic plan was a strong incentive. It left little time for diversion and engaged regional directors and consultants in a growing culture of common professional learning.

Alignment was more problematic with others outside the Department for Education who also had a direct line to schools. The two most significant others were Ofsted with their own field force of school inspectors, and local authorities with their advisory teams and formal responsibilities for school improvement. The first White Paper (DfEE 1997b) had spelled out complementary roles for each and broad priorities were clear but their respective responsibilities, accountabilities and organizational density complicated communication with schools, especially school leaders.

These two lines were further complicated by a directly accountable relationship between Ofsted and each local authority; it inspected the local authorities as well as the schools and held local authorities to account on the performance of the schools. Ofsted also had a relationship with the Strategy through its role as an independent evaluator which was a considerable asset in the early stages. Schools expected to be held to account over the implementation of the Strategy and so tended to comply with its recommendations. Likewise, local authorities promoted the Strategy systematically, all of which helped to get it into place in the first year. However, despite its public commitment to literacy and numeracy, Ofsted did little to develop its own capacity to inspect the Strategy. Formal evaluation of the Strategy was conducted by a small team of primary inspectors sampling 300 primary schools (less than 2 per cent of the nation's 18,500 primary schools) while, at the same time, every school in the country was being inspected[1] by a much larger group of externally contracted 'additional inspectors'.

During the first four years of implementation, these 'additional inspectors' received only one day of compulsory training, which was not completed until the end of the second year. This training was poorly designed, and contracted by Ofsted without reference to the Strategy. Expectations and criteria drawn from the NLS were not built into Ofsted's *Framework for Inspection* used by inspectors as an aide-memoire and handbook of inspection guidance. Some inspectors were expert and supportive but others were unclear about the Strategy's expectations, unfamiliar with the Framework and recommended methodologies, and less informed about the teaching of literacy than the teachers they were charged to inspect. As a result, schools received mixed messages, some of which ran counter to the Strategy's advice and many under-performing schools went unchallenged. A frustrating consequence was the tendency for inspectors to rate mediocre literacy provision positively, while focusing criticism on other aspects of school performance which they saw as weaker, leaving relatively weak schools with lists of action points which diverted attention from the central task of improving literacy.

Local authorities were strongly committed. They saw the Strategy as a practical means of school improvement and valued the additional consultancy resources and training that came with it. Local strategy managers, usually senior advisers or inspectors with wide-ranging responsibilities for primary school improvement, were designated to be first points of reference, act as the Strategy's main conduits into the authority and manage the teams of local consultants. Typically, each school also had a nominated local adviser who was the first point of reference on all school improvement matters including the Strategy. School advisers might be primary specialists, though not necessarily in literacy, or they might be secondary specialists from a variety of subject backgrounds. Over the years, in concert with the growth of Ofsted, local advisory teams had been depleted. Most were over-stretched and had long since abandoned

---

1   Full inspections lasted for four days and took place about every four years. Schools in 'special measures' were re-inspected within the year.

specialist curricular interests for a range of more generic duties centred mainly on monitoring school performance. Some advisers were very able, others were at sea; some systematically visited and supported teachers, others seldom ventured beyond the head teacher's office. The Strategy, with its emphasis on standards, curriculum and pedagogy and leadership was, therefore, a considerable challenge to many.

Because of hierarchies and professional accountabilities, local advisers would normally provide the interface with head teachers, while literacy consultants were dedicated to supporting teachers. This dual input was far from perfect but was outside the Strategy's control. The NLS provided training for Strategy managers but it proved difficult to have them together for more than a day at a time intensively, and near impossible to get local advisory teams into any corporate and systematic mode of training. Dissemination of Strategy training within local authorities to advisory teams was often weak and, as with Ofsted inspections, under-performing schools often got by unchallenged, especially if they had already received an unchallenging Ofsted report. While local authorities accorded due value to the Strategy, primary school literacy was by no means their only priority. Strategy managers had a pivotal role but often had too little weight in the local authority management hierarchy to secure the interests of the Strategy over competing priorities and often, because the Strategy was separately funded, it was hived off and treated as a project rather than a central plank of the local authority's school improvement policy. As a result, while the delivery of consultancy support to teachers became increasingly secure, support for improving literacy leadership was less accountable and more variable. For economic and political reasons the Strategy was committed to working through local authorities and needed their good will and co-operation and, above all, a better structured dialogue with head teachers. Looking back, this was quite a pervasive weakness in the overall strategic approach.

Nevertheless, the Strategy moved forward and by 2000 was described by Chris Woodhead H.M. Chief Inspector of Schools as 'a triumph' (Woodhead 2000). Reporting on the implementation over the first two years, Ofsted reported that:

> the National Literacy Strategy has brought about a transformation in the way in which reading and, to a lesser extent, writing are taught and, through the Framework for Teaching, has provided a common starting point and a common language for everyone who is involved in the teaching of literacy. The strategy has introduced teachers to new methods and materials and has required many teachers to improve substantially their own subject knowledge.
>
> (Ofsted 2000b: §140)

Year by year, the Strategy was building increasingly precise information about what children needed to learn to progress through the National Curriculum levels, based on analyses of the national assessments. This qualitative data was linked to objectives in the Framework and built into training materials and planning guidance. The importance of translating numerical targets into curricular targets was emphasized and teachers were encouraged to use these to set achievable learning targets for children and engage them in self-assessing and recognizing their own progress. This 'assessment for learning' philosophy was new at the time but, nine years after the introduction of the Strategy, it is common practice in primary schools with widespread success.

By the end of 2001, the Strategy was achieving:

- improved standards, particularly in reading
- widespread and strong commitment to the NLS
- transformation of literacy teaching with big improvements in teaching quality
- higher expectations across the system
- improvement and increased challenge for the more able and significant catch-up for low attainers

but also had big challenges to meet:

- maintaining the gains
- developing more effective teaching of writing
- setting and using teaching and learning targets
- improving school leadership for continued growth and sustainability
- getting to the complacent and semi-participating schools
- joining up and refocusing the key messages.

Key messages were clarified and published as an evidence-based aide-memoire to frame the work of everyone involved in leading, supporting, teaching or inspecting during the coming year – see Table 7.2.

By the end of 2000, most of these development priorities were achieved or under way. Still to be implemented were the 'wave 2' programmes *Early Literacy Support* (ELS) for 5- to 6-year-olds and *Further Literacy Support* (FLS) for 10- to 11-year-olds, to complete the suite of catch-up programmes alongside the existing *Additional Literacy Support* (ALS) programme for 7- to 9-year-olds (see Chapter 5). *Developing Early Writing* was also due for completion and implementation in May 2001 to complement the existing *Grammar for Writing* guidance. In their evaluation report on the first four years from 1998 to 2002, Ofsted (2002a: 2, 29) noted that the Strategy 'had a significant impact on the standards attained in English and on the quality of teaching over the last four years' and that 'Headteachers' leadership and management of the NLS continued to improve'. Leadership and management are weak 'in one in ten schools, compared with the first year of the strategy when the equivalent figure was one in five'.

They also commented on its capacity-building potential:

> Overall, the implementation of the NLS has created a virtuous circle: as teachers have recognized that the strategy is working, their confidence in it has begun to rise and they have continued to improve their teaching, building on earlier work. For head teachers it has provided an important lever for change across the curriculum as well as in literacy.
>
> (Ofsted 2002a: 21)

Table 7.2 Development priorities

Unless there are demonstratively more effective strategies in place, every school should provide:

1 a minimum daily hour of continuous, direct and dedicated literacy teaching time for all children;
2 teaching and pupil targets for each class, each term: visible, monitored and assessed;
3 regular shared reading in every class to:
   * enrich,
   * improve fluency and comprehension,
   * provide models for writing;
4 guided reading twice a week for every child in Key Stage 1 and, where needed, in Key Stage 2;
5 regular shared writing (60% as a guide):
   * based on the text-level objectives in the Framework,
   * using the shared writing models from Grammar for Writing,
   * regular Grammar for Writing teaching throughout Key Stage 2;
6 NLS Progression in Phonics or equivalent phonics programme throughout reception and Year 1 classes (5- and 6-year-olds) with continuous reinforcement through Year 2, to habituate, for spelling;
7 systematic use of NLS Spelling Bank through Key Stage 2 and in Year 2, as appropriate;
8 Additional Learning Support (ALS) in place for Years 3 and 4 lower attainers and, also introduced, where appropriate, to Year 2;
9 'booster classes' and post-test continuity of teaching in place for all Year 6 children;
10 literacy beyond the Literacy Hour:
   * cross-curricular, particularly to promote non-fiction writing,
   * additional curricular time e.g. for independent reading, handwriting practice,
   * extra support for children where needed.

The first four years were also marked by a major investment in capacity building (in excess of £600 million) as a result of which it grew exponentially. By 2002 there were around 800 full-time local consultants supporting literacy and numeracy and 4,000 leading teachers who worked in schools and demonstrated teaching to colleagues from other schools, acting as mentors in one of the two subjects. Access to training averaged 20 days per school in 2001, and there was widespread take-up and growing demand. The core of this training had been delivered by consultants, who had a common understanding of the Strategy and its specific priorities through carefully structured prior trainer-training, run by the small but expert national directorate team. A continuing theme of professional learning pervaded this phase of the Strategy, looking forward to a stage of greater sustainability when schools would be increasingly responsible for their own literacy improvement. Also, there had been significant flexing of the original NLS recommendations in response to local needs, new and increasingly refined information from assessment and evaluation about the learning and teaching most likely to contribute to success:

- Schools, while sticking to the principle of the Literacy Hour, had been encouraged to treat it flexibly to suit the needs of their own children. For example, with increasing emphasis on the place of phonics, teachers of younger children commonly planned lessons to start with word level work, while teachers of older children frequently blocked sequences of lessons to get depth and continuity of learning over several days, especially for writing.
- Objectives in the Framework were used in diverse ways. While some schools stuck rigidly to them and tried to cover everything, others treated them as a guide to planning, used and grouped selectively to reflect the needs and priorities for particular individuals, groups or classes.
- Refinements in the target-setting process were providing more opportunity for schools to negotiate targets. Increasing data quality and data literacy at every level were strengthening the position and capacity of school leaders and the precision with which they could define priorities for their own schools.
- A rapid growth in high quality guidance and exemplification materials for schools, particularly for the teaching of phonics and writing, plus the 'wave 2' learning support programmes for lower performing children at different ages (ELS, ALS, FLS) now offered schools a growing structure through which to design and manage their own improvement and professional development strategies.
- The range and organization of training and support varied widely between local authorities in response to local needs and priorities, though the main priorities continued to be determined centrally.
- Although there were clear central messages and national priorities, role definitions, status and deployment of literacy consultants had been substantially devolved to local authorities and were quite diverse, and there was increasing opportunity for regional directors to set priorities and respond to local needs flexibly.

The external evaluation team commented on what had been achieved:

> The early momentum has continued as the strategies have evolved, with a consistent vision that is now supported by more targeted objectives and messages developed in response to performance data and feedback from the field... Developments such as increased policy consistency and coherence, continued emphasis on capacity building and attention to the broader context of schooling will contribute to sustainability.

But they also signalled the central dilemma:

> How can the DfES find and maintain ... an appropriate balance between central direction and local initiative? Over the last year DfES and the NLS and NNS have emphasized local capacity-building through training, networking and sharing good practice. Yet, at the same time central direction and production of resources ... have continued and even increased ... Although DfES is committed to local autonomy, the ever-expanding policy web makes it difficult

to attain. Is there sufficient scope for local input and adaptation to suit unique local circumstances?

(Earl *et al.* 2001: 27)

This is the critical transition for any large-scale programme of this kind, and one about which the Strategy had most to learn. It was clear that the first two phases of implementation and embedding had been worthwhile. They had achieved many of the benefits expected of them: rising standards, changed practices, common transactable approaches, and new professional learning to increase teachers' skills. Schools varied, of course, in the degree to which they made the Strategy their own and there is no doubt that it fostered high degrees of dependency in many, resulting in over-reliance on modelled practices without the accompanying understanding. Fullan (2003) articulates this problem, using the NLS as an example:

All of our examples of phase 1 (literacy and numeracy improvements) success on a large scale had a strong degree of front-end, assertive top-down leadership. This is true for England and for school district successes … In a sense, you can get away with top-down leadership under two conditions: (1) if it turns out you had a good idea (informed prescription) and (2) if you invest in capacity-building (and empowerment) from day one. But this still only brings us large-scale, first steps (not deep or sustainable reform).

(Fullan 2003: 33)

The NLS has been uniquely successful in achieving these 'first steps'. Much has been gained and while the principle of autonomy is clear, there are attendant risks that early gains that required huge effort to achieve can easily be lost. It is a good thing to move from informed prescription towards local autonomy and there is good evidence from spheres of work outside education of the effectiveness of doing so (see Fullan 2003 for reference to this evidence). But the principle is one thing; how to engineer it effectively was new territory. Again, Fullan poses some key questions:

First, does a decade of informed prescription create the preconditions for moving to informed professional judgement? Second, is there a danger that, in moving to informed professional judgement, the gains of valuable prescription will slip away? Put another way, did informed prescription actually hamper the creativeness of teachers, or did it rein in a range of permissive but highly questionable practice that went under the name of creativity and autonomy? Third, how do you move, anyway, from prescription to autonomy? We might be able to portray what informed professional judgement might look like but the pathways for getting there will be enormously complex and different depending on the starting point.

(Fullan 2003: 5)

This was to be the abiding challenge for the Strategy post-2002.

Chapter 8

Devolving the Strategy

The theoretical impetus towards devolving the Strategy came from a number of sources. First, there was the evaluation and research work from Fullan and colleagues in the external evaluation team. Second, this was underscored heavily in the DfES by the appointment of David Hopkins as successor to Michael Barber. Keen to see the principle of deep learning activated, he set the intellectual scene for a radical change in the scope and structure of the Strategy. As in debates about the teaching of reading, the polarization between 'top-down' and 'bottom-up' emerges in relation to implementation and sustainability. In the introduction to a DfES paper about the development of the Strategy, written by Fullan, Hopkins comments:

> Michael makes the futuristic statement that moves beyond the arid polarity between 'top-down' and 'bottom-up'. Here he argues that the future of educational reform lies not only in co-production – the working together of policy makers and consumers towards a common goal but also that the actors are involved not just with making sense of the action but also in leading it. The argument is simple and profound: if a system is striving for both 'high equity and excellence' then policy and practice have to focus on system improvement. This means that a school head has to be almost as concerned about the success of other schools as he or she is about his or her own schools … they need to make sense not just of their own reality and work but to reconceive the system at the same time.
>
> (Hopkins 2004: intro)

A tall order for 18,500 head teachers in small separate institutions across the nation; but this was to be the agenda – moving rapidly towards the ideal of autonomous schools each as a learning community and contributing through corporate thinking about their own improvement to the common good. Third, however, the autonomy theme chimed well with other government priorities on devolution. It fitted comfortably with changing education priorities and the need to move forward urgently on other fronts.

The changing policy context

Following the general election in May 2001, the Labour Government was returned for a third term, marking another phase in the life of the NLS. Although political attention on the Strategies remained high, the imperative now was to sustain and improve earlier gains by shifting the axis of responsibility from the centre to the schools. The 2002 target date was looming and there was real concern about schools' capacity to meet it. National test results for English (reading and writing) had risen by ten points from 65 to 75 per cent over the three years 1998 to 2000 and, at that time, the strategies appeared to be on track to secure, or get close to, the expected 80 per cent. But in 2001 standards stalled at 75 per cent and were destined to remain unchanged in 2002 so that, in the event, the target was not met.[1]

There were also some unwelcome side effects from the target. The relentless focus on level 4 attainment for 11-year-olds was necessary but, despite additional 'wave 2' provision made by the Strategy, concerns were growing about the consequences of this focus for supporting the lowest achieving children. Also, over the previous two years, Ofsted had been picking up quite pervasive weaknesses in the quality of teaching in years 3 and 4 (7- to 9-year-olds), reflecting a tendency for schools to deploy stronger teachers to the target classes in years 5 and 6. Although much had been done to support literacy development among younger children, there was a growing concern that this longer term investment had not been sufficiently deep. For obvious reasons, the messages to schools were positive and encouraging but this, too, had side effects – a point picked up by the external evaluation team in their final report on the implementation of the literacy and numeracy strategies:

> … many teachers believe that the job is done, that they have the knowledge they need and have fully implemented the Strategies – a misconception that makes capacity-building more challenging. In its eagerness to celebrate the early success of the Strategies, the Government may also have added to this sense of there being little more to do, even though it has now committed funding through to 2006.
>
> (Earl *et al.* 2003: 6)

While there was consternation at the target shortfall, it was not the whole story. Underlying the test results, positive qualitative change was continuing:

> An emphasis on failure to reach the 2002 targets may obscure the substantial level of success that has been achieved. Regional directors are convinced on the basis of test data and classroom observation, that pupil learning has improved considerably with the use of the Strategies. Our data indicate that many head teachers and teachers also find that the Strategies have had a positive impact on aspects of pupil learning; a much smaller percentage believe that the Strategies have not. Many LEAs and school staff report that the Strategies have helped to

---

1   Chapter 9 gives a more detailed analysis of results over time.

motivate some pupils, thereby leading to future improvements in learning. Our overall assessment is that increases in pupil learning have been considerable.

(Earl *et al.* 2003: 128)

Nevertheless, with the target date passed and consultation begun on an even more ambitious national target of 85 per cent for 2006, the scene was set to reconfigure the Strategy. Now, the literacy and numeracy strategies would have to take their place in the wider context of evolving education policy which was, itself, part of an even broader policy shift across government departments from old-style command and control models to more devolved decision-making, self-help and front-line accountability, designed to drive continuous improvement. The literacy and numeracy strategies had come thus far and been the centre of attention. Just prior to the 2001 election, David Blunkett, Secretary of State for Education, put it in context:

In this Parliament we said that we would get the basics right in primary schools. We have done so. Standards of literacy and numeracy have been transformed, thanks to an historic partnership for change between teachers, parents and Government. And our pledge to cut infant class sizes of more than 30 will be delivered nationwide by this September. There is further progress to make in primary and early years provision ... but the foundations are secure. Our mission now is to bring about a similar transformation in secondary schools.

(DfEE 2001a: 4)

The focus of attention would shift to Key Stage 3 and the 14–19 sector. The Key Stage 3 Strategy which had been evolving as two separate pilots within the literacy and numeracy strategies now assumed a life of its own under a single national director, developing its own subject frameworks, specialist regional directorate and teams and local consultants. A major effort was already under way by September 2002 to deliver high expectations, training and common approaches to teaching and learning across all secondary schools in the country. Restructuring of the literacy and numeracy strategies into a single national primary strategy was both symmetrical and inevitable. By 2002, three related strategic challenges had emerged:

- maintaining and developing the literacy and numeracy focus with clear key messages, high quality resources and training for every school
- managing the devolution of control to schools, in the expectation that schools would take the strategies on with increasing autonomy
- a new emphasis on embedding literacy and numeracy in the wider curriculum.

Although related, these three objectives are not necessarily connected. For example, continuing to build capacity for literacy and numeracy, while managing devolution to schools, did not require the simultaneous involvement of the national strategy in promoting the development of the wider curriculum. Running all these agendas together smoothly was politically attractive – it was likely to go down well with schools and the professional associations and it began to get ministers off the hook in relation to the growing discomfort with the initial more centralized and prescriptive stance of the NLS. But the changes were extremely complex to communicate and implement, and bound to be difficult to manage.

The first challenge was on the way to being met. There would be further development of guidance, support and training for literacy over the coming years but much of the subject-related provision had been set in place during the first four years. The NLS had directly supported a significant proportion of teachers but more needed to be done to make it sustainable. The big issue for capacity building was to stay focused, reiterate the messages, training and support, get all this to many more teachers, and engage with the relentless task of consolidating and embedding what had been achieved at the school level. It was evident in the course of 2000 and over the following year, that both individual and institutional capacity in primary schools, while developing, was far from secure. The extent to which schools had been able to take the NLS on, learn from it and adapt it, varied hugely between schools and across local authorities. While there was clear evidence of system-wide improvement, there remained a high proportion of schools, head teachers and individual class teachers who were either poorly informed or had become dependent on following the NLS slavishly, with too little regard for the needs of their children. The temptation to talk up the good news also had the effect of under-estimating the level of focus, precision and differentiation needed to move up from the 75 per cent plateau.

It seemed logical that the natural counterpart to the developing Key Stage 3 Strategy would be a national strategy for primary schools, similarly broad in its reach. But this prospect of impending change was also a distraction. New national management structures were to be developed, changes in roles and responsibilities were planned to combine literacy and numeracy, interest grew in planning for wider training and support beyond the specifics of literacy and numeracy, all of which made it harder to keep the Strategy's eye on the ball during the critical capacity-building period from 2000 to 2003, while national standards were flat-lining. In September 2002, somewhat late in the day, a brief but comprehensive document was published to schools summarizing the big messages of the NLS (DfES 2002c). It celebrated the achievements, set out key messages about the teaching and learning of literacy and defined the complementary roles of school staff. It offered guidance on the use of professional support and the NLS 'wave 2' programmes and curriculum organization. It advised schools about developing policy designed to reduce teachers' workload. Nevertheless by now, some of the initial impetus had been dissipated which generated criticism and concern about the effectiveness of the Strategy, and further motivated the change process. The solution seemed to lie in broadening, rather than focusing the Strategy, in the hope that the motivation to be brought by increased local autonomy would fill the gap.

The second strategic challenge was to fulfil the commitment to increasing school autonomy. Earlier talk of pressure and support as the levers for change was superseded by a more sophisticated framework of *high challenge, high support* (Figure 8.1).

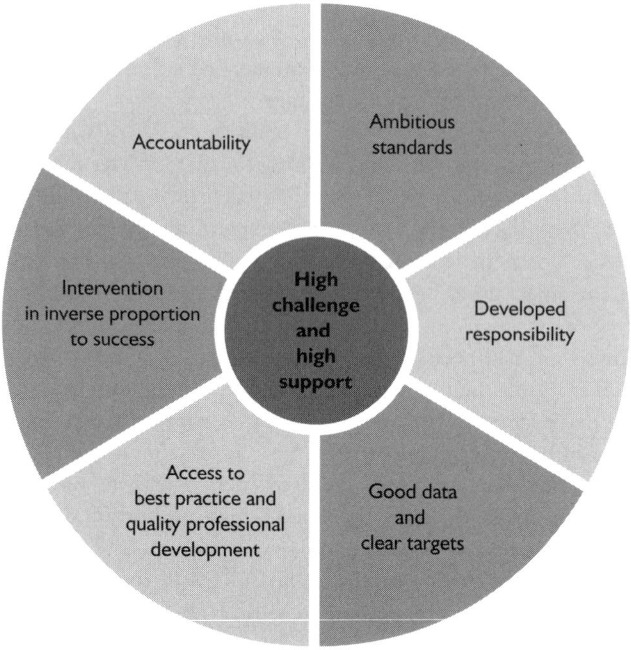

Figure 8.1 High Challenge/High Support diagram (Source: DfEE 2001a: 9)

These principles would drive the secondary transformation and were already establishing themselves in primary schools with varying degrees of security. School autonomy (developed responsibility) was an attractive but challenging prospect. The central push to raise standards had been effective and essential but school level responsibility for the literacy and numeracy strategies was at very different stages across the system. The external evaluation team identified the dilemma facing the Education Secretary. Recognizing that schools, by and large, had been willing to comply with and acquiesce in the NLS recommendations, and that this 'bodes well for implementing the strategies ... in the future', they argued that government cannot sustain this level of intervention indefinitely and might 'paradoxically result in a culture of dependence at the local level' that could prove counter-productive – but how to manage it?

> We are not suggesting that Government bow out of its central role with the Strategies. This is not an either-or situation; both central direction and local initiative are necessary. The challenge is to find a dynamic balance that recognizes that LEAs, schools, head teachers and teachers are at very different points and have different needs.
>
> (Earl *et al.* 2001: xii)

A new paradigm

In 2002, Ofsted published a short but influential survey report *The Curriculum in Successful Primary Schools* evaluating the impact of the literacy and numeracy strategies on the wider primary curriculum, and defining the third big policy challenge. Their investigation focussed on a small sample of 31 schools drawn from the 3,500 inspected in the academic year 2001–2, using two criteria: (a) high standards in English and mathematics and (b) good or excellent grades for the quality and range of learning opportunities. The report struck an optimistic note and had a more formative purpose than their previous evaluation reports. Schools were concerned that the strategies had placed undue pressure on teaching time and narrowed the range and richness of the curriculum. The problem was partly due to pressure on the real time available in the school day or year but due more to workload pressures on teachers. Like time and money, teacher's energy is finite and many said they were putting so much effort into planning and managing the strategies that they had too little left to expend on other subjects. This was a real issue because evidence from the previous two decades of inspection and research strongly indicated that, despite the importance of basics, narrowing the curriculum was likely to be counter-productive. It restricted the range of worthwhile learning, limited opportunities to practise, apply and contextualize basic skills, depressed interest and motivation, especially for reluctant learners and, of course ran counter to the requirements of the National Curriculum which set out statutory rights to learning for all children.

Part of this effect was consequent upon the relaxation, in 1998, of statutory requirements for teaching foundation subjects that we noted in Chapter 1. In practice, it was not that other subjects went untaught but that they received less attention and, more importantly, that they were often reduced to straightforward listening, reading and writing tasks with too little variety of learning. As Ofsted pointed out, often the most vulnerable aspects of other subjects were the very things that bring them to life: enquiry, problem solving and practical work; it was this broader range of active learning that defined the essence of the wider curriculum. Primary teachers in England have always understood this and were instinctively concerned. It was probably no accident that, around the same time, there was a resurgence of interest among primary teachers in the psychological research on multiple intelligences and learning styles. Ofsted (2002b) identified three broad categories of schools:

1   Despite many gloomy messages about impact on the wider curriculum, there were schools which managed to exploit the strategies successfully, achieve high standards in English, mathematics and science, and also give a strong emphasis to the humanities, physical education and the arts. The curriculum in these schools was enriched by first-hand experiences, visits, contributions from adults with knowledge and skills that could enhance children's learning, and an extensive range of extra-curricular activities. Curriculum enrichment contributed positively to children's attitudes, personal and creative abilities. These successful schools had the following characteristics:

- they embraced the strategies and used them confidently and flexibly to achieve high standards in literacy and numeracy
- they managed the wider curriculum effectively and *exploited* other subjects to promote quality learning e.g. through exploration, investigation, problem-solving, critical, creative and imaginative thinking, reflection and self-assessment
- they were well led by head teachers with a clear view of teaching and learning which was strongly promoted throughout the school
- the professional climate was autonomous, accountable, self-critical and self-improving. These schools were prepared to take some 'risks' with the organization and management of the curriculum to ensure successful learning.

2   Such schools were an obvious paradigm for the *high challenge, high support* framework. But they were untypical. Other evidence from Ofsted's broader evaluation indicated that, although the majority of schools had been reasonably successful with the implementation of the strategies, they

- said the strategies took up most of their time and effort
- covered the National Curriculum more or less systematically but were not capitalizing on other subjects effectively to promote pupils' learning and development
- saw the pressures of Ofsted and the DfES as major constraints, lacked the confidence, and sometimes the skills, to move forward
- the professional climate in these schools tended to be hard working but compliant, with the attendant frustrations of a dependency culture where problems and their solutions are too often seen as outside the school's control and attributed to the 'system'.

3   A further, but significant, minority of schools failed to achieve acceptable standards in literacy and numeracy and often did not manage the rest of the curriculum successfully either. These schools under-performed. This group included 'coasting' schools whose outcomes sometimes met or even exceeded the national assessment averages. They were characterized by endemically poor progress and the inability of the school to add value. Leadership was, by definition, weak in these schools and management tended to be reactive. The professional climate was usually hard working but unchallenging, often stressful and sometimes downright depressing.

It is not entirely clear how many schools were in each of the three categories. Informally, Ofsted indicated that it could be up to 20 per cent in the 'very successful' category, 60 per cent in the middle range and a further 20 per cent of under-performing or 'coasting' schools. The figures may have been optimistic; certainly they were very big numbers given the total of 18,500 schools. The expectation of the *high challenge, high support* philosophy was to produce a step-change, by shifting large numbers of schools out of a relatively dependent relationship with the strategies to meet these 'high success' criteria. Estelle Morris, the new Secretary of State, articulated this aim in a White Paper set before Parliament at the start of the Government's second term.

> The last four years have demonstrated that huge progress is possible and this must be the foundation for the next four years. Further radical policy innovation and new programmes are not the key to continued and increasing success in primary schools. Rather, the policy will be to embed the existing strategy in every primary school across the country, continuing to provide a comprehensive programme of professional development and support to schools, making sure that all children benefit from rising standards.
>
> (DfES 2001b: §2.14)

The transformation of primary schools needed to reach beyond literacy and numeracy to embrace the wider curriculum. Literacy and numeracy standards would remain the non-negotiable core with success measured in terms of national and local targets but ministers were also committed to widening and enriching the curriculum with a new emphasis on curriculum breadth, extra-curricular activities, specific pledges on increased access to music tuition, entitlement to two hours of high quality physical education and sport for every child, extended opportunities for the arts and creativity, and the promotion of modern language teaching in primary schools (DfES 2001b). These prospects chimed well with the perceptions of many schools who complained about 'initiative fatigue' and a need for greater stability. The external evaluation team, who had spent the third phase of their evaluation considering implementation perceptions at school level, picked this up:

> After four years, many see the NLS and NNS as needing to be re-energized; the early momentum and excitement have lessened and a new boost would be helpful … continuing improvement will require not only greater individual capacity in head teachers and teachers but also greater organisational capacity in schools and local authorities. In the long run we believe that the commitment to collective capacity building is the most promising direction for addressing the challenges of the future.
>
> (Earl *et al.* 2003: 9)

Other influences were also at work. The call for change was influenced by the need to align and coordinate the early years (Foundation Stage) curriculum with the National Curriculum requirements for primary schools, resulting from a parallel policy to increase early years provision as of right for all 3–5-year-olds. The whole early years structure of curriculum, support and resources were to be brought under the umbrella of a new wider primary strategy. This integration highlighted significant ideological differences between the priorities and values that drove the two curricula, and associated beliefs about the nature of childhood, development, learning and teaching. Chief among these was an antipathy to direct instruction by many early years practitioners and a wide-ranging debate about the age at which a formal curriculum should be introduced. These accommodations brought a new emphasis on the rights and needs of vulnerable children, and a powerful confirmation of the values of breadth, enrichment and active, practical experience in early learning, for which there was much sympathy across the primary school spectrum, particularly among teachers of younger children.

Also, over the previous four years, there had been big improvements in the quality of data at every level, and in the data-literacy of head teachers and other leaders. The strategies had already produced some detailed guidance on planning to teaching objectives, plotting the links between these and expected attainment levels, for teachers of older children, which could be readily extended to cover all year groups. Improved data, combined with our increasing ability to connect numbers to qualitative outcomes (what were earlier called curricular objectives) made it possible to differentiate support more precisely and translate numbers into learning and teaching objectives for children. These improvements were starting to provide practical leadership tools for evaluation, target-setting, identifying curricular objectives and monitoring. Significantly, improved comparative data at school, year group and pupil levels was increasing schools' ability to conduct their own objective self-evaluations, and design targeted improvement strategies. Some key leadership skills that once seemed elusive now began to look more practical and transferable.

These advances were also contributing to improvements in the quality of teaching and learning by helping schools to apply the principles of assessment for learning, linked to growing evidence about the importance of meta-cognition and 'learning how to learn' (Hargreaves and the Learning Working Group 2005). Making children aware of what they are expected to learn and engaging them in assessing their own progress, cultivates transferable competences such as reflection, generalization, ability to plan, self-monitoring and problem-solving as well as positive attitudes and motivation. Assessment for learning helps children see where they are going and marks out progress with successes rather failure. It is a powerful idea that underpinned the early thinking about teaching from objectives in both literacy and numeracy but which was by now clearly articulated and gaining currency through research and advocacy by teachers (Black and Wiliam 1998).

The new national Primary Strategy

In May 2003, following extensive consultation, these evolving ideas came together in the document *Excellence and Enjoyment – a strategy for primary schools*, which set out a vision for the future of primary education built on what had been achieved.

> High standards and a broad and rich curriculum go hand in hand. Literacy and numeracy are vital building blocks, and it is right to focus attention on them. But it is important that children have a rich and exciting experience at

primary school, learning a wide range of things in a wide range of different ways. Our new Primary Strategy will support teachers and schools across the whole curriculum, building on the lessons of the Literacy and Numeracy Strategies, but moving on to offer teachers more control and flexibility. It will focus on building up teachers' own professionalism and capacity to teach better and better, with bespoke support they can draw on to meet their particular needs. There will be extra support and challenge for the schools that need it most.

(DfES 2003b: 27)

The website introduction to the Primary Strategy sets this vision out:

- Empowering primary schools to take control of their curriculum, and to be more innovative and to develop their own character.
- Schools setting their own targets for level 4 and 5 at key stage 2, based on challenging but realistic targets for the progress of each child in the school, with LEA targets being set afterwards.
- Trialling a new approach of supported teacher assessment at KS1, where tests underpin teacher assessment rather than being reported separately.
- Encouraging schools to network together and learning from others in sharing and developing good practice. Partnership with parents, which is vital in helping children to do as well as they can, and making wider links with the community.
- Government acting more and more as an enabler with schools increasingly in control of the support they get to:
  1. strengthen leadership, particularly leadership of teaching, and professional development to help teachers embed the principles of effective teaching and learning both in literacy and numeracy and across the curriculum
  2. help schools design broad and rich curricula which make the most of links between different areas and provide opportunities for children to have a wide range of learning experiences

(PNS Website, accessed December 2006)

In 2003, standards had again flat-lined at 75 per cent. With a similar discrepancy between reading and writing, little had changed from previous years. This outcome was less politically damaging than the results in the 2002 target year and stiffened ministers' resolve to swing the axis of responsibility towards the schools, describing these results as a 'platform for' rather than a 'plateau of' achievement. Based on analysis of the data there was a conviction that the new 85 per cent target was achievable and that this would be best achieved by requiring schools to set their own targets based on detailed comparative school and pupil level data (DfES 2003b: §2.19–2.20). School targets would then be aggregated up to form local authority targets that would be agreed afterwards, as a proportionate contribution to the national target. For schools, it seemed to push all the right buttons: increased autonomy, control of the targets, more attention to the wider curriculum, increased flexibility, a new emphasis on the importance of speaking and listening, more attention to creativity and the wider curriculum, a national workload agreement to increase teaching assistants, guaranteed non-teaching time for planning, assessment and professional development.

Excellence and Enjoyment was created around the principle that the characteristics of successful schools, as Ofsted had described them, could be widely replicated and that, for the most part, there was requisite knowledge about literacy and numeracy in the system to maintain standards. Extensive consultation over the following months with head teachers was positive, though not uncritical. Many saw these new messages as a return to long-held values about the importance of learning, motivation and practical experience; it was also widely perceived to be a relaxing of the pressure that had characterized the strategies hitherto. Much needed to be done to convince schools that the challenge was greater than before and that they would now be expected to take it on for themselves. This radical change required a re-shaped implementation structure with changes at every level to create new levers for improvement that were understood and endorsed by schools.

Thus, the single Primary National Strategy (PNS) was created, amalgamating the literacy and numeracy strategies with a wide remit across the spectrum of primary provision including all subjects, leadership development and the early years (Foundation Stage) curriculum. At national level, a single National Director was appointed, and the separate teams of literacy and numeracy regional directors became primary regional directors. National changes were reflected down the line. Local authority literacy and numeracy strategy managers were augmented by a primary strategy manager as the senior point of reference in each LEA. The new primary strategy managers were expected to take a proactive role, challenging schools to set ambitious targets, planning and managing a comprehensive range of professional development for primary schools and deploying a growing number of professional support staff to maximize benefit to schools. Additional consultants were brought in to serve new project lines alongside literacy and numeracy, bringing the national complement to around 800. Role changes throughout the system were designed to support a range of more generic and different responsibilities.

Finally, changes were made to the structure of accountabilities. Now that one national round of school inspections was complete, Ofsted stepped back from its high intensity programme into a more differentiated pattern with a new 'lighter touch' inspection regime for many schools. They revised the inspection framework from September 2003 to focus on generic features of learning and teaching and to highlight the extent to which the curriculum 'provides a broad range of worthwhile curricular opportunities that caters for the interests, aptitudes and particular needs of all pupils' (DfES 2003b: §2.38). Ofsted's aims were spelled out in *Excellence and Enjoyment*:

> … encouraging schools to use their own professional judgements, and make full use of curriculum flexibilities, in order to take ownership of the curriculum. We want to emphasize that Ofsted is actively encouraging a new culture of innovation through this new framework. …We believe that combined with giving ownership of the target-setting process back to schools, and emphasising the value that

schools add to pupil progress, Ofsted's approach will help empower schools to offer children the rich and exciting curriculum they deserve, and through that rich curriculum to continue to drive standards upwards.

(DfES 2003b: §2.38–2.39)

Local authorities, which Ofsted also inspected, would follow suit. The principle of 'intervention in inverse proportion to success' had already been formalized into a 'Code of Practice' for local authorities and the major part of the new primary strategy managers' role was to monitor school performance. Local authorities were expected to challenge all schools to set targets which made a proportionate contribution to the national 85 per cent target. They identified and intervened in the weaker schools, by deploying consultancy and other local support. Over the next two years, these accountability arrangements were streamlined to create a 'New Relationship with Schools' which would:

- set all schools on three-year financial and development cycles
- establish the 'shorter, sharper' and more frequent inspection regime, giving greater weight to school self-evaluation
- improve information systems and provide public school profiles
- provide challenge and support to head teachers through newly accredited *School Improvement Partners*, most of whom were to be experienced head teachers and who would conduct a 'single conversation' with each school on its priorities for improvement, to replace existing multiple accountabilities.

Changing patterns of accountability were reinforced by new professional standards for teachers linked to their career stages as a basis for performance management and pay. Head teachers were required to set annual objectives, agreed with school governors, which included reference to raising standards. Centrally imposed professional standards were politically sensitive in this new regime so tended to be non-specific on matters of competence in literacy and numeracy.

The revised implementation structure was introduced in 2003 with the twin aims of motivating and challenging schools. As, in the first phase of the Strategy, the support was to be universal (something for everyone) and targeted (intervention in inverse proportion to success). For all schools, existing literacy support was maintained and enhanced with more teaching resources and distance training, including a further programme for early phonics and resources to support speaking and listening. A parallel programme was in place for mathematics. The new primary strategy was launched with a package of distance training materials for every school entitled *Learning and Teaching in the Primary Years* (DfES 2004c) addressing the generic characteristics of learning and teaching:

- planning and assessment for learning
- creating a learning culture
- understanding how learning develops

together with a framework for school self-evaluation and guidance on key aspects of learning in every subject.

2004 also saw the launch of a national structure of Primary Strategy Learning Networks with funding to enable schools to form groups to work and learn together, with the twin aims of (a) raising standards in literacy and mathematics, and (b) increasing the capacity of schools to deliver a rich, broad curriculum (DfES 2004d). Two further support initiatives were directed at lower-performing schools. In 2003 a *Primary Leadership Programme* was introduced to strengthen collaborative leadership and data literacy, and to promote improvements in English and mathematics. Selected schools were assigned a 'consultant leader', usually an experienced local head teacher, to work in a part-time mentoring role (DfES 2003, 2004b). The second initiative was a more rigorous intervention strategy for under-performing schools called the *Intensifying Support Programme* (DfES 2003, 2004a). This provided a structured progression of literacy targets based on the NLS Framework objectives, together with a self-evaluation framework, detailed pupil tracking, and specialized consultancy support to assist implementation, lesson planning, assessment for learning, monitoring and improvement planning. These and numerous other initiatives were combined under the single umbrella of the PNS and designed to improve coherence, sharpen differentiation and target support to primary schools more precisely.

It is not surprising, given the rapid and radical changes of the previous four years, that schools tended to view the reforms as a relaxation of the pressure to improve. For the PNS, there was bound to be a degree of trade-off between motivation and challenge; shifting attention to the wider curriculum came at some cost to the focus on literacy and numeracy. The creation of more generic primary roles and responsibilities changed the patterns of expertise and capacity, weakened the specialist focus and made it harder to fight the literacy cause in competition with other priorities. Ofsted's new focus on its 'successful primary schools' paradigm deflected attention from the inspection of literacy and numeracy on to judgements about the broader curriculum. For example, inspectors were no longer required to observe both subjects during an inspection. The breadth of the new primary agenda also created opportunities for some schools to displace attention on to less challenging, more comfortable priorities. Some schools tended to set targets only by extrapolating from past performance and were over-cautious about the Strategy's potential to add value.

The essence of the change process was to pass the initiative to schools. Evidence from international research had, for some years, pointed to the value of self-directed learning for motivating and embedding professional development. The idea of schools as 'learning communities' had been advocated by the Strategy's external evaluation team, who signalled the need for teachers and head teachers to feel a sense of ownership for the strategies, if the changes were to be sustained (Earl *et al.* 2000: 40). They pointed to the value of professional 'learning cultures' at the school level as a means of securing 'deep change'. A similar theme was taken up by the National College for School Leadership (NCSL) who advocated a 'client-centred' ideology for professional development, contrasting sharply with the more directed and pro-active approach of the strategies. The NCSL stressed learning processes such as motivation, collaboration and negotiation. While it was high on motivation,

> ... the kind of sharing that goes on in educational networks often has the effect of dignifying and giving shape to the process and content of educators' experiences, the daily-ness of their work, which is often invisible to outsiders yet binds insiders together ...
>
> (Lieberman 1999: 3)

it gave little emphasis to the content and precision of learning such as subject knowledge or the specifics of pedagogy. NCSL was clear about *how* schools should be learning but vague about *what* they should be learning. The perceived contrast with the more prescriptive stance of the national strategies echoed older ideological debates about the stand-off between discovery learning and instruction in primary education, and resonated strongly with schools. The rapid shift towards school autonomy with its new emphasis on the processes of professional learning also brought increasing reliance from the centre on schools' capacity to identify their own professional learning needs and fend for themselves. Choosing their own agendas inevitably distracted many from the challenges of improving literacy, while the shift of PNS attention to enrichment and the wider curriculum did little to sharpen the focus.

A new focus on self-evaluation, though welcome in many ways, also had consequences. As national, local and school level data systems improved, the use of data as a lever for challenging schools also increased. This was a good thing strategically but the growing dependence on numbers was also leading Ofsted and local authorities to lose sight of the *practical* consequences of average and poor school performance. Pupil performance targets were identified with increasing precision but the correspondingly precise knowledge about what schools should *do* to improve was not developing commensurately. The new regime expected schools to identify their development needs through self-evaluation and then commission support to meet them, e.g. through buying consultancy, using web-based resources or through collaboration and networking with other schools. 'Blended learning' as it has come to be known is certainly more diverse and may be better motivated because schools choose it rather than having it 'delivered', but whose interests are at stake here? Is the aim to create learning communities or to raise standards? The latter does not necessarily flow logically from the former.

To further complicate matters, in 2003, alongside the launch of the PNS, the government published a major Green Paper, *Every Child Matters* (ECM), inspired by a need to respond to fundamental failures of communication and coordination between health, care and education services, putting the wellbeing and, in some cases even the lives, of vulnerable children at risk. The Green Paper published very worrying statistics showing around 11 million children to be in this potentially vulnerable group. The ECM aims were driven by overwhelming concern for children and, as Paul Boeteng, Chief Secretary to the Treasury, observed in the introduction to the Green Paper, 'creating a society where children are safe and have access to opportunities requires radical reform' (HM Treasury 2003: 4).

The moral case, as ever, was impeccable and immediately swept the PNS into the wider reform as one contributor to a much bigger agenda. Pressure for change was exerted not so much on the newly formed PNS, as on the local authorities charged with implementing ECM policy, and the schools, who were expected to be at the hub of the reforms, providing higher standards and an enriched curriculum, while also transforming themselves into sites for the integrated delivery of services across five all-encompassing objectives:

- being healthy
- staying safe
- enjoying and achieving
- making a positive contribution
- economic well-being.

All these objectives were set in the context of a new emphasis on 'personalized learning' in which 'the system fits to the individual rather than the individual to the system' (DfES 2004d: 7), although within this much more adaptive framework, every primary school must 'offer high standards in the basics'. Charles Clarke, Secretary of State for Education at the time, introduced this new five-year strategy, by setting the literacy and numeracy strategies firmly in the past tense:

> We will never apologise for the directive action we took, for example, on literacy and numeracy in 1997 – it put right a national scandal of low aspiration and poor performance, but once the basics are in place and we want to move beyond them towards excellence, we need a new sort of system that is not based on the lowest common denominator.
>
> (DfES 2004d: 7)

A principal aim of ECM was to get better quality all-round support to children in the lowest quartile. This was the moral imperative and the expected means of continuing improvement towards the targets. The practical implications made sense at school level, e.g. through provision of additional support, access to better coordinated multi-disciplinary support, extended days and wrap-around care for vulnerable children. It is a serious, concerted and highly ambitious effort but it is also complex. Two immediate consequences of the ECM reforms for literacy standards are worth noting. First, the process of absorbing the literacy strategy into ever-widening policy frameworks is likely to contribute to a further loss of political focus. With bigger more encompassing objectives, politicians and senior officials have to step back from the detail of the strategies, relying increasingly on the established capacity of schools and PNS to deliver the continuing improvements in standards. Since 2001, successive Secretaries of State have maintained their concern for standards and worried about the challenge of the 85 per cent target, on which they remain exposed. But increasing concern with the structural reforms of organization and provision diminished attention to the detailed business of maintaining and improving standards. The PNS, of course, remains focused on standards; that is their job. But the job is made harder without the persistent level of political authority, leadership and focus with which the Strategy began.

Second, the ECM reforms have generated major structural changes at the local authority level, with the amalgamation, under a new Children's Services Director for each authority, of care and education services. Many of these high level posts have been new appointments and the new directors have been drawn from both disciplines. In addition to education, directors are required to lead the coordination of other children's services including, for example, social services, health and youth justice. Children's Services Directorates have to balance competing priorities and allocate resources across the five ECM outcomes. At local authority level, the focus on primary literacy remains an important, though relatively small, item on a much bigger agenda. We commented in the previous chapter on the Strategy's heavy reliance on local authorities as brokers in the implementation chain because of the large number of relatively small schools in the primary sector. Diversity in the patterns of local provision, combined with the broader and more complex messages of the PNS, make this task of managing implementation coherently very challenging indeed. If there are other more pressing priorities for which a local authority is accountable, average performance in literacy is likely to be good enough.

Given its ambitions, the PNS was bound to be complex and, in terms of the standards agenda, somewhat risky. The flat-lining of standards at 75 per cent from 2000 to 2003 was a serious blow. Looking back, some of this may be explained by the impact of emerging changes and consequent loss of focus. The scale and speed of change was determined more by the political cycle than by strategic considerations of how best to manage literacy improvement, though that is not necessarily a bad thing. The shift of responsibility to schools was both professionally necessary and politically inevitable, and the rapidity of change had the effect of getting everyone involved, breaking through the growing dependence on centralized support, renewing the professional climate and creating a new relationship between the centre and the schools. These are big achievements in themselves. Added to that, overall English standards have risen to within a point of the 2002 80 per cent target, which many had predicted, in 1998, would take a generation of primary children to reach. These improvements are good but not great. Attainment in writing remains a pervasive challenge and, with a government in its third term and increasingly vulnerable to criticism, there will always be a bad press. Some price may have been paid in standards but, equally, standards did begin to move upwards again with the implementation of *Excellence and Enjoyment*. Capacity established in the earlier stages of the NLS appears to have been sustained and consolidated.

The PNS now has an extensive field force (regional advisors, consultants, leading and advanced skills teachers, consultant leaders) but the lion's share of their effort in most local authorities is still expended on preventing weak schools from tipping over the edge into serious weakness or failure, on the principle of intervention in inverse proportion to success. The English education system has become increasingly intolerant of school failure and there is now a record of significant success in dealing with weak schools. Across the system, compared with a decade ago, mechanisms for identifying and remedying weaknesses have improved to the point where, in its last major revision of the school inspection framework, Ofsted raised the threshold for school failure, stiffening its criteria to challenge more schools. Success in turning weak schools round has been due, in very large measure, to the injection of specific support for literacy and numeracy from the strategies. Overall, a general approach has emerged of targeting resources heavily on raising the floor of achievement in the weakest schools, combined with challenging other, average and good schools through a more arm's length use of data and targets, combined with self-evaluation, school-based needs-identification and access to training and other resources, in a variety of distance learning formats, which schools may choose to use.

Most primary schools, according to Ofsted, continue to prioritize literacy and mathematics, and the majority continue to use the daily Literacy Hour and mathematics lessons which they see as 'central to attaining or maintaining high standards in each subject' (Ofsted 2005a: §29). While schools have embraced the wider aims of the PNS, most are a considerable distance from the successful schools paradigm in *Excellence and Enjoyment*. Climbing the next step up the school improvement ladder will almost certainly require the PNS to transform large numbers of these average schools into good schools while continuing to sustain the improvement of weaker schools. It is an aim few would quarrel with. But there is little evidence to date that simply leaving schools with targets, access to resources and the autonomy to help themselves will deliver the necessary improvements. Like weaker schools, average schools are also likely to need more direct and focused support to move on. There are probably enough resources already in place to achieve this and lessons from the recent and successful *Intensifying Support Programme* for weaker schools might be applied more widely to average and even good schools. However, while further intervention may be necessary to get to 85 per cent, it might also be seen to run counter to current political aspirations, and could prove difficult for the PNS to justify and manage amid the unfolding complexities of new priorities, initiatives and structures, and the emphasis on personalized learning, school autonomy and diversity.

Casting back over this story, it is not surprising that literacy improvement has lost impetus. Autonomy may work if it is informed, led and nourished but for thousands of relatively small primary schools in England, it has led to a plateau. Policy makers, taken up with wider issues, have lost the focus. While data literacy has improved, a new emphasis on measuring school performance against value added criteria has tended to obscure targets and the need to raise standards and, as we shall discuss in Chapter 10, since 2005, there has been a further retreat into redesigning the Strategy, diminishing its credibility and putting everything on virtual hold, instead of getting on with the practical business of implementation.

Overall, as the discussion about impact in the next chapter will show, the NLS has achieved significant gains for thousands of children. It has developed system-wide capacity which is likely to be sustained and can be improved. So there is much good news. However, despite a huge emphasis in recent years on developing leadership at the school level, the loss of focus at the centre has been critical. Failure of leadership at the top goes down the line. Not only has it been evident at the centre, it has been transmitted to local authorities who now manage enormous complexity and have to respect the autonomy of schools, which is commonly taken to mean non-intervention. This, combined with the new emphasis on data as the principle source of information about quality, encourages local authorities to over-emphasize monitoring and pressurizing schools at the expense of systematically supporting them. Reflecting on the question raised by Fullan at the end of the previous chapter:

> how do you move … from prescription to autonomy? We might be able to portray what informed professional judgement might look like but the pathways for getting there will be enormously complex and different depending on the starting point.
>
> (Fullan 2003: 5)

we give the Strategy a mixed report. The autonomy principle is clearly important but it is also seductive, especially to policy makers. It can rationalize political inertia and may leave schools more unaided, frustrated and pressurized than the relatively benign practices of 'informed prescription' with which the NLS set out. The strategic challenge here (as with the debates around the 'reading wars') is not to polarize. School autonomy and informed prescription do not need to compete. There is no either/or choice. It should be obvious, most of all to educators, that autonomy is best fostered where it is managed or 'earned'. Autonomy grows with knowledge and is relatively worthless without it. Fullan argues that sustainability requires 'deep change' through schools as 'learning communities'. The essence of the theory, he says, is that you won't get deep change unless:

- People are interacting
- New knowledge is being produced in the heads of people
- New solutions are being discovered
- People own these solutions in the sense that they are passionately committed and energetic about pursuing them
- There are questioning and critical people so as to avoid locking into weak solutions and to continually seek potentially better ideas.

(Fullan 2003: 47)

This, as we observed at the start of the chapter, is asking a lot. Evidence from inspection and other research shows that the ideal of the 'learning community' applies to a relatively small number of schools like those in the Ofsted paradigm above. For others, especially given the considerable number and variety in England, autonomy may grow and it may recede. Maintaining and developing autonomy requires committed leadership, intellectual competence and stability, none of which can be taken for granted across the system. Autonomy may grow on sustained foundations of effective practice; it is unlikely to be achieved through leaving schools alone or besieging them with the rhetoric of principles and values so characteristic of many publications about leadership. For most schools it is likely to require support, close mentoring, and a good deal of practical information and continuing 'informed prescription' to be maintained and fostered. We shall return to this point at the end of Chapter 10.

Chapter 9

Impact and evaluation

A strategy for evaluation

The expectations and content of the NLS were largely determined by three factors: (a) the values, ambitions and specific policies set by government, (b) evidence of successful practice i.e. what worked and (c) evidence about which practices were most likely to scale up and transfer across a large and diverse number of schools. The regular flow of formative evidence from evaluation was the main driver for decision-making at every stage. Previous chapters describe how the NLS, which began in 1998 as the main focus of attention, had to take its place in the broadening education agenda, alongside the numeracy strategy in 1999, then post-2002 in the wider Primary National Strategy, the developing secondary school strategy, and now in the even broader context of *Every Child Matters* (HM Treasury 2003), which embeds education in a wider framework of objectives related to the care and wellbeing of children. This chapter provides a more systematic overview of the evaluation findings with some concluding commentary on the broader strategic implications.

The importance of evaluation was recognized from the outset and an approach was formed during 1997–8 which would generate a systematic flow of qualitative and quantitative information at a variety of levels including:

- *Test data*: regular and timely information from the Qualifications and Curriculum Authority (QCA) on outcomes from the national assessments at ages 7 and 11. Data was to be analysed in increasingly fine-grained ways to compare local authority, school and pupil level achievement. Each year, QCA also make detailed qualitative analyses of sample papers in English, mathematics and science to provide information to schools about children's learning needs and the implications for learning and teaching. With growing emphasis on school self-evaluation and autonomy, the improving detail and quality of both these analyses have increased their importance and value at every level.
- *Inspection evidence*: Ofsted set up a longitudinal inspection survey of a representative sample of primary schools across the country to evaluate the implementation of the Strategy, paying particular attention to the quality of teaching and school leadership. As the statutory body for quality assurance, Ofsted inspectors had right of access to schools and, as a matter of course, observed teaching and learning in lessons, so were the proper body to take

this responsibility on. Also, Ofsted regularly inspected all schools and a new four-year cycle of school inspections coincided with the implementation of the Strategy. It was agreed that data from these inspections should also feed into the evaluation.

- *External evaluation*: External research teams with experience of large-scale system reform were invited to bid for a four-year contract to evaluate the Strategy with special attention to its structure and effectiveness at policy and strategic levels. In particular, they were asked to provide formative commentary which would help us to shape and steer the Strategy. A team led by Professor Michael Fullan from the University of Toronto was commissioned. They worked closely with the national teams in the first year and then tracked implementation through the system in subsequent years up to the end of 2002.

- *Direct evaluation by the NLS team*: The team of national directors, in collaboration with literacy (later primary) strategy managers in each local authority evaluated and regularly reported on the performance of each local authority, with reference to local implementation strategies. This enabled the national directorate to monitor performance and direct pressure and support where it was most needed. Additionally a number of telephone surveys were commissioned to provide rapid feedback directly from teachers and head teachers on the impact and usefulness of specific aspects of the literacy and numeracy strategies (e.g. CfBT 2000).

- *Anecdotal evidence*: A wealth of anecdotal evidence was also collected from schools and other groups representing a range of interests including authors, publishers, booksellers, library associations, parents, volunteer reading groups, school governors, lobby groups, and various literacy associations and groups supporting particular needs or interests e.g. dyslexia, left-handedness, disabled and handicapped children. There was no shortage of feedback, which was encouraged and used.

There was also a growing body of independent research evidence on the Strategy and its implementation, e.g. through research grants to academics, and professional associations' surveys of members. From 2002, the focused evaluations of the literacy strategy by Ofsted and the external evaluators were discontinued. Since 2003 there have been two evaluations by Ofsted of the Primary National Strategy, broader in scope, encompassing literacy, mathematics and the quality of the wider curriculum, in line with the new agenda set out in *Excellence and Enjoyment*. The latest of these was in February 2005. Additionally, there has been an enquiry into the teaching of reading by a House of Commons Select Committee and a subsequent government-commissioned enquiry into the teaching of early reading – the *Rose Report* – which we discuss in more detail in Chapter 10. The new broader primary agenda encompassing *Every Child Matters* combined with growing devolution of responsibility to schools, has left evaluation of standards increasingly reliant on data, mostly in the form of national test outcomes, but with a diminishing input of specific formative evaluation of the kind used to guide the strategies in the early stages.

Impact on standards

Expectations

The NLS target was clear: by 2002, 80 per cent of 11-year-olds nationally should achieve level 4 in English (reading and writing). Just before the target date in 2002 the projection was increased to 85 per cent for 2006 with an expectation that it would be sustained to 2008. Also in 2003 a further target, that 35 per cent of children should achieve level 5, was introduced. In addition, a floor target of 78 per cent was set for local authorities with the expectation that no authority, however disadvantaged, would fall below this. Since the beginning, level 4 was the established benchmark. The significance of achieving level 4 was set out in 1997 (DfEE 1997b: §19–24) and reiterated in 2003:

> Achieving Level 4 at the end of primary school improves a child's prospects at secondary school and their future life chances. 70 per cent of pupils who achieve Level 4 at Key Stage 2 go on to get five or more GCSEs at grades A*–C. Of those children who did not achieve Level 4 in 1997, just 12 per cent achieved five GCSEs at grades A*–C last summer … Level 4 really is the door to success in secondary school and beyond. A child who is at Level 3 can read a range of texts, but a child who is at Level 4 can read between the lines, use inference and take an overview of the whole story. That is why we have set a nationwide target for 85 per cent of pupils to reach Level 4 at Key Stage 2.
>
> (DfES 2003d: §2.13–2.14)

The 80 per cent target was an intelligent and evidence-based expectation which challenged and supported schools to arrive at a sustainable level of improvement, while providing additional differentiated 'wave 2' support of the kind we described in Chapter 5 to support lower achieving children. At the time, many thought it would take a generation of children moving through their primary school years to achieve a sustainable 80 per cent, which is more or less what has happened. The increase to 85 per cent was extremely challenging. From a moral standpoint, the new target was justified, and it was politically difficult to respond to the criticism that 20 per cent or even 15 per cent of children may not be expected to reach the standard. But the increased target diminished its credibility among the profession and was widely regarded as unrealistic by schools and local authorities.

Children are also assessed at age 7, when they reach the end of Key Stage 1. Although there was no national target for achievement at this stage, it was always reported as a step towards the target. Level 2 is divided into sub-levels a, b and c for measurement and reporting purposes, giving a finer grain to the assessments and helping teachers with feedback on typical needs at each sub-stage. Level 2B+ is a reliable predictor of a level 4 at age 11 and generally regarded as the benchmark for attainment at age 7. As data literacy, collection and analysis has improved, the focus of target setting has shifted from a single national target to more sensitive value-added measures using Key Stage 1 to Key Stage 2 trajectories. In time, as pupil level data continues to improve, trajectories may include baseline data from assessments at the start of children's schooling. These value-added measures provide fairer judgments of school improvement and are sensitive to the needs and capacities of each school. They also create conditions for better focused challenge, intervention and support.

The NLS had two connected aims to raise the bar and close the gap. While literacy standards needed to rise for all children, the standards of the lowest achievers were expected to rise faster. These two aims pervaded everything from the implementation of the Literacy Hour with its aims of 'levelling children up' (Chapter 4), the differentiated 'wave 2' support (Chapter 5), to the focusing of intervention and resources at school and local authority levels.

Raising the bar

Figures 9.1 and 9.2 show the proportions of pupils achieving level 4+ in English. English results are the combined scores of two separate tests for reading and writing. Since the introduction of the NLS in 1998, the proportion of pupils attaining level 4+ in English has improved by 14 points. In common with other international data, boys' attainment is lower than girls'. Despite fluctuations in this difference over the years, it was the same (11 points) in 2006[1] as in 1998. At the same time, there has been a significant improvement of 15 per cent in the proportion of 11-year-olds achieving level 5 in reading and writing, almost doubling from 17 to 32 per cent, i.e. three points short of the government's 35 per cent target.

Taking reading and writing separately, attainment in reading shows significantly higher proportions of pupils at level 4+ than writing (Figures 9.3 and 9.4). While overall English results were 79 per cent in 2006, reading attainment was 83 per cent, two points below the revised government target of 85 per cent for 2006–8 (Figure 9.3). Since 1998, level 4 reading standards have risen by 12 points and the gap between boys and girls reduced by 7 points from 15 per cent in 1998 to 8 per cent in 2006. By 2006, although schools were still three points short of the overall 35 per cent target for level 5 English, they were 12 points ahead of this for reading with 47 per cent of pupils achieving this level.[2]

As we noted in previous chapters, public discussion about literacy tends to focus on reading. Although there is no shortage of awareness about the challenge of teaching writing, the combined reporting of reading and writing scores diminishes the aggregated score. This fosters a widespread public perception that reading standards in England are poor, which is demonstrably not the case. It is of particular significance in the context of international comparisons, where reading attainment tends to be the common comparator. Writing is a different story. Although over the same period the proportion of pupils attaining level 4 in writing rose slightly faster than for reading – by 14 per cent from 53 to 67 per cent – it started from a much

1   All 2006 data in this chapter are based on DfES figures published in August 2006. They are listed as unverified and may be subject to minor final adjustments.
2   In 2006, 53 per cent of girls and 41 per cent of boys achieved level 5 reading at 11 years old.

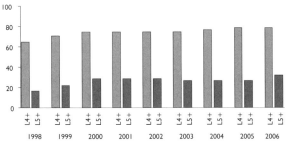

Figure 9.1 Key Stage 2 level 4+ English results, national assessment of 11-year-olds

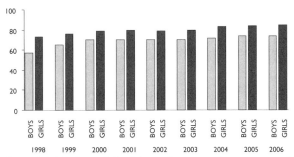

Figure 9.2 Key Stage 2 English results, national assessment of 11-year-olds

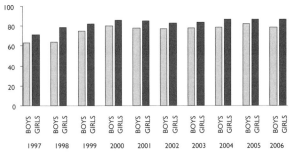

Figure 9.3 Key Stage 2 level 4+ reading results, national assessment of 11-year-olds

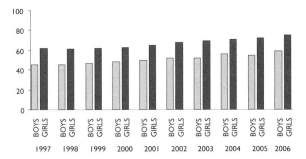

Figure 9.4 Key Stage 2 level 4+ writing results, national assessment of 11-year-olds

lower baseline. Boys' and girls' writing improved over the period but the gap between them has not closed.

Overall, these data are part of an even broader picture of rising standards from the autumn term of 1996 when the National Literacy Project was introduced to the present, where primary schools are working in the context of a wider Primary National Strategy alongside the even greater complexity of the broader standards set out in *Every Child Matters*. Although the NLP affected only about 250 schools at the outset, its impact was much wider. By 1997, positive evaluations of test results and the declared intention of the incoming Labour Government to implement it, in a revised form nationally, had begun a movement in schools towards adopting the NLP's general approach. This helped to create the climate of challenge and higher expectations in which the NLS was launched. The period from 1998 to 2000 saw a steady increase in improvement which was a great confidence builder. By 2000, following a ten point increase to 75 per cent, Ofsted were saying that the Strategy had,

> … helped schools to get within striking distance of the Government's targets for 2002 [and that] it had brought about a transformation in the teaching of reading but had much less impact on writing.
>
> (Ofsted press release, 28 November 2000)

But from 2000 to 2003 there were four years with no increase. We commented on this '75 per cent plateau' in the previous chapter. 2001 was a complex moment for the Strategy. It had built substantial but still quite fragile capacity in the teaching of reading. The tougher challenge of improving writing was at a formative stage; everyone was learning and the new professional demands on teachers in terms of subject knowledge and methodology were much greater. Capacity for improving writing was not secure although the build-up to broadening the Strategy was already under way. Inevitably, there was some loss of focus as new expectations and structures evolved. As the Primary National Strategy settled down, there were the beginnings of further improvements. Reading scores now moved up but appear to be settling at around 83–84 per cent, i.e. comfortably above the target ambition with which the NLS began, and there is a steady but significant improvement in writing with a welcome four point rise between 2005 and 2006.

By comparison, proportions of 7-year-olds attaining level 2+ have fluctuated and not shown a similar improving trend (Figure 9.5). Reading and writing attainment are similar, and in some years, more children achieved the level in writing than in reading. Reading, which has been the focus of recent attention through the Select Committee enquiry and the recent Rose Review (see Chapter 10), has improved by only four points over the period and critics have latched onto this figure in support of their arguments for changing the NLS's approach. However, at the same time, the proportions of children achieving the benchmark level 2B+ have risen by nine points for reading and 12 points for writing since 1998 (Figure 9.6).

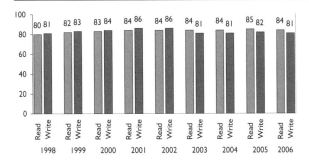

Figure 9.5 Key Stage I level 2+ reading and writing results, national assessment of 7-year-olds

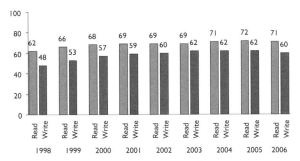

Figure 9.6 Key Stage I level 2B+ reading and writing results, national assessment of 7-year-olds

No one knows what factors are at play here and it is doubtful, despite the research recommendations of the Select Committee, that large-scale further research could determine this conclusively. There are obviously issues of teaching on which the government has taken a particular stand. They are convinced that improving early phonics teaching will bring significant improvements. In a recent response to the one point dip in Key Stage 1 reading in 2006, the Secretary of State said, 'plans to return to a back-to-basics method of teaching reading … would improve results in the future' (*Times Educational Supplement*, August 2006). But, aside from the evident value of phonics, there are other variables impacting on the education and development of young children which may prove more recalcitrant. Not least among these is the growing socio-cultural complexity of modern-day Britain which, over the lifetime of the Strategy, has seen significant increases in the proportions of children from other cultures and language backgrounds with very differing experiences of family, community and schooling.

In 2001, England participated in PIRLS, an international study of reading progress to measure and compare the reading achievement of 10-year-olds across 35 countries (Twist *et al.* 2001). In 1996, reading achievement in England was estimated to be in the middle range by international comparisons and characterized by a 'long tail' of under-achievement. By 2001, Twist and colleagues at NFER reported that:

- Children in England are among the most able readers in the world at about the age of 10. England was ranked third in terms of reading achievement of those countries involved, with only Sweden and the Netherlands higher.
- Pupils in England scored more highly than those in the major European countries of France, Germany and Italy. They also scored significantly more highly than other English-speaking countries in the survey: the United States, New Zealand and Scotland.
- England is one of the countries with the widest span of attainment. Its most able pupils are the highest scoring in the survey but its low achieving students are ranked much lower. This pattern is a consistent one in English-speaking countries but continental European countries are more likely to have a similar standing for their high and low achieving children, leading to a narrower range of attainment.
- Students in England also achieved a high standing in the PISA study of reading for 15-year-olds undertaken in 2000. However there is little correlation between the performance in the two surveys of the countries which took part in both, perhaps illustrating the volatility of educational systems in an age of reform.
- These international comparisons gave good grounds for optimism about the Strategy's capacity to raise standards but also justify the continuing importance attached to the second aim of closing the gap.

Closing the gap

The Strategy has also been closing the achievement gap by raising literacy standards of lower achieving children and lower performing schools. Evidence from the outcomes of the National Literacy Project set the expectations and it was clear that there was big potential for under-performing schools and local authorities to improve. While closing the gap contributes to the national target it is also manifested in other ways. One indicator is the proportion of 7-year-olds achieving the level 2B benchmark (see Figure 9.6). The differentiated *wave 2* programmes, ALS and ELS, designed to support lower achievers (Chapter 5) were not systematically evaluated but Ofsted did monitor the pilot for the *Early Literacy Support* (ELS) programme in 2001. They found that the quality of teaching was good in the vast majority of schools and that pupils' responses were 'overwhelmingly positive' with 'marked gains in their confidence and willingness to contribute to the Literacy Hour' (Ofsted 2001: §150–1). A year later they reported that provision for pupils with special educational needs (SEN) had improved and that intervention programmes such as ELS and ALS had started,

> ... a trend towards greater discernment in the teaching of pupils with SEN, particularly in terms of identifying the pupils for whom short-term intensive intervention might be the most effective approach ... A small number of schools have already found that both ELS and ALS have reduced the number of pupils with SEN related to literacy.

(Ofsted 2002a: §107)

The Further Literacy Support programme (FLS) came on stream after the international evaluation had been completed so the Strategy commissioned an independent evaluation (Beard *et al.* 2004). This found the programme to have been successful in raising standards and improving the attitude of 9- and 10-year-olds to literacy and learning, in general.

> Control group comparisons indicate that FLS children reduced the gap between their average performance and the average performance of non-FLS children in their class.
>
> (Beard *et al.* 2004: 72)

The two more recent school level initiatives, mentioned in Chapter 8, the *Intensifying Support Programme* and the *Primary Leadership Programme*, designed to support lower performing schools, also showed demonstrable effects (Figures 9.7 and 9.8).

Between 1998 and 2002, the proportions of schools achieving at least 80 per cent level 4s doubled, while the proportion achieving below 65 per cent more than halved (Figure 9.7). Although standards had flat-lined at 75 per cent for four years, there had been a significant catching up by lower performing LEAs to reach that point. In 1998, at the start of the National Literacy Strategy, there were only four out of 150 local authorities where 75 per cent of pupils achieved the expected level in English by

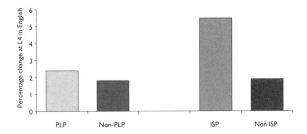

Figure 9.7 Impact of Primary Leadership Programme (PLP) and Intensifying Support Programme (ISP)

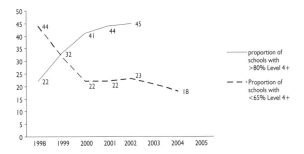

Figure 9.8 Key Stage English results: closing the gap

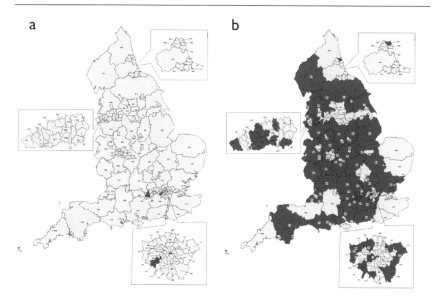

Figure 9.9 a) LEAS achieving 75%+ Level 4 English, 1998; b) LEAS achieving 75%+ Level 4 English, 2002

age 11. By 2004, more than two-thirds of local authorities were in this position. These improvements were graphically illustrated using the map of England (Figure 9.9).

A further indicator of this improvement is the raising of the NLS floor target. At the start of the NLS in 1998 it was set at 70 per cent, but by 2003 it had been raised to 78 per cent.

When the Strategy began, it was made clear to local authorities and schools that the 80 per cent target meant that all of their 7-year-olds who achieved level 2B should progress to level 4 by age 11, and that most schools would also need to 'convert' a significant proportion of lower achieving children as well. Pupil level data was not available at the time, so progress could not be tracked with the sophistication now possible, but it was evident in 1998 that with 62 per cent of 7-year-olds at level 2B and only 65 per cent of 11-year-olds at level 4, the conversion rate was too low. In 2005, Ofsted published conversion rates based on national data (Ofsted 2005b) – see Table 9.1.

These data also give grounds for optimism about the capacity of schools to raise standards for lower achievers – almost 50 per cent of children below the benchmark level 2B are now achieving level 4 by age 11 but, with almost 30 per cent of level 2Bs not reaching level 4, there must also be scope for significant improvement. A further quite telling comparison is between children who achieve level 4 in each of reading, writing and mathematics, which had risen from 43 per cent in 1997 to 60 per cent by 2006. The increase is encouraging but again is dragged down by the relatively lower proportions achieving level 4 in writing. When the English score is

Table 9.1 National conversion rates: Key Stage 1 to Key Stage 2

Key Stage 1	Key Stage 2
English levels achieved by 7-year-olds	% 11-year-olds achieving Level 4
1	11
2c	37
2b	73
2a	94
3+	99

taken (aggregating the combined reading and writing), the proportion of children achieving level 4 is ten points higher, at 70 per cent.

Reading and writing

We commented on the relationship between reading and writing in earlier chapters. Reading remains a challenge but has proved easier to improve than writing. The national assessment of reading in 2006 identified 16 per cent of children who did not achieve level 4 or above. Of these, 9 per cent achieved level 3 and can

> ... read a range of texts fluently and accurately ... read independently, using strategies appropriately to establish meaning. In responding to fiction and non-fiction [they] show understanding of the main points and express preferences. ... [They] use their knowledge of the alphabet to locate books and find information.
>
> (DfEE/QCA 1999: 57)

Of the remaining 8 per cent, 1 per cent were absent, 3 per cent failed to register a level and 4 per cent had teacher's asssessment but had not taken the test. There is certainly scope for improving the reading performance of level 3 children and those below level 3 but, in relation to the national target, further improvements in reading may prove to be marginal.

It is clear from the data over time that, in order to get close to the 85 per cent target for level 4 in English, there have to be big improvements in writing. Writing is a more complex and less researched area of learning than reading. Success in writing draws heavily upon the transfer of knowledge from reading but is equally and, probably more importantly, continuous with speaking. *Excellence and Enjoyment* underlined the importance of speaking which was widely believed to be under-emphasized in the curriculum. Ofsted also drew attention to this in 2003:

> In too many lessons, teachers' talk dominates and there are too few opportunities for pupils to talk and collaborate and enhance their learning. This is a key feature

of the lessons that are satisfactory rather than good and an impediment to raising standards further.

(Ofsted 2003b: §2)

Speaking and writing are language production skills and, in the more mundane sense of the term, both are creative. Under pressure to advance the teaching of writing, the Strategy generated detailed support focused on sentence and text level principles for text composition (see Chapter 4). Since then there has been further development of guidance and resources for teachers, combining creative ideas to motivate children (particularly boys) with the teaching of explicit text knowledge. While schools are evidently improving children's comprehension abilities, there are clear messages here about the fundamental importance of language production and how we promote this effectively in classrooms, especially the more articulated and formal styles associated with context-free communication, including writing. These messages are also important for mathematics where parallel evidence exists about weaknesses in children's abilities to reflect on, explain and justify ideas. We return to this point in Chapter 10.

Longer term effects

Since the introduction of the National Literacy Project almost a decade ago there has been some evidence of longer term effects. The expectations in the NLS framework and the achievement of children at the end of primary school pushed secondary teachers' expectations up. When the Key Stage 3 strategy for 11–14-year-olds was piloted in September 2000, it was modelled on the NLS with a Framework of teaching objectives, a recommended lesson structure, a further suite of catch-up provision, and a parallel infrastructure for support and training. Secondary teachers were encouraged to visit primary classrooms to see what had been achieved. Many observed that 11-year-olds in primary schools were successfully tackling work which, traditionally, they would have covered in the first year or two of the secondary curriculum.

Level 5 is the benchmark at age 14, for which there is a national target of 85 per cent by 2007. The 11-year-old cohort who transferred to secondary schools in 2002 sat the national tests for 14-year-olds in 2005. Figures 9.10 and 9.11 show the overall progress of this cohort.

Precise implications cannot be drawn but these data suggest some hypotheses. By age 14, while overall English scores remain almost the same, the proportions of pupils achieving level 5 for reading and writing are almost reversed. It appears that quite a high proportion of children achieved two levels in writing during the first three years of secondary school and this must have included a significant proportion of boys. Reading appears to have dropped back with an increasing gap between boys and girls, but progress in writing shows a more consistent progression across the years with boys catching up to girls. Some of this variation may reflect differences in the tests and the demands of the Key Stage 3 curriculum but level criteria are supposed to be aligned across the tests at different stages, so comparisons should be valid.

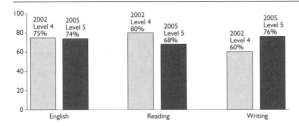

Figure 9.10 2002 Key Stage 2 to 2005 Key Stage 3: outcomes for one cohort by subject

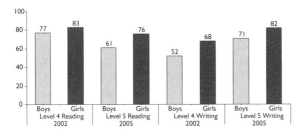

Figure 9.11 2002 Key Stage 2 to 2005 Key Stage 3: outcomes for one cohort by gender

Maintaining and improving standards of reading is clearly a challenge at secondary level, where the demands at levels 5 and 6 for critical and evaluative responses to more complex texts are a major focus. But for writing, it is possible that the reading achievements from Key Stage 2 may be paying later dividends and that for some children, especially boys, it just takes more time to gain confidence and fluency. It is also important not to under-estimate what children have achieved at level 3. In 2002, 43 per cent of 11-year-olds were below level 4. Of these, 31 per cent achieved level 3 (37 per cent boys; 26 per cent girls) in writing. Altogether, in 2002, 94 per cent of children achieved level 3 or better in writing (63 per cent level 4+ and 31 per cent level 3). Although level 3 is below the benchmarked expectation, it still provides a solid foundation for later development. Level 3 writing is

> … often organized, imaginative and clear. The main features of different forms of writing are used appropriately, beginning to be adapted to different readers. Sequences of sentences extend ideas logically and words are chosen for variety and interest. The basic grammatical structure of sentences is usually correct. Spelling is usually accurate, including that of common, polysyllabic words. Punctuation to mark sentences full stops, capital letters and question marks is used accurately. Handwriting is joined and legible.
>
> (DfEE/QCA 1999: 59)

For primary schools, the level 4 target should remain a priority and there is certainly evidence that the gap between boys and girls can be narrowed by better teaching (Ofsted 2003a). Some of this difference is motivational but much of it is down to children's ability to manipulate text and sentence level features of the kind identified in *Grammar for Writing* i.e. language choice for effect, the use of complex sentences and a range of appropriate connecting words and phrases for text cohesion (see Chapter 3). Writing is harder to learn than reading and is likely to take longer for some children. This may also run counter to the broader implication quoted above from *Excellence and Enjoyment* that, without level 4, children's chances of success are seriously diminished. Because of the overriding importance attached to the national target, it is tempting to portray level 3 as a failure. Contrary to intentions, this depresses expectations and fails to do justice to significant levels of competence achieved by the great majority of children.

Two further studies point to possible longer term effects of the Strategy. The first, 'Variation in Aspects of Writing in 16+ Examinations between 1980 and 2004', shows that standards of written English have improved since the same team published a similar study in 1996 (Massey *et al.* 2005). In 1996, samples of 1994 GCSE examinations were considered and found to be of lower quality than equivalent selections of the 1980 English Language O-level examination. The authors, rightly, are extremely cautious about suggesting any causal connections between the national strategies in primary and secondary schools but note that the papers showing these improvements were written by 11-year-olds who were involved in the National Literacy Strategy in 1999, when there had been an eight point increase in English results over the previous two years in primary schools. They found improvements in vocabulary choice, spelling, punctuation and sentence construction. The researchers said 'the positive findings this year reflect initiatives like the National Literacy Strategy and a change of values in society' (BBC 2005).

A second study, by researchers from the London School of Economics, considered the value of the Literacy Hour in relation to the economic value of the policy as a value-for-money investment. Machin and McNally (2004: 27) retrospectively evaluated the Literacy Hour for schools involved in the National Literacy Project (NLP) in the school years 1996–7 and 1997–8. They compared the reading and overall English attainment of children in NLP schools with a set of control schools at the end of primary school education (age 11) and found 'a large increase in attainment in reading and English for pupils in NLP schools as compared to pupils not exposed to the Literacy Hour over this time period'. They comment:

> We find that reading and English Key Stage 2 levels rose by more in NLP schools between 1996 and 1998. Having subjected our identification strategy to a number of robustness checks, we are confident that this constitutes an NLP effect.
>
> These findings are of considerable significance when placed into the wider education debate about what works best in schools for improving pupil performance. They are also of considerable significance for education policies in countries which have problems with their levels of literacy skills … Indeed, as the effects we identify come from a government policy aimed at improving literacy, the evidence we report suggests that public policy aimed at changing

literary instruction can significantly raise pupil achievement and can do so in a highly cost-effective manner.

Impact on the quality of teaching

When the Literacy Hour was launched, most schools gave priority to reading. They needed to tackle the NLS recommendations in sequence, and priority for reading was underlined in the structure of the introductory training sent to schools. What no one fully realized at the time was the extent of the challenge that writing would present. Despite the evident priority schools gave to writing, there was a widespread assumption that, given stimulus and opportunity to write, well-developed reading competence would pull writing along in its wake. We now know that, while reading competence is necessary for effective writing, it is far from sufficient. Writing needs to be taught in quite systematic ways from the earliest stages (Chapters 3 and 4). Also, many schools believed reading was harder to teach than writing. But this was due more to the relative difficulties of *managing* reading and writing lessons than challenges inherent in the subject matter and teaching methodologies. Because reading teaching tended to be highly individualized and time-consuming it was harder to organize, monitor and tutor than the established writing lesson where, typically, class discussion of a topic was followed by supervised individual work to be marked and returned later.

Despite the importance of rapidly establishing word level work, especially the teaching of phonics, probably the most influential early change was the adoption of shared reading across the whole primary age range. At the time, a large proportion of children were attaining level 3 towards the end of their primary careers. Many had reasonably fluent reading but relatively poor comprehension. They knew too little about texts and could not 'read between the lines'. This under-achievement was reflected in the prevailing teaching methods prior to the Strategy which often focused more on book choice and monitoring than on teaching. Shared reading was new to a lot of older classes and immediately challenged teachers to engage children with texts and teach to specific comprehension objectives from the Framework. For many children this was enough to open the door to more reflective and critical reading. In turn, good responses from children led to better teaching and so generated something of a 'Matthew effect' with success engendering success. By the end of the second year, Ofsted observed that 'pupils' response to the Literacy Hour was satisfactory or better in nine in ten lessons, and that

> ... the NLS continues to have a major impact on the teaching of English in primary schools. The teaching of reading ... has undergone a transformation, particularly in the amount of effective whole-class work at both Key Stages. This has had a very positive effect on standards of pupils' reading, both of boys and girls. By contrast, the teaching of writing remains much more limited.
>
> (Ofsted 2000b: §5, 13)

Issues about management of Literacy Hour time emerged in the first year and many schools adopted a practice of suspending one Literacy Hour per week to make time for teaching creative and extended writing – christened by some as 'the Friday armistice'. Writing was better assimilated in the second year of implementation when shared writing was more clearly seen as a counterpart to shared reading. Though shared writing was a lot more challenging, it resulted in a better balance of time for reading and writing over the teaching week and began to forge the important link between the teaching of reading and writing.

A further important and related change, discussed in Chapter 4, reversed the shared reading and word work elements in the first half of the Literacy Hour. This sequence was more coherent because (a) it underlined the value of teaching phonics and spelling systematically and separately and (b) it improved continuity between shared text work, and the group or individual work that followed. Many schools saw the logic of this and adopted the change. It also fitted in well with the recommended structure of the new daily mathematics lesson introduced in 1999, where on each day teaching began with a brief, fast-paced episode of mental mathematics. This changed pattern rapidly became the accepted form for the Literacy Hour. It was reinforced by Ofsted and through subsequent training and guidance from the NLS. Today it is common to find word level work taught separately from the Literacy Hour as well as within it.

The teaching of guided reading in the Literacy Hour has improved progressively. Inspectors judged the teaching as good in 60 per cent of lessons and satisfactory in a further 30 per cent (Ofsted 2002a). But guided reading still presents a big challenge. It requires careful classroom management, as well as close monitoring of, and interaction with, children as they read. This in turn requires a good understanding of how the NLS 'searchlights' should be used and applied (see Chapter 4 for more detailed discussion).

Plenary sessions, somewhat to everyone's surprise, also presented problems. At the end of the first year Ofsted judged these to be the weakest part of the lessons inspected (Ofsted 1999). This short session at the end of each Literacy Hour was designed as the fore-runner to the later, more articulated, practices of assessment for learning, now integrated into the Primary National Strategy (Black and Wiliam 1998). Teachers were expected to use this ten-minute session for discussion and reflection to 'provide opportunities for teachers to monitor and assess the work of some of the pupils [and] … develop an atmosphere of constructive criticism and provide feedback and encouragement to children' (DfEE 1998b). Problems of time management robbed some Literacy Hours of this important element but the bigger challenge to teachers lay in the dialogue itself. Often, these sessions would become ritual 'show-and-tell' events with little discussion of what had been learned and too few opportunities for children to engage in dialogue with each other or the teacher. It was, of course, one tip of the speaking and listening iceberg, and signalled a need to improve the quality of classroom interaction, touching on what Alexander (2004) more recently referred to as 'dialogic teaching'. Also, it pinpointed the need for teachers to be clear about their objectives, share them with children and use them for continuous and reflective assessment. Thus, plenaries set teachers a considerable challenge. According to Ofsted, the quality of teaching in plenaries improved significantly over the first four years of the Strategy, but remained one of the weakest elements (Ofsted 2002a). Subsequent emphasis on Assessment for Learning has led to further improvement but it remains the 'least successful element of teaching' (Ofsted 2005a: 23).

The teaching of phonics

When the NLS was launched in Autumn 1998, Ofsted reported that phonics was taught well in only 25 per cent of lessons and not taught at all in a third of the lessons inspected. Two terms later, inspectors judged the teaching of phonics to be satisfactory or better in 80 per cent of lessons with the proportion of good teaching doubling to 50 per cent, although the scale of this improvement was obscured by the somewhat negative tone in which it was reported:

> Although this aspect of the work has improved throughout the year, the teaching of word level work remains one of the weakest elements of the Strategy; good teaching of word level work took place in only about half of the lessons and was poor in one in five.
>
> (Ofsted 1999: §55)

By the end of 2002, the teaching of phonics was included in virtually all lessons for 5–7-year-olds where the quality of teaching was good in two-thirds of lessons, reflecting the 'significant shift which has taken place ... since the report in 1998' (Ofsted 2002a: §48–54). Ofsted reported a measurable impact of phonics on children's spelling at age 7 but registered concern about the quality of phonics teaching to older children aged 7–9 years. Notwithstanding substantial improvements in the teaching of phonics and a persistent emphasis on this over the previous four years by the NLS, Ofsted continued to worry about it. In their final report on the NLS, despite much good news about the teaching of phonics, they criticized the 'searchlights' metaphor as

> ... not effective enough in terms of illustrating where the intensity of the 'searchlights' should fall at different stages of learning to read. While the full range of strategies is used by fluent readers, beginning readers need to learn how to decode effortlessly, using their knowledge of letter–sound correspondences and the skills of blending sounds together. The importance of these crucial skills has not been communicated clearly enough to teachers. The result has been an approach which diffuses teaching at the earliest stages rather than concentrating it on phonics.
>
> (Ofsted 2002a: §58)

In a report that was positive and uncritical of the teaching of phonics in the 'earliest stages', this criticism appears unwarranted. The implication that teaching which does not 'concentrate on phonics in the earliest stages' is 'diffused' also carries the dangerous implication that teaching which concentrates *only* on phonics may be preferable. Predictably this observation combined with pressure from others of a phonics-first persuasion, helped to re-ignite the rumbling literacy debate. This in turn sparked the Parliamentary Select Committee enquiry in 2005, an ensuing government enquiry and the abandonment of the 'searchlights' in favour of a new 'simple model' of reading promoting the 'phonics fast and first' ideology (see the discussion in Chapter 10). During the same period, however, Ofsted published a further reading report based on survey evidence of successful practice, endorsing the 'searchlights' principles and reflecting the long-standing advice of the NLS:

> The teaching of phonics was good in schools with high standards. Rapid, early coverage of phonic knowledge and skills ensured that pupils had a strong foundation for decoding … the schools which were successful in raising reading standards and tackling underachievement taught a broad range of strategies early on, including the use of words recognized on sight, context and grammar.
>
> Head teachers in the most effective schools recognized the importance of introducing pupils to a broader range of reading strategies alongside phonics. Many saw the early introduction of the NLS's reading 'searchlights' model as a way of broadening pupils' strategies which enabled them to read not only accurately but also with understanding and enjoyment. One head teacher said: 'We try to teach all the reading skills from the word go – then you are building upon existing foundations and not changing the architecture halfway through the house.'
>
> (Ofsted 2004: §26)

Obviously reading can and should be further improved but, given the evidence, it is doing well and writing should be the obvious priority. A detailed discussion of the searchlights and their rationale can be found in Chapter 2. So far, we see no persuasive grounds in the recent debates to abandon it.

Impact on school leadership and improvement

The NLS was designed as a policy to promote school improvement generally, as well as the specific improvement of literacy. Since the introduction in 1998, this influence on school improvement has grown through the National Numeracy Strategy and in 2002, the National Primary Strategy. All these developments depended crucially on a widespread improvement in school leadership skills and the quality of communication with school leaders.

Because of the number of schools, communication with school leaders was heavily dependent on the skills of local authorities and the quality of their relationships with primary schools which varied considerably from one authority to another. Good communication also depended on how well the key messages were understood by local authorities and the fidelity with which they were communicated. In all these respects, communication was porous. Local authorities also had to balance the need for head teachers to take responsibility for the Strategy with the pressures on them from Ofsted and the government, to deliver school improvement results. This worked well where constructive professional relationships had been cultivated but, in some authorities where leadership was less confident, it was a big challenge which generated uncertainty and dependency, as local authorities pressed schools to meet targets and comply with the recommendations of the Strategy. Also, as we noted in Chapter 8, there was a strong tendency under the principle of 'intervention in inverse proportion to success' for local authorities to leave the average and good schools with very little support on the assumption that they were sufficiently able to fend for themselves. Aside from the local authority interface, the National Strategy tried to maintain a continuous engagement with head teachers, for example through the introductory distance learning materials, a national programme of local conferences, local training and conferences for language coordinators, surveys and telephone polls of school leaders. As the Strategy grew, a similar pattern was initiated for mathematics and, again, to initiate the broader National Primary Strategy.

There is little doubt from available evaluation evidence that the strategies have enhanced leadership competence and quality. Prior to the Strategy, there was a widespread tendency for school leaders to focus on the management of schools: finances, maintenance, resources, provision etc., but to pay less attention to the leadership of the curriculum and the quality of teaching. The structures provided by the literacy and numeracy strategies were a support and a tool for many head teachers who used them with varying degrees of flexibility to set expectations, improve progression and secure greater continuity of practices. The NLS structure provided a common language which enabled heads and literacy coordinators and teachers to work together coherently, while the political authority behind the Strategy provided the impetus to get it implemented, and the motivation to get on with the business of monitoring the quality of teaching and learning in classrooms. In 2000, Ofsted reported:

> Leadership and management of the implementation of the Strategy have improved and by the end of the year, were at least satisfactory in almost nine in ten schools. Over the course of the year there was a significant increase in the amount of monitoring by head teachers of the teaching of literacy.
>
> (Ofsted 2000b: §22)

By 2002, they reported sustained improvement, judging the quality of leadership to be satisfactory or better in 80 per cent of schools with the proportion of weak leadership halved over the same period. By 2005, they said that leadership and management were satisfactory or better in 'almost all schools' (Ofsted 2005a: 5). Nevertheless, there remain serious challenges for head teachers, particularly in relation to their knowledge about literacy. In the early stages, training had been directed mainly at teachers to impact on the classroom and probably gave insufficient weight to the learning needs of head teachers. Certainly the levels of subject knowledge by head teachers was a distinguishing feature of the strongest and most effectively led schools, while the weaker head teachers tended to see the Strategy 'as a classroom initiative and, as a result their knowledge of it was weak and they did not see it as a tool for whole school improvement' (Ofsted 2002a: §151). The external evaluation team also investigated leadership quality from the standpoint of the teacher. Through questionnaires they sought teachers' and head teachers' views on questions about school leaders' expectations and the degree of support, encouragement, feedback and professionalism they demonstrated. Responses were positive:

> The majority of teachers and head teachers clearly felt that their school leaders were giving useful feedback, encouraging collaboration and new ideas for teaching, demonstrating high expectations for pupils and modelling good professional practice in relation to the Strategies.
>
> (Earl *et al.* 2003: 100)

Improvements in the leadership of literacy and numeracy went hand in hand with improvements in the levels of data literacy across the system. This was partly due to the changing school improvement culture which has become increasingly data-led, placing more responsibility on schools to set their own targets and take responsibility for targeting and tracking children, and was greatly facilitated by improvements in the quality and detail of data available to schools to do the job. Even more important has been the structured guidance provided through the Strategy for translating numbers into teaching and learning objectives. This structure has great potential for supporting and steering schools while leaving considerable latitude for each to tailor the strategy to their own needs and ambitions. The Intensifying Support Programme provides a codified example of this structure, designed to support weaker schools. Its effectiveness provides a lesson in how to support leadership effectively. The clear practical focus on assessment, teaching and learning objectives with linked support from the Strategy's resources focuses squarely on curriculum and instructional leadership as the key levers for change. The fact that it has raised standards and improved leadership competence in so many weaker schools demonstrates well how it is possible to support leadership in a very focused way and promote greater autonomy, confidence and professionalism in the process.

Chapter 10

Politics and practice

The literacy game

Literacy education is inextricably bound up with politics because literacy, like language itself, is part of a nation's cultural identity and a fundamental concern for governments in the pursuit of equity and excellence. The consequences of literacy education, for better or worse, are visible and affect the lives of everyone. Literacy is one of the most public and internationally compared measures of a nation's educational, economic and cultural development and an important indicator of the competence of governments – England is no exception. It was no surprise therefore to find literacy standards and the teaching of literacy at the heart of education policy, when the new Labour government was elected in 1997; its palpable sense of urgency borne out in phrases like 'zero tolerance of failure' and 'whatever it takes'. One of the most politically attractive aspects of the NLS was its infra-structure of full-time specialist regional directors and local literacy consultants. Nothing like this had previously existed. It gave the DfEE a direct line of communication with local authorities and schools, massively increasing its powers of influence and accountability. The combination of this field force along with the common structures and expectations embedded in the *Framework for Teaching* and the Literacy Hour, the context of a widespread concern about literacy and professional frustration with the previous fatigued conservative administration, proved to be a winning combination. Much was at stake and risks were high but the NLS, as it turned out, was a strategy for its time, and can stand on its record of success.

The teaching of literacy was bound to be controversial. High stakes generate opposition, disagreement and controversy, placing teachers and others with responsibility for literacy in the public eye. All this is integral to the business of literacy improvement and should be no surprise. The effort to evolve and implement a rational and practical framework for teaching, and to develop support and deliver improvement, had to be played out against a background of continual political manoeuvring by interest groups.

In Chapter 2 we discussed the NLS rationale which was based on a broadly constructivist approach to learning and made use of a 'searchlights' metaphor to characterize the process of reading and, by inversion, writing. The rationale was constructed on the basis of evidence about learning in general and literacy in particular, to meet a number of conditions. First, and fundamentally, the Strategy was committed to promoting learning principles which would engage and motivate children as well as encouraging reading for meaning and the application of thinking skills and problem-solving strategies to reading and writing. Similar skills were promoted by the numeracy strategy and have become progressively more embedded in the principles of the wider post-2002 Primary National Strategy: activating prior knowledge, developing reading and writing strategies, questioning, inferential and analogical thinking, self-monitoring, error recognition, self-correction.

Second, we were, and remain, convinced about the importance of synthetic phonics teaching i.e. the separate and direct teaching of phonics and spelling, which were explicitly structured into the NLS *Framework for Teaching*, and the Literacy Hour, and progressively refined, as understanding of this important area evolved. Third, and linked to the point about phonics, there was equal determination to avoid the trap of opting for sides in the so-called literacy wars. The rationale for the NLS was based on neither a 'top-down' nor a 'bottom-up' theory but provided a balanced and theoretically sound framework, which sought to bring the factional interests together. Finally, it was essential that all the recommendations about literacy teaching connected with the teachers who would need to implement them. Recommendations had to be recognizable and described in sufficiently teacher-friendly language to take root. Such language is bound to be non-theoretical and relatively simple because it is addressed to an audience of variable expertise – teachers, local authority personnel, school inspectors, politicians and the wider community. But language designed to be helpful to the teaching community can also be problematic because it is open to misinterpretation by accident and on purpose, and may fail to please some in the academic community who baulk at its imprecision and use of everyday terminology.

A detailed explanation of the NLS rationale, together with our concerns about replacing the broader 'searchlights' rationale for *literacy* development with the so-called 'simple model' of early reading, are given in Chapter 2. Chapter 3 raises related concerns about the way this model has been used to restructure the Framework and the consequences of this for deconstructing the three conceptually linked strands, *word*, *sentence* and *text*. The restructuring has also reinforced a hypothetical and contentious disconnect between decoding and comprehension in reading, deleted reading strategies and their development from the curriculum, de-coupled the learning and teaching of reading from writing, and broken a carefully engineered continuity with the secondary English framework, which, at the time of writing, remains structured in line with the original three strands.

As ever, ideology mixed with reason to colour debates about literacy and the manner in which opponents chose to portray the NLS over the years. The Labour government had set out its stall, committing itself to specific literacy targets and expectations and the opposition was ready to capitalize on the first signs of failure. Behind this, a broader and long-standing history of ideological differences between 'new' conservative radicalism of the 1980s and the public perception of Labour as 'old-style' socialist liberalism also played its part. Though Labour was at pains to shed this image and had done so successfully by winning the election in 1997, opposition parties were quick to capitalize on the chance to reinforce it. Debates about phonics provided one such opportunity. The Ofsted report (1996b) had already been used to pillory three Inner London LEAs for their failure to raise reading standards. The political implication of Ofsted's criticism was that these schools were failing because they did not get on with the job of systematically teaching phonics, and this reflected a general sloppiness in the administration of schools borne of old-style laissez-faire Labour values. The values of more formalized instruction, already proving their worth in the Pacific Rim and Eastern Europe, were aligned with the teaching of phonics in English primary schools and it was clear that anyone out of step with this would be in line for criticism.

Advocates of phonics-first approaches were always the most strident voice among critics partly because of their clear commitment to the teaching of early phonics but also because of their strong right-wing political support, for example through the Conservative Centre for Policy Studies, and via Chris Woodhead, then Chief Inspector of Schools and a declared supporter of both phonics and the political right. For this reason, a high proportion of energy was devoted to negotiations with advocates of early phonics programmes, the Reading Reform Foundation and the dyslexia lobby – who often scarcely agreed among themselves – in an effort to secure this important element. At an early stage Ruth Miskin was invited to play an influential part in writing the phonics objectives, mainly because of her close association with Chris Woodhead. Jim Rose, one of Ofsted's deputy directors and later to chair the enquiry into early reading which led to the 2006 revision of the Framework, was also closely involved, and party to the final agreed text. Between them, they were largely responsible for the draft of the phonics section of the Framework that was published to schools in 1997.

As soon at the NLS was launched it became clear that those that the Strategy had tried to accommodate were not about to be silenced. They were not content to have synthetic phonics teaching included in the NLS. Their opposition remained undiminished when, in 1998, a detailed programme *Progression in Phonics* was agreed with Ofsted and launched through a nationwide training programme for teachers and NLS advice was strengthened with unequivocal recommendations about early, explicit synthetic phonics teaching. Nor were they to be satisfied by the NLS recommending to schools that they should adopt either *Progression in Phonics* or one of a variety of established, commercially produced programmes, including those authored by the Strategy's critics.

A necessary but disproportionate amount of energy was devoted to managing this debate behind the scenes in an effort to keep the messages to schools clear and consistent. The argument that it would be best for everyone, not least the children, if opponents could agree some practical compromises, cut little ice. In 1999 and again in 2003, conferences were organized, bringing protagonists together to discuss research and its implications. They arrived at more or less the same conclusions i.e. that alphabetic knowledge was essential to successful early reading in English and that systematic (synthetic) phonics teaching was the best known way to achieve this. Both conferences exposed detailed differences in research perspectives and recommendations about how phonic teaching should be sequenced and paced. By 2002, a general consensus had emerged that phonics teaching could be introduced at an earlier stage and accomplished more rapidly than recommended in the Framework. The fact that this could be done led inexorably, though not logically, to the conclusion that it would be right to do so – a serious bone of contention with early years lobby groups who saw introduction of explicit instruction for young children as antithetical to other important values associated with childhood and child development.

There were also strong and politically aligned commercial interests at work. Over the years, commercial programmes and projects of various kinds were promoted, generating waves of media interest in the fairly obvious phenomenon that children who are taught phonics can read phonically regular words more easily than those who are not. Opportunities were not lost for these more commercially-minded interests to add their criticism. These included *Jolly Phonics* which had good publicity and developed a strong market share in schools. Phonographix, sponsored by Penguin Books in 1998, made a bid to take over the phonics programme in the NLS. *Success for All*, promoted by David Hopkins among others, came forward with further programmes and recommendations, while Ruth Miskin's phonics programme *Best Practice Phonics* received quite extensive national newspaper and TV coverage and considerable implicit support from Ofsted. All, except *Success for All*, which was subject to independent piloting and evaluation, were endorsed by the NLS and recommended, along with a number of other programmes, for use in schools. The different approaches all had appropriate credentials; there was no single preferred approach, nor is there today.

On the research front, a number of studies were being conducted to investigate the effectiveness of synthetic phonics teaching on learning to read and spell. In particular, a longitudinal study of Scottish primary schools in Clackmannanshire, begun around the same time as the NLS in 1997, was receiving increasing attention partly because of its methodology which allowed the authors to plot progress over time but mainly because it was increasingly, and perversely, portrayed as a test of the NLS. The emerging findings from this study were important and were taken seriously. In 1999, Tom Burkard, in a polemical pamphlet for the Center for Policy Studies aligned the recommendations in the Framework with the least successful practices in this Scottish study (Burkard 1999). In fact, as John Stannard pointed out in an anecdote to the first of the Ofsted phonics seminars on 29 March 1999, the more successful practices in this study were well aligned with the recommendations of the NLS. The main difference was that many more schools were working in this way across England than apparently was the case in Clackmannanshire.

> The other day I met a headteacher and teacher. Their school was not involved in the National Literacy Strategy but they were teaching literacy in very similar ways. The headteacher described what they did somewhat as follows:
>
>   They taught phonics in infant classes, using *Jolly Phonics* as a basis but adapting the progression and using some of the materials but not all. The essence of the programme was to teach about six phonemes a week along with their

spellings and to learn to manipulate these phonemes through segmentation and blending to read and to write. They also had shared reading sessions and did lots of language play with nursery and other rhymes. They taught the alphabet, the letter names and the upper and lower case letters simultaneously. They had word recognition for tricky words and throughout the teaching they emphasized the importance of reading for meaning. They said, 'the children do not necessarily learn in a sequential way and they quickly begin to work out new connections for themselves'. When children read, if they got stuck on a word, they were encouraged to sound it out and if that failed, to re-read the text to predict and then check the word back visually. When I asked how they dealt with spelling choices for long vowel phonemes they said they had no systematic way of teaching them but the children seemed to make progress mainly through writing, where they tested out and corrected spellings with the help of the teacher. The school used a 'look-and-say' rather than a phonics-based reading scheme because they could not afford to change it. 'All aspects of literacy need to come together', said the headteacher, and 'far from distracting the children, these different aspects are mutually reinforcing.' The children made rapid progress in reading and spelling, were confident early writers and the approach had proved particularly beneficial to the lower attainers.

I relate this small vignette for two reasons:

a. because this seems an eminently sensible head who understands the principles of direct phonics teaching and the importance of keeping it within a context of reading and writing for meaning. And she has understood the power and significance of inferential thinking in generating early autonomy. This is exactly the kind of work that is going on in the best of our NLS schools and it is what we are working to establish more widely;

b. because this head and the class teacher are from one of the *synthetic phonics* schools in the Clackmannanshire study that has been widely reported recently. One can only guess at what was happening in other schools in the name of the NLS where, as one observer commented, '*they had to police sounding out to ensure it did not creep into the teaching of reading*'! It certainly bears no resemblance to what is written in the NLS Framework.

(Address by John Stannard at Ofsted phonics conference, Strand Palace Hotel, 29 March 1999)

Despite this, the Burkard comparison stuck, and was progressively exploited by the opposition in an effort to 'prove' that the NLS was failing. For its part, in the face of determined opposition, the NLS proved less than adequate in presenting its own position. This was partly due to a political need to keep everyone on side and avoid public and potentially damaging arguments with critics. It was also due to the mistaken impression that, because systematic, synthetic phonics teaching was already strongly recommended by the Strategy, the concerns of opponents should have been met. Also, as we noted in Chapter 8, during the second term of the Labour government there was an over-optimistic assumption that the issues of literacy teaching were sufficiently met and that, while the NLS still needed sustaining, the time had come for other priorities. Thus the political focus shifted to Key Stage 3 and the NLS was absorbed into a broader Primary National Strategy (see Chapter 8). Inevitably, the specific focus on literacy, and phonics in particular, diminished. As well-intended policy initiatives multiplied, so too did the complexity of the central PNS agenda. This, in turn, made it increasingly hard to manage at local authority and school levels. Local authorities found themselves enriched with regional directors, additional consultants, funding for specific projects and a growing number of government priorities competing for attention. Good ideas from the centre filtered unevenly down an increasingly complex implementation chain where literacy had to take its place as one important option among many others.

Alongside these structural changes the systematic, national evaluations of school and local authority performance in literacy were drawing to a close. The Canadian external evaluation team completed its work in 2002 and Ofsted published its final report on the Strategy in the same year.

Also the political pendulum was swinging away from its original focus on standards towards the relative safety of structures, reorganizing schools to manage extended days and integrated on-site children's services. Specific indicators on which local authorities had been accountable for literacy were absorbed into broader 'balanced scorecard' indicators across the five big outcomes of *Every Child Matters* where, in judgements of overall performance, limited literacy achievement might be compensated for by a better performance on other indicators, for example health or social care. Political leadership of the original standards agenda diminished and ministers knew progressively less about the state of literacy in schools and what specifically might be needed to improve it. By the time of the election in 2005, with attention focused on an ambitious new education agenda, the Government had pretty well lost the literacy plot, creating a political and intellectual vacuum waiting to be filled.

The battle for control

In Autumn 2004, a House of Commons Select Committee on Education and Skills convened to consider the NLS and its approach to the teaching of early reading, taking particular account of the arguments being advanced by the most vocal critics of the NLS. Presentation of evidence was less than objective. Debbie Hepplewhite of the Reading Reform Foundation claimed the NLS led to under-achievement, failed a third of children and was a cause of dyslexia:

> I am suggesting that the National Literacy Strategy, with its promotion of getting from pictures, from context, from initial letter clues leads to people manifesting this dyslexic symptom.
>
> (Hepplewhite evidence to House of Commons Select Committee, 15 November 2004)

Sue Lloyd, the inventor of *Jolly Phonics*, said the NLS was failing children, but in her view, by requiring them to:

> … memorize words just by looking at them … If we ask them to try to memorize all these books, which they do in the NLS, … then that is where they start to fail.
>
> (Lloyd evidence to House of Commons Select Committee, 15 November 2004)

Morag Stuart, advocate of the 'simple model' of reading, made her position on the 'searchlights' rationale clear:

> The model of reading which is presented to teachers which is this black hole of four things operating and disappearing into a text is completely and utterly misleading and bears no relation to any research on reading that I know of. This is tragic because it has missed an opportunity to get a generation of teachers who understood about reading. I should like to see different models of reading adopted in the National Literacy Strategy guidance to teachers which were in accordance with research evidence and knowledge about reading.
>
> (Stuart evidence to House of Commons Select Committee,15 November 2004)

In its final report, the Select Committee characterized the NLS approach as 'analytical phonics' which:

> …does not necessarily break words down into their smallest units or phonemes. The onset-rime method, for example divides words into openings (onset) and endings (rime)… In contrast, synthetic phonics … breaks words into the smallest units of sound then teaching children to blend these sounds together to form words.
>
> (House of Commons Education and Skills Committee 2005: 13)

In fact, the NLS had been putting the case for the systematic, focused teaching of phonics persistently and unambiguously in the Framework and guidance since 1997 and its definition of phonics was almost identical to that given by Stuart to the Select Committee in 2004:

> pupils should be taught to:
> - discriminate between the separate sounds in words;
> - learn the letter and letter combinations most commonly used to represent these sounds;
> - read words by sounding out and blending the separate phonemes;
> - spell words by segmenting the phonemes and using their knowledge of letter–sound correspondences to represent phonemes.

...phonics consists of the skills of segmentation and blending, knowledge of the alphabetic code and understanding of the principles which underpin how the code is used in reading and spelling.

(DfEE 1999b: 4)

... children need to understand the alphabetic principle to know three things. They need to know the correspondences between letters and their sounds and that goes beyond the single 26 letters of the alphabet ... They need to be able to blend sounds that they recover from translating letters into sounds in order to form words for reading and they need to be able to segment spoken words into their sounds in order to translate them into letters for spelling.

(Stuart evidence to House of Commons Select
Committee, 15 November 2004)

In the event, and not by accident, the Committee's enquiry generated a convenient political storm just prior to the election. Ruth Kelly, Secretary of State for Education, agreed to a formal enquiry into the best ways of teaching phonics. Jim Rose who, as a previous director of inspection at Ofsted, had watched and participated in the development of the NLS, was invited to chair it. Its main terms of reference were to advise on the best practice in teaching phonics, how this should bear on the renewal of the literacy and early years' frameworks, and to consider how best to meet the needs of the lowest achieving young children. Unlike the Select Committee, Rose gave some credit to the NLS for what had been achieved and set the record straight on what the NLS had said. But his interim report raised a number of issues about the rationale, saying the 'searchlights' were in danger of leading teachers to underestimate the priority of phonics and emphasizing how crucial it was to teach phonic work systematically: 'it cannot be left to chance, or for children to ferret out, on their own, how the alphabetic code works' (Rose 2005: §27).

More controversially, he implied that early reading experiences which encourage the use of other strategies in addition to phonics can, 'for many beginner readers ... amount to a daunting and confusing experience' (Rose 2005: §34) – a claim we have challenged in Chapter 2 and not borne out by evidence that 85 per cent of 7-year-olds were meeting national expectations for reading at the time (achieving level 2 or better in national tests in 2005).

Predictably, Rose's interim findings were reported with heavy negative spin, in a well-orchestrated opposition press campaign. Seizing on pejorative phrases like 'ferreting out', the *Daily Telegraph* described the NLS as 'a lesson in failure' with a front page headline announcing that the Strategy 'was to be torn up after report condemns 30 wasted years of trendy teaching'. Phonics, the public was told, had been successfully used in schools 50 years ago but long since abandoned by teachers whose:

... steadfast refusal to reintroduce the method in the face of overwhelming evidence of sharply falling reading standards, represents the greatest educational betrayal of the past 20 years, reducing the life chances of an estimated four million children.

(*Daily Telegraph*, 2 December 2005)

In a similar vein, the *Daily Mail*, reported that the government had been forced to make a u-turn, 'ditch trendy methods of teaching' and adopt the Conservative's policy on reading. Nick Gibb, leading Conservative member of the Select Committee, urged the Secretary of State, 'not to be put off by recalcitrant Labour backbenchers or those in the education establishment still wedded to failed sixties approaches'. Chris Woodhead added that 'it was about time too' that phonics was made the chief method of primary school teaching lessons (*Daily Mail*, 2 December 2005).

The public message was abundantly clear. The NLS was trendy, out-dated, typical old-Labour thinking and opposed to phonics, while phonics was effective, traditional, rigorous and Conservative. Secretary of State Ruth Kelly, seriously weakened by the Select Committee's attack, with a long agenda of other pressing worries and little understanding of the issues, was not prepared to defend or justify the Strategy. Anxious to get off the political hook, she shouldered the criticism and promised that Rose's prescription would replace the core of the Strategy from September 2006. The attack on the NLS had been carefully timed and well stage-managed. The publication of the Select Committee and Rose reports marked the culmination of a long-standing bid for control of the NLS by those of a phonics-first persuasion, who represented a powerful alliance of political, academic and commercial interests, all of which are well served by pushing phonics teaching even further into the limelight. The group has since exercised a controlling influence in the restructuring of the Framework and will be largely responsible for a new wave of training to disseminate the credentials of the 'simple model' of reading to teachers and teacher trainers. The uncompromising effort to bring phonics to the fore-front did little to build up the fragile confidence of teachers and could have inflicted considerable harm. In the final report, which received much less attention than the interim version, Rose worked hard to calm the debate, appease the critics, build on what the NLS has achieved and produce an acceptable political compromise (Rose 2006).

Nevertheless, as we noted in the previous chapter, according to Ofsted's last report on the NLS, phonics was included in virtually all lessons for 5- to 7-year-olds and was good in two-thirds of them. Most teachers, it seems, are already converted and need little persuasion. Bringing phonics teaching into the curriculum for 4-year-olds is a different challenge. Convincing a large and varied population of early years practitioners about the importance of synthetic phonics and how to teach it will require sensitivity and some persuasion. However, so far as schools are concerned, it is likely that the prevailing model of teaching reading will be similar to the Clackmannanshire vignette above and, if increasing numbers of teachers work in that way, we may expect to see further improvement. More extreme recommendations from phonics evangelists to teach children *not* to use other reading strategies alongside phonics, should be treated with great caution. They over-estimate the efficacy of phonics and carry the dangerous implication that children should be discouraged from using their own knowledge of language when learning to read. Nevertheless, an increased commitment to phonics from everyone along with some intelligent compromise could go a long way. If Rose can achieve that, well and good.

A perspective on priorities

Improving early reading

There is clearly a case for continuing to improve early reading and no one should be complacent about it, but it is nothing like the catastrophe portrayed in the press. In 2006, 84 per cent of 7-year-olds achieved the expected NC level 2:

> … [their] reading of simple texts shows understanding and is generally accurate. They express opinions about major events or ideas in stories, poems and non-fiction. They use more than one strategy, such as phonic, graphic, syntactic and contextual, in reading unfamiliar words and establishing meaning.
>
> (DfEE/QCA 1999: 57)

Evidence justifies the expectation that more systematic phonics teaching should increase the numbers of 7-year-olds achieving level 2 though, as we argued in Chapter 2, phonics alone is unlikely to bring this about. Level 2 requires reading for meaning by using and integrating more than just the phonics 'searchlight', as reflected in the level description itself. Nevertheless, it is evident that young children will benefit from being taught phonics and, though some may benefit more than others, the simplest and most foolproof solution as far as schools are concerned, is to have every child taught phonics from an early stage. There are three good reasons for doing this.

First, it will benefit some children greatly. These are the children most likely to experience reading difficulties, many of whom are failing later because they lack understanding of the alphabetic system. Second, for a greater number of children, good early phonics teaching is likely to accelerate reading progress and establish the conditions for faster literacy development overall. Third, and most significantly, early phonics learning has much potential for learning to spell. This point was stressed strongly in the early stages of the Strategy and was persuasive with teachers. It may well be the greater benefit for the majority of children. The Rose report and the new literacy framework re-emphasize this and teachers of young children need to take it seriously. Phonics is a substantial asset to children in the early stages of becoming writers and fits comfortably with established early years practices in 'developmental writing' by providing the proper tools for them to experiment with.

Developing comprehension

However, phonics is by no means the only game in town, and evidence of reading attainment by 11-year-olds tells a different tale. In 2006, reading results for 11-year-olds stood at 83 per cent (down a point from the previous year), only two points short of the revised 85 per cent target for English i.e. the combined reading and writing scores. In 2006, 91 per cent of 11-year-olds achieved level 3 and could

> … read a range of texts fluently, accurately and independently, use strategies appropriately to establish meaning, show understanding of the main points, express preferences and use their knowledge of the alphabet to locate books and find information.
>
> (DfEE/QCA 1999: 57)

Of the remaining 9 per cent, just over 5 per cent did not sit the test, and around 3.5 per cent failed to register a level. In other words, discounting absences and those children with the most serious reading difficulties, almost all the 2006 cohort of 11-year-olds reached at least level 3. And there is even better news: in the same year, 83 per cent achieved level 4 or above, and more than half this group (almost 57 per cent) achieved level 5 or above. By any standards, the teaching of reading in England is good; by international comparisons, it is world class.[1] Almost all 11-year-olds can read 'fluently, accurately and independently'. They can do everything that the best phonics teaching is capable of delivering. The great majority of schools now have the capacity to maintain these levels, and there is sufficient expertise in the system to intervene and successfully support those that under-perform.

Continuing to make this happen is largely a matter of implementation, and better phonics teaching will help. But we also know that while good phonics teaching can improve word recognition, reading accuracy and spelling, it has much less measurable impact on comprehension. This is brought out in the evidence of the Clackmannanshire study where improvements in word reading abilities were not matched by similar improvements in comprehension, and reinforced by the approaches commended in the Rose report and the 'simple model', which disconnect comprehension from decoding. On the evidence, the difference that more phonics can make to attainment at age 11 is likely to be marginal and will not, in any case, have an impact for another six years, by which time another generation of children will have passed through our schools. The evidence does suggest, on the other hand, that the aim of universal reading *fluency* is almost met and, though it can be improved upon, the big challenges relate to comprehension and critical literacy, which were outside the terms of reference of the Rose enquiry.

The moral case for improving reading is unassailable. Ability to read is taken for granted in every aspect of children's lives. At one time, children unable to read would be unable to participate as adults, now they cannot participate as children. Today, reading fluency is so basic that it is almost like a 'sixth sense'. Technology has exponentially increased the demand to read and its influences – internet, mobile phones, the media – are not lost on children. Business and bureaucracy are intolerant of reading failure and, daily, step up demands to transact and communicate by written text in all its forms, mainly because it is cheaper, less interactive than talk and

---

1   See the discussion of the PIRLS findings in the previous chapter.

reduces their accountability. Such is its pervasiveness that today it is a selling point for a bank or an insurance company to advertise the presence of actual people to speak to on the other end of a telephone line. An individual can do almost nothing today without quite high levels of reading fluency.

These cultural pressures have surely played a big part in raising standards by increasing children's awareness and motivating reading during the past decade. But while fluency can empower children it also leaves them open to persuasion, control and conditioning – soft targets for the manipulative forces of advertising and propaganda. As reading skills improve, so too does the vulnerability of the young. If children do not learn to read between the lines or fail to understand how language can be manipulated, then becoming 'merely' a fluent reader in today's world may turn out to be a handicap of similar proportion to being a non-reader 50 years ago. While getting better phonics must be part of the improvement picture, especially for the lowest achievers, the most urgent challenge for reading must be getting some 54,000 level 3 children up to level 4 and beyond, and increasing the numbers of level 5s. What distinguishes these levels is not speed and accuracy of word reading but critical literacy: interpretation, inference, response and evaluation.

The challenge of writing

In 2006, English results for 11-year-olds (reading and writing combined) stood at 79 per cent overall – unchanged from the previous year. The 85 per cent target for 11-year-olds is the key measure. Due to be met in 2005, the timescale has already been extended. The government was six points short of the target for English overall (combined reading and writing) though it was only two points short of that target for reading. Although improving reading will always be important, the greater challenge, as we have argued repeatedly in this book, is the teaching of writing. Compared with the 83 per cent of level 4 readers in 2006, only 63 per cent of 11-year-olds achieved level 4 in writing. Even more worrying was a 17-point gap between girls and boys; only 55 per cent of boys achieved level 4. As schools have assumed greater responsibility for setting their own targets, the importance of the 85 per cent national target has receded. It still matters to the press and the opposition and, though it may be a bed of nails for government, it matters very much for children. Moreover, as reading has improved over the years, it makes a decreasing contribution to the overall target, such that getting to 85 per cent now requires significant improvements in writing. There is now a strong case for setting and committing to separate reading and writing targets designed to deliver the broader 85 per cent over a limited time.

The NLS was launched in 1998 amid high levels of public concern about reading standards. Adult illiteracy rates, a key economic measure, were worryingly high, and the line between socio-economic advantage and disadvantage correlated strongly with the ability to read. The NLS invested heavily and successfully in improving reading. Today, as children leave primary schools, they expect to be able to read. Most can, and we confidently predict that rates of adult reading literacy in years to come will be significantly higher for those educated in England since 1997. But, while reading has been improving, the scale of the writing challenge has become more apparent: differences between reading and writing attainment have increased, the gap between boys' and girls' writing is unacceptably wide and the correlation between social disadvantage and poor achievement in writing is stark. Every year, as test results are published, Secretaries of State pronounce on the need to improve writing and every year the results step up a point or two, but the gaps are not closing and variations between schools do not diminish. In the circumstances, it is hard to understand why a Secretary of State should choose to invest in a protracted enquiry into the teaching of early reading and exclude writing from its terms of reference.

A contingent but related problem, which we noted in Chapter 6, arises from the way reading and writing assessments are reported in England. Although the two aspects are assessed and reported separately, they are also combined into a headline figure for English. Because this is the measure against which national targets are set, it is the most widely reported and influential in forming public opinion. As a result, successes in reading are easily obscured, because they are 'pulled down' by lower writing outcomes, while writing often fails to get the attention it deserves because of a tendency to construe the overall shortfall as a problem with the teaching of reading. There are three of reasons for this. First, there is a widespread public perception of literacy as reading. Second, there is a common assumption that, because children are unlikely to be good writers if they are poor readers, reading must be the core skill from which competent writing will surely follow. Third, reading is more amenable to assessment and research than writing so has always had a higher academic and public profile.

But ten years on, this perception of literacy as reading is out of date. When employers and those in higher education criticize the literacy standards of school leavers, it is not reading but writing competence that concerns them. Writing is *the* fundamental skill for progress through higher education and into success and promotion in the workplace. The working environment for most people is structured, controlled and driven by writing. Writing is visible literacy. If an employee cannot communicate coherently in written English, or a student cannot write a decent essay, it is there for all to see. Writing is the key to participation and control. Business at every level is conducted through writing, and few get promoted who cannot write competently. Ten years ago, inability to read was the dividing line between success and failure. Today reading is the assumed baseline of competence. In terms of rights, equity, the economic potential of literacy and the future of educational investment, writing is where the political challenges need to be met.

And it is not handwriting and spelling which are at the root of the concern. These transcriptional skills need to be a focus of attention in the school curriculum of course, but the growth of word-processing technology has completely changed the landscape of writing. When the NLS began, though word-processing was established and widely used, it was nowhere near as prolific as it is today. Part of the Government's strategy, in common with governments around the world, has been heavy investment in technology for schools. Word processing has overtaken handwriting as the principal means of transcription. Today, spelling is more like using a calculator. Most writers depend on spell-checking to save time and effort. A spell-checker can locate errors and almost always give the correction, so long as the writer knows enough about how words are spelt to make the right choice when the options pop up. Not only does this change how we deal with spelling, it changes what we need to know in order to spell efficiently. It also strengthens the case for phonics. Good phonic knowledge can produce phonologically sensible approximations while the spell-checker can often do the rest. Any accurate, fluent reader with basic keyboard skills should today be able to transcribe and spell efficiently and neatly using a computer. This changes the perspective from handwriting and spelling, which used to define the skills of writing, to the much more challenging focus on the content of what is written and how to compose it.

Writing presents a qualitatively different challenge from reading because, like speaking, its focus is on language production rather than comprehension. The early emphasis in the NLS on reading did much to develop comprehension and it is almost certain that most of the improvement in standards gained was due to improvements in teaching which led children to better and more critical understanding of texts. From the start, there was a strong emphasis on interactive, class-based instruction to promote active learning, and the majority of teachers in England now do this well. These principles were further reinforced in the numeracy strategy through its emphasis on mathematical thinking and problem-solving and, later, in relation to the cross-curricular agenda of the broader primary strategy. But while teachers got better at encouraging discussion, collaboration and active learning, most of the emphasis stayed on the comprehension rather than the production of language. It is a common feature of the school curriculum, most of which is delivered through class-based instruction and the comprehension but assessed through independent language production, most often some form of writing. Reading fluency and reflective comprehension may be necessary for writing but they are far from sufficient. Many good readers are poor communicators, and worse writers. It is one thing to appreciate a narrative, grasp an explanation or follow an argument but a very different challenge to compose any of these.

As awareness of the writing challenge grew, the NLS responded with some formative guidance on teaching writing, *Grammar for Writing* and *Developing Early Writing* (see Chapters 3 and 4), which were introduced to schools through a national training programme in 1999 and 2000. This guidance has since been supplemented and extended, and is alive and well in many schools. But its potential is not yet realized. Schools are well aware of the writing challenge and it is more common than not to find writing as a priority in their improvement plans. In response, many local authorities have initiated projects, training and deployed school-based consultancy into support for writing. But overall, at a national level, while attention has been on early reading, too little has been done strategically to promote better teaching of writing. Despite the national target, expectations are not ambitious enough and many schools are still making too little difference. There are serious shortcomings in teachers' knowledge and effective strategies for teaching composition are not widely established. There is scope for more research and development work, which should be sponsored. But we believe there is already sufficient knowledge and training capacity in the Strategy to make a major difference, if it were more strategically led.

A strategic scenario

Ordering the priorities

The above three priorities, early reading, comprehension and writing, sound like the whole literacy agenda all over again but they are not. Our argument is that while early reading and reading comprehension need some refining, schools already do them well. In fact there is a serious danger that continued drilling down into the fine grain of early reading pedagogy will just become a diminishing return. The challenge for reading today is not about how to teach it but about how to accelerate progress. We need to accelerate reading progress because reading and writing are interdependent. Efficient decoding is a necessary condition of fluent reading; fluent reading, in turn is the foundation upon which analytic and critical literacy skills are built. Both fluent and analytical reading are necessary, though not sufficient conditions, for effective writing. This interdependency does not, of course, constitute a sequence. The connections are logical not chronological, and it would be utterly wrong to conclude that the teaching of writing should wait until comprehension skills are developed or, indeed, that reading for meaning should be delayed in the cause of phonics-first-and-only, as some might argue.

If our argument is valid, the priority for everyone over say, the next four to five years, should be to improve progress and achievement in writing; for example to aim for 75 per cent level 4 for 11-year-olds by 2010, maybe with a floor target of 90 to 95 per cent level 3s. In other words, to get writing to the level achieved in 2000 for reading, by the end of the decade. To do so would be the biggest single contribution to educational success the Strategy could make and it is, in our view, achievable. It implies, in turn, that reading attainment would probably need to rise to, say, 75 per cent at level 5 which would at the same time reduce further the small proportion of level 3s. We predict that, with advances in early reading and a stronger focus on the teaching of writing, reading comprehension would be pulled along to achieve these levels. Writing improvement would, of necessity, provide the leverage needed to advance reading as a consequence of the way it is taught, using text analysis and texts as models. So beyond the re-emphasis on early phonics, schools could be recommended to *maintain* their efforts on reading, for which capacity is already well established, and refocus the whole national effort over a defined period on the teaching of writing.

A fresh look at implementation

It is one thing to identify improvement priorities but something else to deliver them. Recent events raise questions about how to manage the balance between design and implementation strategically to get the best results for children. The design of the strategy must be theoretically sound, practical and user-friendly. It should also be sufficiently robust to bring disparate points of view together, anticipate and accommodate change and deliver the Government's major goals. Above all, it must be defensible in the face of criticism. Design and implementation are reciprocally linked. Design is nothing if it cannot be implemented but, if implementation weakens or fails, it opens the door to criticism of the design. Sticking to the design, making sure everyone understands it properly, and refining it only with the greatest care, is essential. Moving the design goalposts can be disruptive and depict the strategy as confused or misguided. It dissipates energy, frustrates those who implement it and creates opportunities for non-participation. For these reasons great care had been taken over the years to maintain, explain and justify the framework and structure of the Strategy. Maintaining stability also depended on continuously improving its implementation, fidelity to the core messages by those responsible for implementation, and adapting structures to meet challenges and solve problems. We set these implementation principles out in Chapter 6. The strength of the NLS was that it started out with both robust design and strong, persistent implementation. But they would always be tough to maintain.

Growing weaknesses in the implementation of the Strategy contributed to questions about its design, which were bubbling up by 2001. With hindsight, these questions might have been better anticipated. Had the NLS done so, criticism and revision of the Framework might have been managed with more continuity and less disruption. It was not and, as a result, there has been a major shift of effort from implementing to redesigning the Framework, which now looks very different from its predecessor. At the time of writing, over a year has been devoted to this with more to come. Whatever its merits, it has been a major distraction, taking up the energy of key personnel and sending a message to schools that the NLS was about to be 'radically reformed' and was, for the time being, on hold (*Times Educational Supplement*, Aug 2006). Despite assurances that it should be 'business as usual', the effect was bound to discredit the strategy and undermine public and professional confidence in it.

We noted in Chapter 8 how the implementation of the Strategy changed through a combination of multiplying priorities, increasing school autonomy and the assimilation of the specific literacy focus into a broader cross-curricular agenda. This tended to distance the Strategy from the 'front-line', making direct communication with primary teachers more difficult. Unlike the secondary strategy which is more hierarchical with a relatively clear line of communication from specialist regional staff through school leaders to heads of departments and teachers, the primary implementation chain is complex, diffuse, clogged by competing priorities and heavily dependent on local authorities with diverse, often opaque, structures. Local agendas, now driven by the wider objectives of *Every Child Matters*, create a multitude of priorities for schools to respond to, and literacy may not be high on the list. In concert with these changes the assertive and pro-active stance, with which the Strategy began, has given way to a more facilitative role. Today, schools set their own improvement agendas. Apart from those identified as the weakest, who may benefit from various forms of intervention, most schools are the architects of their own improvement. They make the choices while the Strategy acts more as a resource bank for them to draw upon. The government is increasingly dependent on the good will and competence of individual schools to deliver its ambitions.

A key implementation principle with which the NLS began was 'intervention in inverse proportion to success' (DfEE 1997b). The principle was designed to differentiate and target resources according to need, and bring weak schools up to an acceptable standard. We noted in Chapters 8 and 9 how successful this has been. The number of schools going into 'special measures' diminished and the threshold of acceptability was raised as a consequence. Through the first phase of the NLS, this worked well. The messages were clear, the strategy focused, the political leadership unequivocal and persistent, and the challenge obvious. Everyone needed to get better at reading, and this involved defined changes in practice.

Today, things are more complex. Many more schools are achieving at, or close to, the old 80 per cent target. Most regard 85 per cent as a national ambition but do not see it as directly relevant to them. In any case the target-setting process is no longer driven by this figure but by school-based added value measures. As a result, while many schools may be sustaining and adding value on their own account, they are making little difference to the national improvement picture. At the same time, targeting most of the Strategy's resources at a minority of weak schools contributes only marginally to raising national standards. On a purely economic analysis, this looks like a poor return. It is highly likely that, if the present regime persists, the best that can be expected is a continuing plateau with little significant improvement; 85 per cent still looks a long way off.

It is not the 'inverse proportion' principle per se which creates the problem but the level at which the threshold for intervention is set, which is currently too low to make a difference. The strategic point about improvement in 2007 is that under-achievement is not confined to the minority of weak schools. Low-achieving children are spread across schools throughout the system, many of which are rated as average on the data though, collectively, they are failing large numbers of children and not making a proportionate contribution to overall improvement. Many of these children are achieving level 4 in reading but not in writing and define quite precisely a population that should be capable of significant improvement.

School autonomy is an important principle. It engages schools, helps them to take responsibility, gives them a stake in their own improvement and motivates professional learning. With guidance and support available from the central resource bank, school networks to call upon, plus the challenge and leverage from targets, monitoring and inspection, it should be a recipe for continuous improvement. However, self-improvement also depends on each school's capacity to help itself and the degree of challenge it is prepared to set itself. The principle of autonomy should be compatible with the principle of intervention but, too often, autonomy is interpreted by local authorities as *non*-intervention, partly because it smacks of prescription and interference, and partly because of a general nervousness about challenging and intervening in more successful schools. Some authorities say the practice is reinforced by Ofsted's 'zero tolerance' policy, which makes the reduction of weak schools a criterion of effectiveness in local authority inspections. Whatever the reason, it is a misunderstanding. Intervention should be designed for improvement. It should increase schools' capacity and strengthen rather than weaken autonomy. It is surely the purpose of intervention in weak schools so why not in average and even good schools as well?

As we implied at the end of Chapter 8, climbing the next step up the school improvement ladder may require the primary strategy to re-invent itself to focus more on the business of delivery and implementation. It will almost certainly need to raise the threshold for intervention significantly to transform large numbers of average schools into good schools, while, at the same time, sustaining the improvement of weaker schools. It will certainly need to take a stronger and more proactive lead. The Rose enquiry took the view that system-wide intervention is needed to improve phonics. We agree. However, while we expect investment in phonics to be worthwhile, particularly for an important minority of children at risk of reading failure, we do not expect it to make a significant difference to the bigger 85 per cent target. But there may also be contingent benefits. Implementing the changes in phonics could help the Strategy to re-shape itself and sharpen its focus on literacy improvement. It could help create more direct lines of communication with schools and simplify the raft of central priorities and projects that make it so hard to manage at the local level.

So here it is. We should get things into perspective: phonics is supposed to be time-limited for children; make it time-limited for teachers too. Get it secured without delay and settle the arguments. If Rose achieves this, it will be a start. At the same time, get strategic attention back on the bigger picture: how to improve critical literacy and, most of all, writing. Treat writing as the Strategy treated reading in the early stages when schools needed to learn. As with phonics, define clear, precise messages, common practices, a national training and support programme for schools, then implement it systematically and persistently. Those responsible for monitoring and inspection should be trained in precisely what to expect, to harness their support, strengthen accountability all round, and leave no doubt for schools about the priorities and what they mean. Most importantly, get the politicians back on the case because none of this will be possible without clear focus, persistence and leadership from the top.

Primary school literacy has been high on the government's agenda for a decade. It has been through periods when attention was deflected, notably post-2002 when it was assimilated into a wider primary strategy and again into the even wider *Every Child Matters* agenda. More recently there has been a resurgence of attention and public interest through the phonics enquiries. As a policy, it has proved remarkably resilient and much of this has been due to the careful and persistent efforts of all those associated with it to keep challenging local authorities and schools, continue developing and providing high quality training and support, and to stay focused on the practicalities of teaching and learning. Over its ten years the NLS has evolved and changed as have the priorities and needs in schools. Today it is very different but still important and highly relevant. In the face of the evidence, no one but the most churlish could deny that it has had a major impact both on literacy standards, teaching quality and, more widely, on school improvement. It has been at the leading edge of a transformational process in primary education in England. The government has an opportunity now to make a step change which could secure the early gains and advance educational opportunity for many more children. We hope they take it.

References

Adams, M.J. (1990) *Beginning to Read*, Cambridge, MA: MIT Press.

Alexander, R. (1991) *Primary Education in Leeds*: *Final Report of the Primary Needs Independent Evaluation Project*, Leeds: University of Leeds, School of Education.

Alexander, R. (2000) *Culture and Pedagogy*, Oxford: Blackwell.

Alexander, R. (2004) *Towards Dialogic Teaching: Rethinking Classroom Talk*, Cambridge: Dialogos.

Alexander, R., Rose, J. and Woodhead, C. (1992) *Curriculum Organisation and Classroom Practice: A Discussion Paper*, London: Department for Education and Science.

Baddeley, P. and Eddershaw, C. (1994) *The Not So Simple Picture Book*, Nottingham: Trentham Books.

Barber, M. (1996) *The Learning Game: Arguments for an Education Revolution,* London: Gollancz.

Barber, M. (2002) From good to great: large-scale reform in England, paper presented at Futures of Education Conference, 23 April, University of Zurich, Zurich.

Barber, M. and Phillips, V. (2000) *Fusion – How to Unleash Irreversible Change: Lessons for the Future of System-wide School Reform*, DfEE Conference on Education Action Zones, March.

BBC education website *Today's Teenagers 'More Literate'*, http://news.bbc.co.uk/ (accessed 30 October 2005).

Beard, R. (1999) *National Literacy Strategy: Review of Research and other Related Evidence*, London: DfES.

Beard, R., Pell, G., Shorrocks-Taylor, D. and Swinnerton, B. (2004) *National Evaluation of the National Literacy Strategy, Further Literacy Support Programme*, Leeds: University of Leeds.

Black, P.J. and Wiliam, D. (1998) Inside the black box: raising standards through classroom assessment, *Phi Delta Kappan,* 80 (2), pp. 139–48.

Brooks, G. (2002) *What Works for Children with Literacy Difficulties? Effectiveness of Intervention Schemes*, London: DfES.

Brown, G.D.A. and Ellis, N.C. (1994) *Handbook of Spelling*, Chichester: John Wiley and Sons.

Bruner, J. (1986) *Actual Minds, Possible Worlds,* Cambridge, MA: Harvard University Press.

Burkard, T. (1999) *The End of Illiteracy? The Holy Grail of Clackmannanshire*, London: Centre for Policy Studies.

Burns, C. and Myhill, D. (2004) Interactive or Inactive? A consideration of the nature of interaction in whole class teaching *Cambridge Journal of Education*, 34 (1), pp. 35–49.

CfBT (2000) *Comparison of the National Literacy and Numeracy Strategies: Survey of Head Teachers*, Prepared by BMRB Social Research. London: BMRB.

Clarke, K. (1991) Primary Education, *DES News 412/91*, London: Department of Education and Science.

Clarke, M.M. (1984) Literacy at home and at school: insights from a study of young fluent readers, in Goelman, H., Oberg, A. and Smith, F. (eds) *Awakening to Literacy*, London: Heinemann Educational Books.

Clarke, S. (1998) *Targeting Assessment in the Primary Classroom*, London: Hodder and Stoughton.

Clarke, S. (2001) *Unlocking Formative Assessment*, London: Hodder and Stoughton.

Clay, M.M. (1979) *Reading: The Patterning of Complex Behaviour* (2nd edition), Auckland: Heinemann.

Clay, M.M. (1991) *Becoming Literate*, Auckland: Heinemann.

Clay, M.M. (2001) *Change Over Time*, Auckland: Heinemann.

Clay, M.M. and Tuck, B. (1991) *A Study of Reading Recovery Subgroups: Including Outcomes for Children who did not Satisfy Discontinuing Criteria*, Auckland: University of Auckland.

Crévola, C. and Hill, P. (1996) *CLaSS Children's Literacy Success Strategy: An Overview*, Melbourne: Catholic Education Office.

Cripps, C. and Peters, M. (1990) *Catchwords: Ideas for Teaching Spelling*, London: Harcourt Brace Jovanovich.

DES (1967) *Children and Their Primary Schools* (The Plowden Report), London: HMSO.

DES (1978) *Language for Life* (The Warnock Report), London: HMSO.

DES (1988) *Report of the Committee of Inquiry into the Teaching of English Language* (The Kingman Report), London: HMSO.

DES (1989) *A Guide to the National Curriculum*, London: Department of Education and Science.

DES (1990) *HMI Survey of the Teaching of Language in Primary Schools*, London: Department of Education and Science.

DES (1992) *Curriculum Organisation and Classroom Practice: A Discussion Paper*, London: Department of Education and Science.

DfE (1995) *Key Stages 1 and 2 of the National Curriculum*, London: Department of Education.

DfEE (1997a) *The Implementation of the National Literacy Strategy: Final Report*, London: Department for Education and Employment.

DfEE (1997b) *Excellence in Schools*, London: Department for Education and Employment.

DfEE (1998a) *The National Year of Reading*, London: Department for Education and Employment.

DfEE (1998b) *The National Literacy Strategy: Framework for Teaching*, London: DfEE. Online. Available HTTP: http://www.standards.dfes.gov.uk/primary/publications/literacy/nls_framework (accessed 2 April 2007).

DfEE (1998c) *NLS Framework for Teaching: Additional Guidance*, London: DfEE. Online. Available HTTP: http://www.standards.dfes.gov.uk/primary/publications/literacy/63281 (accessed 2 April 2007).

DfEE (1999a) *Additional Literacy Support (ALS)*, London: DfEE. Online. Available HTTP: http://www.standards.dfes.gov.uk/primary/publications/literacy/63457 (accessed 2 April 2007).

DfEE (1999b) *Progression in Phonics*, London: DfEE. Online. Available HTTP: http://www.standards.dfes.gov.uk/primary/publications/literacy/63305 (accessed 2 April 2007).

DfEE (1999c) *Spelling Bank*, London: DfEE. Online. Available HTTP: http://www.standards.dfes.gov.uk/primary/publications/literacy/63313 (accessed 2 April 2007).

DfEE (2000a) *Grammar for Writing*, London: DfEE. Online. Available HTTP: http://www.standards.dfes.gov.uk/primary/publications/literacy/63317 (accessed 2 April 2007).

DfEE (2000b) *Grammar for Writing Leaflets*, Online. Available HTTP: http://www.standards.dfes.gov.uk/primary/publications/literacy/63321 (accessed 2 April 2007).

DfEE (2000c) *Grammatical Knowledge for Teachers*, Online. Available HTTP: http//www.standards.dfes.gov.uk/primary/profdev/literacy/571599 (accessed 2 April 2007).

DfEE (2000d) *Target Statements for Writing*, Online. Available HTTP: http://www.standards.dfes.gov.uk/primary/publications/literacy/63333 (accessed 2 April 2007).

DfEE (2000e) *NLNS Guidance on Teaching Able Children*, London: DfEE. Online. Available HTTP: http://www.standards.dfes.gov.uk/primary/publications/inclusion/63377 (accessed 2 April 2007).

DfEE (2000f) *Supporting Pupils with SEN in the Literacy Hour*, London: DfEE. Online. Available HTTP: http://www.standards.dfes.gov.uk/primary/publications/literacy/63373 (accessed 2 April 2007).

DfEE (2001a) *Schools Building on Success*, London: Department for Education and Employment.

DfEE (2001b) *Developing Early Writing*, London: DfES. Online. Available HTTP: http://www.standards.dfes.gov.uk/primary/publications/literacy/63337 (accessed 2 April 2007).

DfEE/QCA (1999) *The National Curriculum for England Key Stages 1–4*, London: Department for Education and Employment/Qualification and Curriculum Authority. Also online. Available HTTP: http://www.nc.uk.net/webdav/harmonise?Page/@id=6001&POS[@stateId_eq_main]/@id=5875&POS[@stateId_eq_at]/@id=5875 (accessed 2 April 2007).

DfES (2001a) *Schools Achieving Success*, London: Department for Education and Skills.

DfES (2001b) *Illustrative Target Statements for Reading*, London: DfES. Online. Available HTTP: http://www.standards.dfes.gov.uk/primary/publications/literacy/63325 (accessed 2 April 2007).

DfES (2001c) *Early Literacy Support Programme (ELS)*, London: DfES. Online. Available HTTP: http://www.standards.dfes.gov.uk/primary/publications/literacy/63469 (accessed 2 April 2007).

DfES (2002a) *Supporting Pupils Learning English as an Additional Language: Revised Edition*, London: DfES. Online. Available HTTP: http://www.standards.dfes.gov.uk/primary/publications/literacy/63381 (accessed 2 April 2007).

DfES (2002b) *Further Literacy Support (FLS)*, London: DfES. Online. Available HTTP: http://www.standards.dfes.gov.uk/primary/publications/literacy/63449 (accessed 2 April 2007).

DfES (2002c) *Implementing the National Literacy Strategy*, London: Department for Education and Skills.

DfES (2003&2004a) *Primary National Strategy: Intensifying Support Programme*, London: Department for Education and Skills.

DfES (2003&2004b) *Primary National Strategy: Primary Leadership Programme, Information for Participating Schools*, London: Department for Education and Skills.

DfES (2003a) *An Example of NLS Medium-term Planning*, London: DfES. Online. Available HTTP: http://www.standards.dfes.gov.uk/primary/publications/literacy/63385/ (accessed 2 April 2007).

DfES (2003b) *Excellence and Enjoyment: A Strategy for Primary Schools*, London: Department for Education and Skills.

DfES (2003c) *Primary National Strategy*, London: DfES. Online. Available HTTP: http:// www.standards.dfes.gov.uk/primary/about primary national strategy (accessed 2 April 2007)

DfES (2003d) *Speaking, Listening, Learning*, London: DfES.

DfES (2004a) *Literacy Planning CDROM*, London: DfES.

DfES (2004b) *Playing with Sounds: A Supplement to Progression in Phonics*, London: DfES. Online. Available HTTP: http://www.standards.dfes.gov.uk/primary/publications/ literacy/948809 (accessed 2 April 2007).

DfES (2004c) *Learning and Teaching in the Primary Years: Professional Development Resources*, London: DfES. Online. Available HTTP: http://www.standards.dfes.gov.uk/primary/ publications/learning_and_teaching/1041163/ (accessed 2 April 2007).

DfES (2004d) *Primary Strategy Learning Networks: An Introduction*, London: Department for Education and Skills.

DfES (2004e) *Putting People at the Heart of Public Services: Department for Education and Skills: Five Year Strategy for Children and Learners*, London: Department for Education and Skills.

DfES (2005) *Boys' Writing Fliers*, London: DfES. Online. Available HTTP: http://www. standards.dfes.gov.uk/primary/publications/literacy/1128197/ (accessed 2 April 2007).

DfES (2006a) 'Literacy'. Online. Available HTTP: http://www.standards.dfes.gov.uk/ primaryframeworks/literacy/ (accessed 2 April 2007).

DfES (2006b) 'Guidance papers'. Online. Available HTTP: http://www.standards.dfes.gov. uk/primaryframeworks/literacy/Papers/ (accessed 2 April 2007).

Earl, L., Fullan, M., Leithwood, K., Watson, N. with Jantzi, D., Levin, B. and Torrance, N. (2000) *Watching and Learning: NLNS First Annual Report*, Toronto: Ontario Institute for Studies in Education, University of Toronto.

Earl, L., Levin, B., Leithwood, K., Fullan, M., Watson, N. with Torrance, N., Jantzi, D. and Mascall, B. (2001) *Watching and Learning: NLNS Second Annual Report*, Toronto: Ontario Institute for Studies in Education, University of Toronto.

Earl, L., Watson, N., Levin, B., Leithwood, K., Fullan, M. and Torrance, N. with Jantzi, D., Mascall, B. and Volante, L. (2003) *Watching and Learning 3: Final Report of the External Evaluation of England's National Literacy and Numeracy Strategies*, Toronto: Ontario Institute for Studies in Education, University of Toronto.

Earl, L., Watson, N. and Katz, S. (2003) *Large-scale Education Reform: Life Cycles and Implications for Sustainability*, Reading: CfBT Research and Development Publications.

Education Department, Western Australia (1994) *First Steps*, Sydney: Longman.

Ehri, L.C. (1988*)* Movement into word reading and spelling: how spelling contributes to reading, in Mason, J. (ed.), *Reading/Writing Connections*, Boston, MA: Allyn Bacon.

Ehri, L.C. (1998) Grapheme-phoneme knowledge is essential for learning to read words in English, in J. Metsala and L. Ehri (eds), *Word Recognition in Beginning Literacy* (pp. 3–40), Mahwah, NJ: Erlbaum.

English, E., Hargreaves, L. and Hislam, J. (2002) Pedagogical dilemmas in the National Literacy Strategy: primary teachers' perceptions, reflections and classroom behaviour, *Cambridge Journal of Education*, 32 (1), pp. 9–26.

Fletcher-Campbell, F. (ed.) (2000) *Literacy and Special Educational Needs: A Review of the Literature*, Slough: National Foundation for Educational Research.

Fountas, I.C. and Pinnell, G.S. (1996) *Guided Reading*, Portsmouth, NH: Heinemann.

Fullan, M. (1999) *The Return of Large-Scale Reform*, Ontario: Ontario Institute for Studies in Education.

Fullan, M. (2003) *Change Forces with a Vengeance*, London: RoutledgeFalmer.

Galton, M., Simon, B. and Croll, P. (1980) *Inside the Primary Classroom*, London: Routledge and Kegan Paul.

Goodman, K. (1970) Unity in reading, in Singer, H. and Ruddell, R.B. (eds), *Theoretical Models and Processes of Reading*, Newark, DE: International Reading Association.

Hargreaves, D. and the Learning Working Group (2005) *About Learning*, London: Demos.

Hatcher, P. (1994) *Sound Linkage: An Integrated Programme for Overcoming Reading Difficulties*, London: Whurr Publishers.

Heath, S.B. (1983) *Ways with Words*, New York: Cambridge University Press.

HM Treasury (2003) *Every Child Matters (Green Paper)*, London: Her Majesty's Treasury.

Holdaway, D. (1979) *The Foundations of Literacy*, Sydney: Ashton Scholastic.

Holt, J. (1969) *How Children Fail*, New York: Pelican.

Hopkins, D. (2004) Introduction, in Fullan, M., *Systems Thinkers in Action: Moving Beyond the Standards Plateau,* London: Department for Education and Skills.

House of Commons Education and Skills Committee (November 2004) *Teaching Children to Read*, Minutes of evidence.

House of Commons Education and Skills Committee (March 2005) *Teaching Children to Read*, London: HMSO.

Huxford, L.M. (2006) Phonics in context: spelling links, in Lewis, M. and Ellis, S. *Phonics: practice, research and policy*, London: Sage.

Institute of Education (2002) *Guided Reading Key Stage 2: A Handbook for Teaching Guided Reading*, London: Institute of Education.

Lewis, M. and Wray, D. (1995) *Developing Young Children's Non-fiction Writing*, Leamington Spa: Scholastic.

Lieberman, A. (1999) Networks, *Journal of Staff Development,* 20 (3). Published on NCSL website: Online. Available HTTP: http:// www.ncsl.org.uk (accessed 2 April 2007).

Literacy Task Force (1997) *A Reading Revolution: How We Can Teach Every Child to Read Well; Interim Report of the Literacy Task Force; Consultation Document*, London: Literacy Task Force.

Machin, S. and McNally, S. (2004) *The Literacy Hour*, London: Centre for the Economics of Education, London School of Economics.

Massey, A.J., Elliott, G.L. and Johnson, N.K. (2005) Variation in aspects of writing in 16+ examinations between 1980 and 2004, *Research Matters: Special Issue 1*, University of Cambridge Local Examinations Syndicate.

Meek, M. (1982) *Learning to Read*, London: Bodley Head.

Miller, G., Galanter, E. and Pribram, K. (1970) *Plans and the Structure of Behaviour*, London: Holt, Rinehart and Winston.

Mortimore, P., Sammons, P., Stoll, L. and Ecob, R. (1988) *School Matters: The Junior Years*, London: Open Books.

Mroz, M., Hardman, F. and Smith, F. (2000) The discourse of the literacy hour, *Cambridge Journal of Education*, 30(3), pp. 373–90.

NAHT (1999) *National Literacy Strategy Survey*, London: National Association of Head Teachers.

NFER (1998) *Literacy Hours: A Survey of the National Picture in the Spring of 1998*, Slough: National Foundation For Educational Research.

NUT (1999) *Primary Teachers on the Literacy Hour: A Report of a Survey by the National Union of Teacher: December 1998–January 1999*, London: National Union of Teachers.

Ofsted (1996a) *Annual Report of Her Majesty's Chief Inspector of Schools*, London: Office for Standards in Education.

Ofsted (1996b) *The Teaching of Reading in 45 Inner London Primary Schools*, London: Office for Standards in Education.

Ofsted (1998) *The National Literacy Project: An HMI Evaluation, November 1998*, London: Office for Standards in Education.

Ofsted (1999) *The National Literacy Strategy: An Evaluation of the First Year of the National Literacy Strategy*, London: Office for Standards in Education.

Ofsted (2000a) *The National Literacy Strategy in Special Schools, 1998–2000*, London: Office for Standards in Education.

Ofsted (2000b) T*he National Literacy Strategy: The Second Year*, London: Office for Standards in Education.

Ofsted (2001) *The National Literacy Strategy: The Third Year*, London: Office for Standards in Education.

Ofsted (2002a) *The National Literacy Strategy: The First Four Years, 1998–2002*, London: Office for Standards in Education

Ofsted (2002b) *The Curriculum in Successful Primary Schools*, London: Office for Standards in Education.

Ofsted (2003a) *Yes He Can: Schools Where Boys Write Well*, London: Office for Standards in Education.

Ofsted (2003b) *The National Literacy and Numeracy Strategies and the Primary Curriculum*, London: Office for Standards in Education.

Ofsted (2004) *Reading for Pleasure and Purpose: A Survey of the Teaching of Reading in Primary Schools*, London: Office for Standards in Education.

Ofsted (2005a) *Primary National Strategy: An Evaluation of its Impact in Primary Schools 2004/5*, London: Office for Standards in Education.

Ofsted (2005b) *National School Improvement Data Summary for Maintained Primary Schools*, London: Office for Standards in Education.

Polanyi, M. (1969) *Personal Knowledge*, London: Routledge and Kegan Paul.

Popper, K. (1972) *Objective Knowledge*, London: Oxford University Press.

QCA (1998) *Standards at Key Stages 1 and 2: Report on the 1998 National Curriculum Assessments for 7 and 11 Year-olds*, London: Qualifications and Curriculum Authority.

Ramsden, M. (1996) *Rescuing Spelling*, Crediton: Southgate Publishers.

Reading Recovery National Network (2000) *Book Bands for Guided Reading* (revised edition), London: Reading Recovery National Network.

Reynolds, D., Stringfield, S. and Schaffer, E. (2003) The High Reliability Schools Project: some preliminary results and analyses, conference paper presented at New Connaught Rooms, London, 6 June.

Rose, J. (2005) *Independent Review of the Teaching of Early Reading: Interim Report,* London: Department for Education and Skills.

Rose, J. (2006) *Independent Review of the Teaching of Early Reading: Final Report,* London: Department of Education and Skills.

Rumelhart, D.E. (1977) Towards an interactive model of reading, in Dornic, S. (ed.), *Attention and Performance VI*, Hillsdale, NJ: Lawrence Erlbaum Associates.

Sainsbury, M., Schagen, I., Whetton, C. with Hagues, N. and Missis, M. (1998) *Evaluation of the National Literacy Project: Cohort 1 1996–8*, Slough: National Foundation for Educational Research.

Share, D. (1995) Phonological recoding and self-teaching: sine qua non of reading acquisition. *Cognition*, 55, pp. 151–218.

Smith, F. (1971) *Understanding Reading*, New York: Holt, Rinehart and Winston.

Smith, F. (1997) *Reading Without Nonsense*, 3rd edition, New York: Teachers College Press.

Stanovich, K.E. (1980) Toward an interactive-compensatory model of individual differences in the development of reading fluency, *Reading Research Quarterly*, 16, pp. 32–71.

Stanovich, K.E. (1986) Matthew effects in reading: some consequences of individual differences in the acquisition of literacy, *Reading Research Quarterly*, 21, pp. 360–407.

Stanovich, K.E. (2000) *Progress in Understanding Reading*, New York: Guilford Press.

Stanovich, K.E. and Stanovich, P.J. (1997) Memorandum: UK Literacy Strategy, 6 November, Toronto: OISE, University of Toronto.

Stuart, M. (2003) Fine tuning the National Literacy Strategy to ensure continuing progress in improving standards of reading in the UK: some suggestions for change, paper presented to DfES Phonics Conference, March.

Tizard, B. and Hughes, M. (1984) *Young Children Learning, Talking and Thinking at Home and at School*, London: Fontana.

Turner, M. (1994) Sponsored reading failure, in Steirer, B. and Maybin, J. (eds), *Language, Literacy and Learning in Educational Practice*, Milton Keynes: Multilingual Matters with Open University Press.

Turner, M. and Burkard, T. (1996) *Reading Fever: Why Phonics Must Come First*, London: Centre for Policy Studies.

Twist, L., Sainsbury, M., Whetton, C. and Woodthorpe, A. (2001) *Reading All Over the World*, Slough: National Foundation for Educational Research.

Vygotsky, L.S. (1978) *Mind in Society: The Development of Higher Psychological Processes*, London: Harvard University Press.

Wade, B. (1979) *Reading for Real*, Milton Keynes: Open University Press.

Waterland, L. (1985) *An Apprenticeship Approach to Reading*, Stroud: Thimble Press.

Wells, G. (1986) *The Meaning Makers*, Portsmouth, NH: Heinemann Educational Books.

Woodhead, C. (2000) Radio interview on BBC *Today* programme with Chris Woodhead, 23 November, London: BBC.

Index